Cultural Algorithms

Cultural Algorithms

Tools to Model Complex Dynamic Social Systems

Robert G. Reynolds
Department of Computer Science
College of Engineering
Wayne State University
Detroit, Michigan 48202

and

Visiting Research Scientist
Museum of Anthropological Archaeology
University of MIchigan-Ann Arbor
Ann Arbor, MIchigan 48107-1259

IEEE
**Computational
Intelligence**
Society

IEEE Press Series on Computational Intelligence

IEEE PRESS
WILEY

Published by John Wiley & Sons, Inc., Hoboken, New Jersey.
Published simultaneously in Canada.

For general information on our other products and services or for technical support, please contact our Customer Care Department within the United States at (800) 762-2974, outside the United States at (317) 572-3993 or fax (317) 572-4002.

Wiley also publishes its books in a variety of electronic formats. Some content that appears in print may not be available in electronic formats. For more information about Wiley products, visit our web site at www.wiley.com.

Library of Congress Cataloging-in-Publication Data:

Names: Reynolds, Robert G., author.
Title: Cultural algorithms : tools to model complex dynamic social systems / Robert G. Reynolds.
Description: Hoboken, New Jersey : John Wiley & Sons, [2020] | Series: IEEE Press series on computational intelligence | Includes bibliographical references and index.
Identifiers: LCCN 2020001817 (print) | LCCN 2020001818 (ebook) | ISBN 9781119403081 (hardback) | ISBN 9781119403098 (adobe pdf) | ISBN 9781119403104 (epub)
Subjects: LCSH: Social systems–Mathematical models. | Culture–Mathematical models. | Algorithms. | Social intelligence. | Computational intelligence.
Classification: LCC H61.25 .R49 2020 (print) | LCC H61.25 (ebook) | DDC 300.1/5181–dc23
LC record available at https://lccn.loc.gov/2020001817
LC ebook record available at https://lccn.loc.gov/2020001818

Cover Design: Wiley
Cover Image: © engel.ac/Shutterstock

Contents

List of Contributors

Anas AL-Tirawi
Department of Computer Science,
Wayne State University, Detroit,
MI, USA

Rami Alazrai
Department of Computer Engineering,
German Jordanian University,
Amman, Jordan

Mostafa Z. Ali
Department of Computer Information
Systems, Jordan University of Science
and Technology, Irbid, Jordan

Mohammad I. Daoud
Department of Computer Engineering,
German Jordanian University,
Amman, Jordan

Samuel Dustin Stanley
Computer Science Department,
Wayne State University, Detroit,
MI, USA

Mehdi Kargar
Ted Rogers School of Management,
Ryerson University, Toronto,
ON, Canada

Khalid Kattan
Computer Science Department,
Wayne State University, Detroit,
MI, USA

Leonard Kinnaird-Heether
Department of Computer Science,
Wayne State University, Detroit,
MI, USA

Ziad Kobti
School of Computer Science,
University of Windsor, Windsor,
ON, Canada

Thomas Palazzolo
Department of Computer Science,
Wayne State University, Detroit,
MI, USA

Robert G. Reynolds
Department of Computer Science,
Wayne State University, Detroit,
MI, USA
The Museum of Anthropological
Archaeology, University of Michigan-
Ann Arbor, Ann Arbor,
MI, USA

Kalyani Selvarajah
School of Computer Science,
University of Windsor, Windsor,
ON, Canada

Faisal Waris
Department of Computer Science,
College of Engineering, Wayne State
University, Detroit, MI, USA

About the Companion Website

This book is accompanied by a companion website:

www.wiley.com/go/CAT

The website includes:

- Supplementary materials

1

System Design Using Cultural Algorithms

Robert G. Reynolds

Computer Science, Wayne State University, Detroit, MI, USA
The Museum of Anthropological Archaeology, University of Michigan-Ann Arbor, Ann Arbor, MI, USA

Introduction

By and large, most approaches to machine learning focus on the solution of a specific problem in the context of an existing system. **Cultural Algorithms** are a knowledge-intensive framework that is based on how human cultural systems adjust their structures and contents to address changes in their environments [1]. These changes can produce a solution to the new problem within the existing social framework. Beyond that, the system can adapt its framework in order to produce the solution for a larger class of related problems. Cultural Algorithms are able to mimic this behavior by the self-adaptation of its' knowledge and population components.

In other words, we are participating in the Cultural learning process right now. However, as part of the process it is hard to assess what progress, if any, is being made by the system. The Cultural Algorithm provides a framework by which we can step outside of the system so that we can assess its trajectories more clearly. This issue is addressed somewhat by the notion of "human-centric" learning. However, such an approach suggests that we are ultimately in control of the learning activities. In reality, we are embedded in a performance environment that we have partially created on the one hand, and have been passed down as the result of millions of years of evolution on the other.

The framework for the Cultural Algorithm is given in Figure 1.1. A networked population of agents interact with each other in the population space. The network of agents is termed the **social fabric**. Agents are connected with each other in the network based on their level of interaction. If the level of interaction between a pair of agents falls below a certain level, that connection can be lost. In that sense, the network is like a piece of cloth where a stress on some portion of the fabric can lead

This work was supported by grant NSF #1744367.

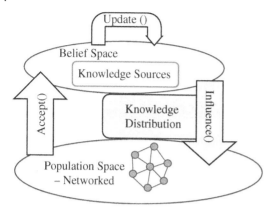

Figure 1.1 Cultural Algorithm framework.

to a disruption or tear in the fabric. Such tears can be mended over time if interactions resume. It is a key feature of Cultural Algorithms since they need to be able to simulate not only the growth but also the decline of social systems [2].

The results of agent interaction within the performance environment in which they are embedded can be accepted into the Belief Space. The Belief Space is a repository of the knowledge acquired by the system so far. It is viewed as a network of different knowledge sources. The accepted knowledge is then integrated into the network through the use of learning procedures that make focused adjustments to the cultural compendium of knowledge. The Information "cloud" can be viewed as the current manifestation of the Belief Space using current technology.

These knowledge sources in the Belief Space can be "active" and or "passive." Active knowledge sources directly select individuals based on their location and history in the social fabric (network). Passive knowledge sources are selected by individual agents in the network. A knowledge source can be both active and passive. The influence function in a Cultural Algorithm has two stages. In the first stage, each individual is assigned a **direct influence**, either actively or passively. Next, comes the knowledge distribution stage. Each individual's direct knowledge source is compared with a subset of its neighbors in the network in the **knowledge distribution stage**. If the knowledge sources are the same, then nothing more needs to be done for an individual. On the other hand, if there is a disagreement, then there is a conflict that needs to be resolved. This conflict is mitigated by a **knowledge distribution mechanism**. Currently, the mechanisms used are taken from traditional approaches to conflict resolution including drawing straws, majority win, weighted majority, win, various auction mechanisms, and various game frameworks including the Prisoners Dilemma and Stackleberg games.

The resultant distribution ranges from static, to moderate, to viral in nature. Individual agents then use their knowledge source(s) to direct their actions in the performance environment. The results of the actions are then sent to the Accept function to decide what will be used to update the Belief Space, and then the cycle continues.

The knowledge sources themselves can support exploitative, exploratory, or stem behaviors. **Exploratory** mechanisms produce new knowledge about the search space, while **exploitative** mechanisms focus the search within already discovered regions. A knowledge source that exhibits a **"stem"** behavior is one that can either produce exploitative or exploratory behavior dependent on the context. The term itself derives from the biologic notion of "stem cell." It is a useful transitional device since in the solution of a complex multiphase optimization problem knowledge sources that are useful in one phase may become less useful at the onset of another. The stem knowledge source can help expedite the transition from one set of knowledge sources, say exploitative, that are dominant at the end of one phase to a set that are more useful in the start of the next phase, such as exploratory ones.

This ability to transition from the use of one set of knowledge sources to another as problem dynamics change is one of the key features of cultures in general. The goal of a Cultural System like that of an operating system for a computer is to continue to provide resources for its active agents. The features inherent in the Cultural Algorithm that support this notion of process **sustainability** are as follows:

1) Cultural Algorithms inherently support **multiobjective** approaches to problem solving. A multiobjective problem is when there is some conflict in an agent's goals, such that the achievement of one goal takes resources away from achieving the other. Since conflicting objectives can reside simultaneously in the Belief Space, agents working on one goal may need to resolve conflicts with agents working on complementary ones. So Cultural Algorithms do not need to be restructured to explicitly deal with multiobjective problems, whereas other machine learning algorithms may need to do so.

2) Cultural Algorithms inherently support population **co-evolution**. Stress within the social fabric can naturally produce co-evolving populations. New links can be created subsequently to allow the separate populations to interact again.

3) Cultural Algorithms also support alternative ways to use resources through the emergence of subcultures. A **subculture** is defined as a culture contained within a broader mainstream culture, with its own set of goals, values, practices, and beliefs. Just as co-evolution concerns the disconnection of individuals in the agent network, subcultures represent a corresponding separation of knowledge sources in the Belief Space into subcomponents that are linked to groups of connected individuals within the Population Space.

4) Cultural Algorithms support the social context of an individual by providing mechanisms for that individual to resolve **conflicts** with other individuals in the population space through the use of knowledge distribution mechanisms. These mechanisms are designed to reduce conflicts between individuals through the sharing of knowledge sources that influence them. This practice can be used to modulate the flow of knowledge through the population. The use of certain distribution strategies can produce viral distributions of information on the one hand or slow down the flows of the other knowledge sources dependent on the context. This feature makes it a useful learning mechanism with regards to design of systems that involve teams of agents.

5) Cultural Algorithms support the idea of a **networked performance space**. That is, the performance environment can be viewed as a connected collection of performance functions or performance simulators. This allows agent performance to potentially modify performance assessment and expectations.

6) Cultural Algorithms can exhibit the flexibility needed to cope with the changing environments in which they are embedded. They were in fact developed to learn about how social systems evolved in complex environments [3].

7) Cultural Algorithms facilitate the development of distributed systems and their supporting algorithms. The knowledge-intensive nature of cultural systems requires the support of both distributed and parallel algorithms in the coordination of agents and their use of knowledge.

All of these features have been observed to emerge in one or more of the various Cultural Algorithm systems that have been developed over the years. In subsequent chapters of this book, we will provide examples of these features as they have emerged and their context.

The Cultural Engine

While there is wide variety of ways in which Cultural Algorithms can be implemented, there is a general metaphor that describes the learning process in all of them. The metaphor is termed the "Cultural Engine." The basic idea is that the new ideas generated in the Belief Space by the incorporation of new experiences into the existing knowledge sources produce the capacity for changes in behavior. This capacity can be viewed as entropy in a thermodynamic sense. The influence function in conjunction with the knowledge distribution function can then distribute this potential for variation through the network of agents in the Population Space. Their behaviors taken together provide a potential for new ideas that is then communicated to the Belief Space and the cycle continues.

We can express the Cultural Algorithm Engine in terms of the entropy-based laws of thermodynamics. The basic laws of classical thermodynamic concerning systems in equilibrium are given below [4]:

Zeroth Law of Thermodynamics, About Thermal Equilibrium

If two thermodynamic systems are separately in thermal equilibrium with a third, they are also in thermal equilibrium with each other. If we assume that all systems are (trivially) in thermal equilibrium with themselves, the Zeroth law implies that thermal equilibrium is an equivalence relation on the set of thermodynamic systems. This law is tacitly assumed in every measurement of temperature.

First Law of Thermodynamics, About the Conservation of Energy

The change in the internal energy of a closed thermodynamic system is equal to the sum of the amount of heat energy supplied to or removed from the system and the work done on or by the system.

Second Law of Thermodynamics, About Entropy

The total entropy of any isolated thermodynamic system always increases over time, approaching a maximum value. Therefore, the total entropy of any isolated thermodynamic system never decreases.

Third Law of Thermodynamics, About the Absolute Zero of Temperature

As a system asymptotically approaches absolute zero of temperature, all processes virtually cease, and the entropy of the system asymptotically approaches a minimum value.

We metaphorically view our Cultural Algorithm as composed of two systems, a Population of individual agents moving over a performance landscape as well as a collection of knowledge sources in the Belief Space. Each of the knowledge sources can be viewed statistically as a bounding box or generator of control. If we look closely at the second law, it states that over time an individual system will always tend to increase its entropy. Thus, over time the population should randomly spread out over the surface and the bounding box for each knowledge source expand to the edge of the surface, encompassing the entire surface. Yet this does not happen here. This can be seen in terms of a contradiction posed by Maxwell relative to the second law. This Contradiction is the basis for **Maxwell's Demon**.

In the 1860s, the Physician Maxwell devised a thought experiment to refute the second law [5]. The basis for this refutation was that the human mind was different than pure physical systems and that the universe need not run down as predicted by the second law. In his thought experiment, there were two glass boxes. Within each box was a collection of particles moving at different rates. There was a trap door connecting the boxes controlled by a demon, see Figure 1.2. This demon was able to selectively open the door to "fast" particles from A and allow them to go to B. Therefore, increasing the entropy of B and reducing that of A.

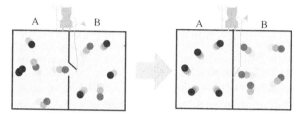

Figure 1.2 An example of Maxwell's demon in action. The demon selectively lets particles of high entropy from one system to another. Reducing the entropy in one and increasing it in the other.

This stimulated much debate among physicists. Leo Szilard in 1929 published a refutation of this by saying that the "Demon" had to process information to make this decision and that processing activity consumed additional energy. He also postulated that the energy requirements for processing the information always exceeded the energy stored through the Demon's sorting.

As a result, when Shannon developed his model of information theory he required all information to be transported along a physical channel. This channel represented the "cost" of transmission specified by Szilard. He was then able to equate the entropy of physical energy with a certain amount of information, called negentropy [6] since it reduced entropy as the Demon does in Figure 1.2.

We can use the metaphor of Maxwell's Demon as a way to interpret the basic problem-solving process carried out by Cultural Algorithms when successful. We will call this process the **Cultural Engine**. Recall that the communication protocol for Cultural Algorithms consists of three phases: vote, inherit, and promote (VIP). The voting process is carried out by the acceptance function. The inherit process is carried out by the update function. The promote function is carried out through the influence function. These functions provide the interface between the Population component and the Belief component. Together, similar to Maxwell's Demon, they extract high entropy individuals first from the population space, update the Belief Space, and then extract high entropy Knowledge Sources from the Belief Space back to modify the Population Space like a two-stroke thermodynamic engine.

Thus, the evolutionary learning process is viewed to be directed by an engine powered by the knowledge that is learned through the problem-solving process. While the engine is expressed here in terms of Cultural Algorithm framework, it is postulated that any evolutionary model can be viewed to be powered by a similar type of engine.

Outline of the Book: Cultural Learning in Dynamic Environments

Earlier it was mentioned that one thing that differentiates Cultural Algorithms from other frameworks is that it is naturally able to cope with changes in its environment. In Engineering, dynamic environments are typically modeled in three basic ways. One approach is to take a general problem such as bin packing and make changes to that application problem over time. A second approach is to generate changes in a multidimensional fitness landscape over which the search problem is defined [7]. A third way is to use large-scale problems whose solution takes place in multiple phases such as the design of a cloud-based workflow system. In the design of a complex system such as this, the knowledge used in dealing with one phase may be different from the knowledge needed in subsequent phases.

The focus of this book is on the design of Cultural Algorithm solutions for the development of complex social and engineering systems for use in dynamic environments. Chapter 2 introduces the Cultural Algorithm toolkit (CAT). That system contains a Cultural Algorithm that is connected to a dynamic problem landscape generator. The generator, the ConesWorld, is an extension of the work of Dejong and Morrison [7]. It was selected because its dynamics were described in terms of entropy, which makes it a good fit with the Cultural Engine model discussed above. It is written in Java and available on the website associated with the book. Examples of its application to problems in the simulated landscape along with some benchmark engineering design problems are presented.

A second feature of Cultural Algorithms mentioned earlier is their ability to provide a social context for an individual and facilitate the movement of knowledge through a network. Chapters 3 and 4 investigate the use of several knowledge distribution mechanisms using that platform. Chapter 3 by Kinniard-Heether et al. shows when an auction mechanism can be a useful tool in expediting the solution to optimization problems generated in the ConesWorld at different entropy levels. Al-Tirawi et al. in Chapter 4 investigates the extent to which allowing the knowledge sources' specific information about an individual's location in a social network can improve performance in dynamic problems with high entropy. The approach is called common valued auctions. The common value related to the shared knowledge that knowledge sources have about the location of individuals in a network. The Common value approach is then applied to ConesWorld landscape sequences that range from low entropy to highly chaotic systems.

Auctions can be viewed as competitive games, but the strategies available to bidders are by definition limited. In Chapter 5, Faisal Waris et al. investigate the use of competitive and cooperative games in CA problem solving. First, examples are presented within the ConesWorld environment and compared with other knowledge distribution mechanisms. The latter half of the paper investigates the use of a CA in the design of a real-world application for autonomous vehicles. The real-world system to be designed is an Artificial Intelligence pipeline for a pattern recognition component. Such pipelines consist of a series of components, and each of the components is tuned initially by their manufacturer. However, when placed within a pipeline, the parameters for all of the participating stages need to be tuned to optimize pipeline execution. Such pipelines can consist of 50 or more stages. In the paper, it is shown that the CA that uses a competitive game framework provides a statistically more efficient solution than alternative approaches. In addition, maps of how knowledge sources that are distributed within a successful network are provided. Unsuccessful networks are more conservative with more homogeneous regions and possess overall less diversity in their distributions than those produced with games.

As stated earlier, another feature of Cultural Algorithms is their ability to produce effective designs of networks for team-based systems. The next two chapters focus specifically on team-based design. Chapter 6 by Kobti et al. describes the use of Cultural Algorithms in the design of a variety of real-world networks. They are interested in how CAs can be applied to the team formation problem, TFP. The TFP is in general NP-hard. Efficient team formation is key to the success of large-scale industry projects that employ a number of different individuals, each with their own expertise and skills. The first example used is a coauthorship network in which individuals collaborate to produce a specific product or outcome. A second example application is that of a palliative care network, where a team of healthcare providers are networked with each other and a number of patients. Cultural Algorithms are shown to be advantageous in each of these cases in comparison to traditional techniques in terms of producing efficient solutions to each of these different problems.

Chapter 7 by Ali et al. addresses the design of a competitive robot soccer team. It employs a population model based on Evolutionary Programming (EP) to evolve offensive and defensive strategies. First, Evolutionary Programming and Genetic Algorithms were each used to develop the offensive and defensive skills of a team. Next, EP was embedded into a CA as the population component. As it turned out, the CA enhanced the EP to beat both the unenhanced EP and GA teams as well as a hard-coded default team. In other words, it was able to produce an increase in team performance beyond that of a human expert and was able to beat the unenhanced versions as well.

The following two chapters focus on the use of Cultural Algorithms in the solution of multiobjective problems. Chapter 8 by Kattan et al. employs Cultural Algorithms to assess the impact that climate change has on artisanal offshore fishing in Peru. Artisanal fishermen of the Pacific coast of Peru use traditional equipment to catch fish, unlike the large-scale deep sea vessels. Marcus [8] collected the data for all fishing trips, over 6000, conducted from a specific coastal Peru port, Cerro Azul. During this period, the ecosystem was affected first by warming of the waters due to an El Nino, then by a subsequent cooling called La Nina, and finally a back to normal phase. A biobjective model of fishing behavior was produced that traded off quality catches versus investment in resources. On the one hand, a goal is to produce the highest payoff in terms of quality catches. On the other hand, since each fisherman is an independent producer, the goal is to minimize the resources needed to produce catches.

Pareto fronts were produced for each of the three phases and the results analyzed and compared statistically by a parallel Cultural Algorithm, CAPSO. CAPSO is short for **C**ultural **A**lgorithm **P**article **S**warm **O**ptimizer. The results indicate that the changes in the ecosystem produced by the warming and cooling of the regional waters resulted in statistically significant changes in the fishing behavior of the individual fishing agents. In the El Nino phase, individuals favored catch quality over resource investment. In the La Nina phase, they emphasized resource investment to insure producing any catch at all. The back to normal phase produced a more balanced set of fronts that represented the knowledge obtained over hundreds of year of fishing in the area, now that the requisite food chains were back to normal.

Chapter 9 by Stanley et al. describes the design of the parallel Cultural Algorithm, CAPSO. While CAPSO was designed initially to deal with the intensive parallelism inherent in the Peru Fishing computations, they were interested in how parallelism was actually needed to support the efficient solution of benchmark problems in multiobjective optimization. Often algorithms are tweaked to produce better results relative to existing benchmarks. That way, individuals can compare their approach with the solutions provided by other systems. This often results in algorithms that may be more tailored to the needs of the benchmark problems than those of the real world.

When CAPSO was applied to a representative set of benchmark problems, two basic patterns emerged. First, very little parallelism was needed to find an efficient solution of each of the problems. At most, around 30 parallel threads were needed as compared to the hundreds required for the fishing example. Second, the knowledge sources most frequently used to guide the search were exploitative in nature, rather than exploratory. The mathematical formulations of the examples were such that once explorations found a piece, the exploiter knowledge sources were able to fill in the rest. So the parallelism that was observed was primarily due to the exploration portion, which contributed to the overall computational time in a limited way.

Like Chapter 8, Chapter 10 also deals with cultural change. However, Chapter 8 dealt with relatively local and short-term change, but the scale of change is markedly different in Chapter 10. The paper by Palazzolo et al. examines the use of Cultural Algorithms on a much larger scale project, one that involves hundreds of square miles and thousands of years. The Land Bridge project is an NSF supported cooperative project between the University of Michigan-Ann Arbor and Wayne State University [9]. The project used AI technology to create a virtual world model of an ancient environment, now submerged under over a hundred feet of water in Lake Huron. The goal of the project is to predict the location of archaic hunting sites that existed over 10 000 years ago. This was done by producing a model of caribou behavior and using Cultural Algorithms to guide the production of optimal migration paths for large caribou herds across the ancient landscape;

the assumption was that hunting sites and activities were positioned relative to these migration pathways. Cultural Algorithms were then employed to produce a system that used knowledge from the anthropological literature to predict hunting site location. The results were used to guide researchers to previously undiscovered sites.

References

1 Reynolds, R.G. (1999). An overview of Cultural Algorithms. In: *Advances in Evolutionary Computation* (eds. D. Corne, M. Dorigo and F. Glover), 367–378. New York: McGraw-Hill.

2 Jayyousi, T.W. and Reynolds, R.G. (2014). Extracting urban occupational plans using cultural algorithms [application notes]. *IEEE Computational Intelligence Magazine* 9 (3): 66–87.

3 Reynolds, R.G. (1978). On modeling the evolution of hunter-gatherer decision-making systems. *Geographical Analysis* 10 (1): 31–46.

4 en.wikipedia.org Laws of Thermodynamics, 2020.

5 Reynolds, R.G. (2018). *Culture on the Edge of Chaos.* Springer.

6 Woodward, P. (ed.) (1957). Entropy and negentropy. *IRE Transactions on Information Theory.* 3 (1): 3–3.

7 Morrison R., De Jong K. (1999). A test problem generator for non-stationary environments. Proceedings of the Congress on Evolutionary Computing, pp. 25–31.

8 Marcus, J. (ed.) (2016). *Coastal Ecosystems and Economic Strategies at Cerro Azul, Peru. The study of a Late Intermediate Kingdom.* Ann Arbor, MI: Memoirs of the Museum of Anthropology, University of Michigan.

9 O'Shea, J.M. (2002). The archaeology of scattered wreck-sites: formation process and shallow water archaeology in western Lake Huron. *The International Journal of the Nautical Archaeology* 31 (2): 211–247.

2

The Cultural Algorithm Toolkit System

Thomas Palazzolo

Department of Computer Science, Wayne State University, Detroit, MI, USA

CAT Overview

The Cultural Algorithm Toolkit (CAT) System is a test bed toolset environment designed to exhibit the implementation of the Cultural Algorithm across a wide variety of mathematical problems. These problems can vary from multivariable equations, to optimal dimensions of a machined component, to a three-dimensional landscape comprising simple conical shapes.

A major component of the system's use in analyzing the implementation of the Cultural Algorithm has to do with its visualization capabilities. For problems that yield up a landscape, such as the ConesWorld example, a full three-dimensional model can be produced that shows the position of agents in this virtual world. For those problems that deal with abstract mathematical problems, the scored results of a knowledge source's progress during each generation of the run can be stored (Figure 2.1).

In addition to visualizing the Cultural Algorithm as it works to find an optimal solution to a given problem, the CAT system also serves to make a number of aspects of the Cultural Algorithm modular and readily redefined by the user. The interface offers a panel that can display a number of variables, such as generations, landscape, and social network topology, and allows the user to alter them to suit a given experimental framework.

In Figure 2.2, a number of variables can be seen on the left panel. These variables control the operational parameters of the Cultural Algorithm. The Year Limit represents how many subsequent generations the system will run for, each year being a singular "tick" in the simulation. The Population Size is the number of agents that will take part in the simulation, those agents being divided up among the five Knowledge Sources that will either gain or lose influence on them as the simulation proceeds.

This work was supported by NSF grant #1744367.

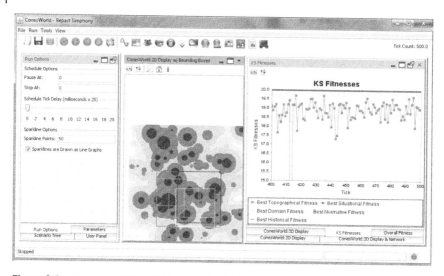

Figure 2.1   A sample of the CAT System displaying a visualization of the ConesWorld problem.

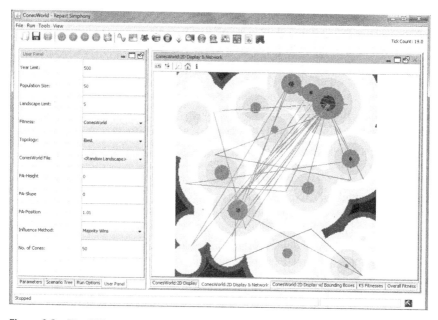

Figure 2.2   The CAT system's user interface panel.

The Landscape Limit allows some of the possible mathematical problems in the CAT System to update their topography. While some problems have a static form which is unchanging, some problems, such as ConesWorld, allow for a dynamic landscape which can, during the course of the simulation, change its shape, resulting in alternate optimal points created later in the simulation. The simulation will run its user-defined number of generations (the Year Limit) repeatedly for each of these updating Landscapes with continuous agents and knowledge spaces retaining their data across the updates. An example of this setup of a Year Limit of 500 and a Landscape Limit of 5 would run for a total of 2500 generations, the topography of the problem changing 5 times during this simulation.

The Fitness option dictates which problem will be the focus of a given simulation. It is here that the user can switch between the mathematical problems available in the CAT System. Each Fitness Function has its own unique aspects and will be more closely detailed in the section "Fitness Functions". Visualization options will change based on which Fitness option is selected, as visualizations such as the 2D Display and 3D Display are restricted to ConesWorld problems only, while Fitness displays are available to all Fitness Functions.

As the Cultural Algorithm is a replication of the social networks that exist among human beings and other social creatures, it too has a social network that links together its agents and allows them to exert influence on one another. The topology of this network can be altered to allow for different numbers of connections between agents, and this can be adjusted with the Topology setting. In Figure 2.2, the social network topology is being visualized and can be seen as a series of lines connecting agents to one another.

While ConesWorld itself spawns a randomly generated landscape comprising conical shapes with each new simulation, it is possible to choose for it to use a presupplied landscape for repetition across a given sample. This can be chosen in the ConesWorld File option.

One major aspect of the CAT System's ability to update the topography of some problems has to do with a logistics function that generates a fluctuation rate that can be controlled by the user. It is possible to deal in minor fluctuations, which produce steady, smooth transitions from one topography to another, and it is also possible to induce erratic fluctuations, which create seemingly disjointed topographies.

The scale on which it goes from smooth to erratic can be controlled by the user with the input of a variable ranging from 0 to 4. This variable controls the fluctuation rate and will be looked at in greater detail in later in the logistic Function section. It is enough for now to point out that in the ConesWorld problem, the height, slope, and position of the cones can be separately set so that one aspect is smooth while another is erratic, and if the user sets the input variable at 0, it will result in no change to a given aspect with each update of the system's landscape.

The Influence Method affects how each Knowledge Source gains or loses influence with each subsequent generation of the simulation. This can vary across methods, such as winning a majority vote, taking up varying percentages of a roulette wheel, or winning an auction. These can be selected from the Influence Method section of the user interface.

Finally, the number of cones utilized in the ConesWorld simulation can be altered to create greater numbers of possible optimal outcomes or more local maximals to attempt to sway the system's exploration and exploitation.

With this combination of user variable input and visualization, the CAT system allows for rapid testing of multiple configurations of the Cultural Algorithm across a wide variety of problems and environments. The numerous visualization options also allow for greater discussion of results than could previously be produced by endless lists of numbers without visual aid or reference.

Downloading and Running CAT

The CAT System can be downloaded from the following location: https://drive. google.com/open?id=161wpeNQIkEcR9gAWRDazPUaKX3wHCA7B

On downloading the CAT Kit zip file and extracting its contents, please install the included Repast Simphony v1.2.0 for Windows. This is the required version of Repast Simphony that the included code is optimized to run with. Once installation of Simphony is complete, run Repast Simphony IDE. It will ask for a workspace to utilize. Please navigate to where you have extracted the CAT files, and select the folder labeled CAT3. Once Repast's version of Eclipse Ganymede finishes opening, you can immediately run the software in one of two ways. To see the visual interface detailed in this chapter, select the circular green "Run" icon from the toolbar. This will immediately run the visual interface version of the CAT. If you click the small arrow immediately next to the green icon, you will be given the option to choose either "ConesWorld," which is the visual interface or "CATnG," which runs an interface-free version of CAT. Open-source coders who are unfamiliar with the Repast Simphony visual interface may wish to utilize this latter option.

Once the visual interface has begun, the "User Panel" tab can be accessed to allow the alteration of various attributes of the run, including population size, the number of different landscapes used, and how many years/generations the system should run over. These attributes are discussed in greater detail in later sections. On pressing the blue "Start Run" button, the system will begin processing with the given attributes. A right clicking within the visual ConesWorld display window will allow a drag interface to move the visuals, and a mouse wheel can be used to zoom in and out. The left and right mouse buttons pressed in unison can be used instead of the mouse wheel to zoom. Different attributes of the run can be viewed via the tabs located at the bottom of the screen.

The Repast Simphony System

Simphony is part of a suite of software known as the Repast Suite. This software is distributed by the Argonne National Laboratory. Repast Simphony is an agent-based modeling software designed to organize, monitor, and record the movements of agents in a given environment.

The system works as a shell, in that Simphony first executes its own visualization system, and then executes the provided environmental code within its own framework. Simphony also provides its own feedback for errors in code running within its environment for the purpose of debugging. It should be noted that errors in environmental code will not propagate out to the Java environment being used to run Simphony, so users should be aware of locating the feedback within Simphony itself.

Knowledge Sources

The Cultural Algorithm's implementation within the CAT system relies on a collection of Knowledge Sources, which can influence the behaviors of the agents as they work toward optimization. Each Knowledge Source analyzes the data in a different way, trending toward either widespread explorative style or tightly focused exploitative style. As the knowledge sources learn more about the problem being analyzed, their suggestions can improve performance resulting in more agents being influenced by that particular Knowledge Source. There are five Knowledge Sources used by the CAT system: Topographical, Normative, Domain, Historical, and Situational.

The Topographical Knowledge Source influences agents to seek new possible feasible solutions by making predictions given the performance landscape of the scoring mechanism. By analyzing trends in certain regions, it can then make suggestions where it is likely that these trends may reach a maximum and influence agents to move toward those locations. Because it sends agents into unexplored areas based on its predictions, it falls into the Explorative category.

In the CAT System, Topographical Knowledge takes the shape of a tree made up of the cells that contain information about the problem's topography. The topographical map can be composed of N-dimensions, based on the number of variables within the given problem, plus the fitness function. For example, as seen in Figure 2.3, ConesWorld is a three-dimensional topographical map, with the X and Z variables for location, and the Y value representing the fitness at a given location denoted by X and Z. The domain of X and Z is limited between the values of 0 and 250 for each of them, resulting in an area of 62 500 units for the given problem domain.

Each cell in the tree assumes its place in the hierarchy of the tree based on the feasibility gathered from the agents that exist within that cell. An agent's position is considered within feasible constraints if that position's fitness registers higher than or equal to a specified fitness gate, which is calculated as half of the sum of the minimum fitness and maximum fitness in the most highly ranked cell.

The Normative Knowledge source experiments with the extension of norms. As the system progresses, clear standards begin to emerge that lead toward likely optimal solutions. If a new, greater optimal solution is found that exceeds the standards, then the knowledge source will readjust its constraints to encompass the new optimal solution.

In the CAT System, the Normative Knowledge is represented by restricted ranges within the available ranges of the inputs. These ranges are adjusted over successive steps, with less optimal subsections of the ranges on the edges of the constraints discarded, and the intersections of these ranges of value are where all of the predictions from the Normative Knowledge source will be found. In ConesWorld, this can be visualized as two rectangular subsections of the topography that intersect, each subsection representing a single variable of the domain, within which agents will be placed.

The Domain Knowledge is reflective of the world in which the problem itself exists. For example, a stock market program would be aware of seasonal trends, a system that works to determine optimal speed around a track would need to understand feasible speed around a curve, and a system that analyzes ConesWorld would need to understand the nature of the sloping topography. It examines the relationship between the objects that exist in a problem domain and how their interactions can lead to solutions.

In the CAT System, the Domain Knowledge of which the system is aware is the nature of a cone. Through the use of a collection of agents and the slope of the area the agent is placed at, they can attempt to calculate where these different slopes would place a possible peak to be sought and a valley to be avoided. The more widely spread the agents are, the more inaccurate the prediction, yet the more tightly packed the agents, the more likely they are to be trapped in a suboptimal local maximum.

To move the agents, the knowledge system influences them to gradually advance via a set step size in the direction that their current location's slope indicates, or along the direction indicated by the overall group's slope with regards to how many agents' slope directions point toward a common point. This is repeated for each dimension in the problem domain, with a small element of randomization included with the step size.

When the agents are spread out, the Domain Knowledge acts in an explorative manner through the combined efforts of all of its agents. When they converge on a given point, it acts in an exploitative manner and agents can even become trapped if they all converge on a suboptimal point with a slope of zero at the peak of a cone.

If this is a suboptimal point, then the actions of another knowledge source can rescue the trapped agents. When the rank of a knowledge source drops in comparison to the other knowledge sources, then agents previously under its influence can come under the influence of a different knowledge source. This will move them away from the suboptimal trap, at which point it is possible that Domain Knowledge will begin to exert influence again.

For this reason, the Domain Knowledge acts as a buffer between the Exploitative and Explorative Knowledge sources. It adapts to the nature of the problem domain via exploration, focuses in via exploitation, can then become trapped due to suboptimals, and then return to its explorative stage when another knowledge source provides it with fresh knowledge. It explores the possibilities of the system's governing rules and exploits them as well.

Historical (or Temporal) Knowledge exploits past knowledge to guide agents in future predictions. By analyzing successful agents of the past and making cautious refinements on their variables, it is possible to predict a new optimal solution near to a high-ranking solution of the past.

To achieve this in the CAT system, a population of successful agents is recorded, in addition to a drift variable. The drift is the tolerance within which an agent must variate from the past recorded agent to be deemed worth the attempt. Even though this knowledge source exploits past successes, its drift ensures that it will not simply repeat the exact scenario of a past success for any given agent.

As the CAT system also has a dynamic update for the landscape, the Historic Knowledge source has the ability to update itself in this situation as well. In a typical run, the historic record is kept and pruned as some past achievements are outpaced by a significant degree. The drift of the Historic Knowledge source can allow the prediction of a newly created optimal on the dynamic landscape if the new optimal location is a slight variation of a previous historic scenario.

The most exploitative of all of the knowledge sources, Situational Knowledge finds an agent with a highly scored combination of variables and uses it as an exemplar for all other agents to follow in all subsequent scenarios.

Situational Knowledge is highly vulnerable to false-positives, and in a large enough landscape it can become absolutely impossible for it to detect other possible maximums on its own. However, it is excellent at refining local solutions, often variating only the smallest of feasible changes in any one variable in its search for an improvement to the best known result.

In the CAT System, this is achieved by a tightly clustered local search of areas that deviate only slightly from the position of the best-known agent. While the Situational Knowledge focuses on the position of agent with the highest fitness, it has a voting system based on different agents and different scores. For example, if a newly discovered agent is found at a tremendous distance from the currently focused-on position of the Situational Knowledge source, and the increase in performance is minimal, then the Situational Knowledge may vote to remain and more closely examine the immediate area around its currently selected agent.

This influence function is carried out using a roulette wheel, where each piece of the wheel is composed of subsets of elite agents. With regards to the distance between agents described above, agents near possible optimal solutions are subdivided into elite groups, and the roulette wheel's wedges are composed of the best agents from the best subsets. Each agent then spins the wheel and moves to the location given by the best agent selected, plus a randomized position variable addition of the smallest variation possible in the scenario.

Fitness Functions

Each problem available within the CAT System is contained within a Fitness Function, which not only dictates the domain of the problem but also the means by which it can possibly be updated, the metrics by which it can be judged, and any possible cutoff that could be reached by discovering a sought-after goal.

First basic initialization is performed in which the domain of the problem is established, such as any necessary variables or placeholders, predefined boundaries or caps, or even a maximum possible fitness that the system is to work towards. There are also two functions called CalculateFitness and CalculateFunctionValue. In some cases, it is entirely possible that to get the fitness of a given fitness function, calculating the function itself will yield its fitness. Some other cases have a fitness which is separate from the function value calculated by the fitness function itself. Both Fitness and FunctionValue are calculated by being passed a point in N-dimensional space, containing the given values for the variables that can alter the results of the system.

If a fitness function has a dimensional input smaller than three (meaning either two or one dimensional inputs), then it is possible for the system to display it in a manner used by the ConesWorld Fitness Function, where the two components of the input represent the X and Z coordinates, and the fitness at that location comprises the Y coordinate (Figure 2.3).

Following these commands are a collection of queries for data such as the constraints of the problem which returns a simple Boolean to denote if an input dimensional point falls within the previously defined domain of the problem. It is also possible to query for the size of the problem's dimensions and the domain constraints themselves.

For some problems that may be defined within the CAT System, it is possible for the actual answer to be known; however, in these cases the system is not aware of how it might reach this particular answer. For example, in an optimization problem, the system may attempt to alter the sizes of various interconnected machinery, each of which has its own constraints it must exist within. The system knows the answer

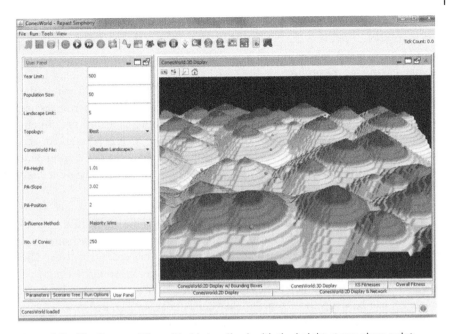

Figure 2.3 The fitness of ConesWorld visualized, with the height at any given point representing that point's fitness.

it wants, but not how the parts might be modified to achieve this answer. Another example from ConesWorld has to do with the known dimensions of *N*-cones that exist within it, and that it is efficient to query the list of cones for the one with the maximum height. Again, the system knows what the height of the cone is, but it does not need to share the location of that cone with any of the active agents.

Finally, there is a Change function within each fitness function. While the *N*-dimensional points contain all of the variables of the function and can be altered repeatedly throughout the course of the simulation, the purpose of the Change function is to change the domain of the fitness function itself. It could change the structure of an equation, which variables are being used, and the topography of the fitness function itself. This will be further explored in the ConesWorld example given in the following section.

ConesWorld

As previously stated, each problem in the CAT System is represented by a fitness function. The example fitness function here concerns the problem of seeking a maximum point across a two-dimensional landscape made up of a variable number of cones. Each cone is defined as a pair of coordinates, a height, and a radius.

The number of cones can be defined by the user as denoted in the overview, and the more cones there are, the greater the possibility that there could be multiple cones with an equal, maximum value, as well as more local maxima to hinder the agents seeking the maximum.

The constraints defined during the initialization of ConesWorld include the dimension variables of the two-dimensional landscape which neither the cones nor the agents can exceed, the maximum and minimum values for the dimensions of the cones, and the rate of change for updates. As it is possible for the ConesWorld fitness function to update its topography, changing the location and dimensions of the cones, these constraints serve to limit what changes can take place in the cones.

In addition to the constraints and basic domain knowledge of the ConesWorld problem, there is also a series of flags for each cone. These flags indicate the directional change a cone may take during an update. There are strict maximum and minimum values that the dimension variables of a cone may change between. The movement between these extremes is cyclical in nature, moving the cone first toward one extreme and then back toward another, similar to how the pistons in an engine can move up and down. Should a cone undergoing an update exceed its dimensional limits, its flag is switched to denote its new increasing or decreasing status, and the amount by which it exceeding its limit then becomes additional change in its new dimension.

For an example of this, assume the cone height limits are set between 1 and 3, and the rate of change is restricted to 0.25 at the most for any single update. If a cone's height is already at 2.80 with its directional flag indicating that it should increase, it will have 0.25 added to it, and it will exceed the height limit of 3 by 0.05. In this case, its flag will be triggered to indicate that it is now decreasing, and the overflow of 0.05 will be taken away from the height of the cone, resulting in a cone of 2.95 height. The next update to the cone, for example 0.20, will result in the cone's height being updated to 2.75, as its directional flag is still indicating that it is decreasing. This decrease will continue until the cone hits the lower limit, at which point the flag will be toggled, the overflow will be added back in, and the cycle will continue again.

While the rate of change is a fixed value, during an update it is not necessarily the only possible rate of change. It simply defines the maximum possible rate of change, but not how wildly the rate of change can vary between any two cones. For that, there are a set of user-defined variables which are known as the A-values, one for each of the variables of all cones, height, radius, and spatial dimension. It is entirely possible to specify that one particular aspect, such as the height of the cone, should wildly vary between a set minimal rate of change and a set maximum rate of change, while another aspect should change at a set rate, while a third aspect should predictably variate between one extreme to the next (Figure 2.4).

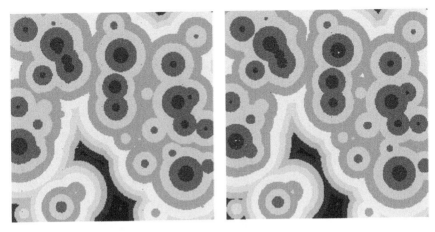

Figure 2.4 A small ConesWorld topography update of position only.

As the topography of ConesWorld is subject to change if the user defines multiple landscapes for it to generate during a given run, it is entirely possible that new maximum values for the function would be created. At the same time past maximum values might vanish as the cones lower in height. Due to this process of vanishing and reappearing maximums, agents need to adjust their movements and mechanisms to explore the environment for new viable maximum points. This can result in a dramatic downturn in the scoring for a group of agents during an update cycle.

As seen in Figure 2.5, those points on the graph where an upward trend is suddenly interrupted by a dramatic drop in score, followed by a rapid ascension to a steady upward trend is a clear indication of a topographical update occurring in the system. Here what had been a maximum suddenly becomes a non-maximum, and the agents need to branch out to find the location of the new maximum point. Depending on how dramatically the landscape changes, the reclamation of the previous score may be instantaneous or take several generations to rediscover. For example, a topography where the height and radius of all cones remains static but their positions gradually change places, as seen in Figure 2.4, will result in momentary drop-offs and then rapid return to the maximum score.

It should also be noted that as there is no guarantee that the absolute allowable maximum height for a cone will be present in any simulation. In fact, it is entirely possible for the overall maximum score to lower over the lifespan of a simulation given multiple topographical updates, as depicted in Figure 2.6. In this case, the height of the cones varied with each update resulting in lower possible maximums due to the shifting nature of the overall possible maximum.

To control this shift, a logistics function is utilized, which produces a change variable that fluctuates between a range of 0 and 1, and this rate of fluctuation may be controlled by the earlier described A-values that may be set by the user.

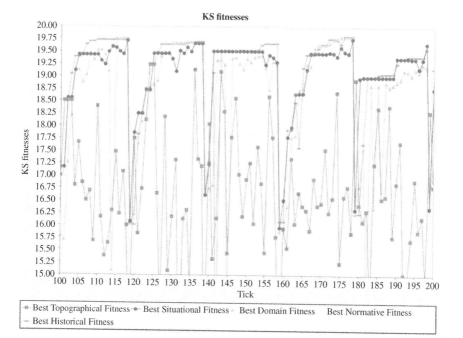

Figure 2.5 The Knowledge Source fitness of a ConesWorld simulation undergoing regular topographical update every 20 ticks.

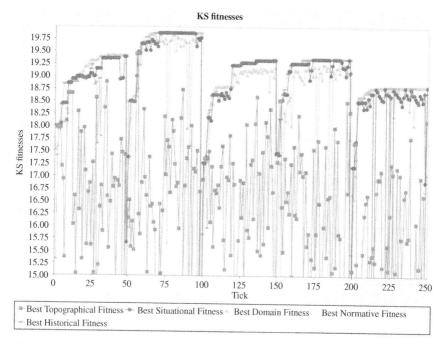

Figure 2.6 ConesWorld KS Fitness with a regular topographical update at every 50 ticks, with variable cone heights.

The Logistics Function

The logistics function (Figure 2.7) utilized by the CAT System, notably in the update mechanism for the topographic of the ConesWorld fitness function, is a recursive function that generates a value between 0 and 1. This value is then used by the update mechanism to select a fractional amount of the allowable rate of change that the system specifies.

Given an A value between 0 and 4, successive iterations of the logistics function will generate a fluctuation between the values of 0 and 1. The frequency of this fluctuation is dependent on the size of the A value. Due to the recursive nature of the function, low values of A will result in subsequent values of $Y_{(n)}$ approaching a steady output that will cease to fluctuate after a sufficient number of iterations. For this reason, using lower values of A in the ConesWorld simulation will result in the appearance of smooth, predictable, near-linear transitions from one update to the next.

However, as the A value approaches 3, the resulting fluctuations becomes more self-sufficient and will maintain a steady, regular frequency between two absolutes, which its peaks and valleys will trend toward. For these cases, it is possible to have subsequent steps of the logistics function vary, but in predictable ways. As each cone in the ConesWorld simulation freshly calculates the logistics function with the next iteration of $Y_{(n)}$, alternating cones querying it for their rate of change will receive alternating high and low rates from it.

After exceeding an A value of 3.33, the logistics function enters into a self-sufficient, non-maintaining erratic frequency with relatively unpredictable shifts in frequency, without ever stabilizing to a constant, repetitive cycle. As seen in Figure 2.8, the lower values of A, ranging from 0 to 3 in the forefront, quickly reduce to a singular output after a brief initial period. After A reaches 3, the frequency does not reduce, but rather becomes a self-perpetuating frequency that continues indefinitely without diminishing.

In those rows of the graph beyond 3.33, the pattern becomes erratic, with each subsequent iteration of the logistics function taking a dramatic, seemingly unpredictable movement that bears little relation to the patterns produced by lower values of A. It should also be noted that even with this erratic fluctuation the resulting $Y_{(n)}$ values are still within the range of 0 and 1. However, should the A value exceed 4, then the system will destabilize and quickly break out of the given range.

$$Y_{(n)} = A * (Y_{(n-1)} * (1 - Y_{(n-1)}))$$

Figure 2.7 The CAT System Logistics Function.

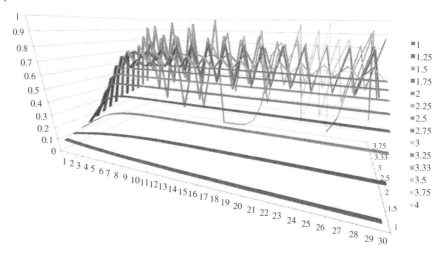

Figure 2.8 A three-dimensional visualization of successive iterations of the logistics function across increasing values of *A*.

CAT Sample Runs: ConesWorld

The following data are the result of two separate runs of the CAT system's ConesWorld simulation. Both runs use similar parameters for their initializations. The population consists of 50 agents in each of them; the social topology between them is represented by lBest (each agent having a connection to 2 agents, resulting in a circular chain); the influence is calculated by Majority; the number of cones is 150 (it must be noted that some smaller cones can be consumed by larger cones and not be visible during the simulation); and the *A*-values for height, radius, and position are all 3.5

The difference between the two runs is the usage of the system's dynamic landscape. For the first run, the landscape remains static across 20 generations. For the second run, the landscape dynamically updates every 5 generations, for 4 separate landscapes. This combination results in both simulations running for 20 generations, with the second run using (5 generations * 4 landscapes) for its 20. The agents present in each run are persistent in their respective runs, meaning that those agents in the static landscape carry the continuous knowledge of the landscape from initialization until the system stops on the twentieth generation. Similarly, those agents in the dynamic landscape are also persistent, so even though the landscape changes every 5 generations, they continue to possess their past knowledge of the landscape.

The initialization step of each run occurs when the system takes the data used to establish the parameters of the simulation, and generates the given number of

·cones. While the number of cones is set at 150, a number of these cones are not readily visible, as they are absorbed by the larger cones. Whenever two or more cones overlap, the system is designed to take the maximum of those cones at the given points where they overlap. Those cones subsumed by larger cones in the static landscape will remain hidden throughout the entirety of the run, while those hidden cones in the dynamic landscape have a chance of becoming visible when the dynamic landscape is updated and the dimensions of the cones are altered.

The A-values fed into the logistics function are used to determine the relative dimensions of each cone. For a given acceptable range of values for the cones to have, each cone will be individually defined based on repeated initial calls of the logistics function as a means of seeding the function, followed by subsequent calls to the function for each newly generated cone. This means that a low A value, which results in the linear results seen in The Cones World section, used for initialization will result in a number of cones that are not terribly dissimilar from one another, the changes in their dimensions being gradual and slight. Using a higher A value, such as 3.5 which was used in these two runs, will result in subsequent calls to the logistics function returning a more chaotic frequency. For this reason, subsequently generated cones can differ dramatically from one another.

A point of interest in Figure 2.9 is the distribution of agents at the time of initialization. They are homogeneously distributed across the landscape, evenly spaced out from one another as well as along the borders of the landscape. With the lBest social network topology visualized, they can be seen connected to one another by a zig-zagging line and each agent connected to two neighbors. For the purposes of finding a maximum, the early configuration provides a unique sampling of early information for each of the knowledge sources to use. It is for this reason that later we may observe that, once the agents begin to cluster around likely candidates, the dynamic updates can result in a slower ascent back to the maximum. This is because the agents are now tightly clustered and thus yield less relevant data back to their respective knowledge sources.

When viewing the network connections across successive steps, it is possible to see the agents begin to concentrate on a maximum via the convergence of lines. In Figure 2.10, the first two steps depicted on the static landscape on the left indicate that some of the agents have located a local maximum and are investigating it. But as more information is gathered, notice that the large cone towards the right side of the static landscape is abandoned by step 3, as the agents converge more on the overall maximum that has been located. The network takes a denser appearance as more agents gather, and other agents are sent out to explore with the majority remaining with the highest scoring locations.

The shape of the network varies based on the selection made by the user, varying how each agent is able to communicate with its neighbors, and how far information can penetrate the social network. As we can see in Figure 2.11, in a

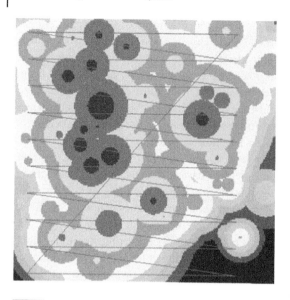

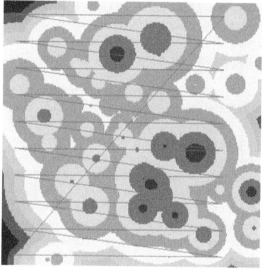

Figure 2.9 The initialization stage of the static (above) and dynamic (below) landscape runs.

homogeneous topology, all neighbors have an equivalent level of connectedness to all other neighbors. If any given agent has four connections in a homogeneous network topology, then ALL agents have four connections in a homogeneous network topology. Heterogeneity in network topologies can be seen in the uses of

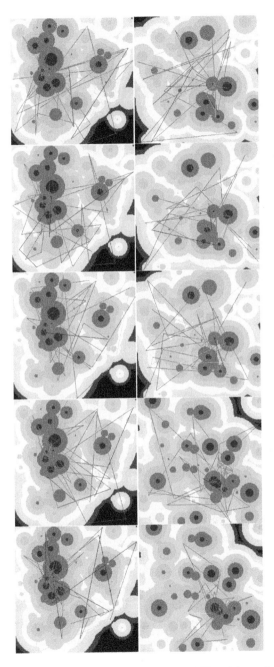

Figure 2.10 Five steps of the static (left) and dynamic (right) landscape networks.

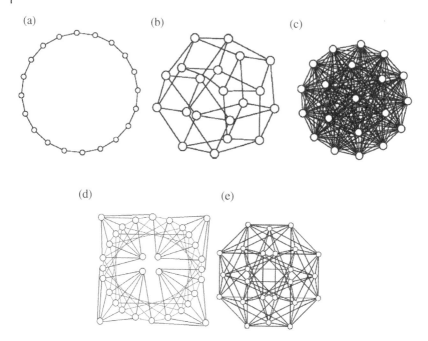

Figure 2.11 The homogeneous topologies. (a) Ring topology, (b) square topology, (c) global topology, (d) hexagon topology, and (e) octagon topology.

subcultures, in which network connections are awarded based on agent merit, and in randomization, in which each agent has access to a random number of others as discussed next in Chapter 3.

Meanwhile in the dynamic landscape, it is possible to see in Figure 2.10. that they are just beginning to cluster as the agents in the static landscape did, when the first dynamic change occurs to the landscape. The agent cluster, which had previously begun congregating on the overall maximum for the dynamic landscape, is suddenly clustered near a new overall maximum, although the centroid of the cluster is not on it. But because the loosely clustered group was near the overall maximum, they were able to then cluster on the maximum and send out exploratory agents to investigate the newly changed landscape. As the A-value for the dynamic landscape is 3.5, this means that each dynamic shift will be a radical update which can result in the total possible maximum being significantly lower as no cone approaches a height similar to those of a pre-updated landscape. This will be displayed later in the scoring results of the agents working in the static and dynamic landscapes.

The movement of the social clusters, with regards to the network topologies displayed in Figure 2.11, gives us an idea of how the mass of agents moves, with new, more rewarding locations, being disseminated among the other agents at varying rates depending on the shape of the network topology. As the network change will not only produce new information but will make some old information obsolete. For example, overabundance of connections may be both beneficial and detrimental depending on which information is discovered first. Therefore, any poisonous data introduced into a network can take longer to be purged from the system based on how it is able to move through said network (Figure 2.12).

While continuing the simulation, it is possible to view not only the agents and their network shared network topology, but also the area which each influencing knowledge source encompasses. By identifying each agent with the knowledge source which is influencing it, and then compiling the coordinates of each agent, it is possible to draw a bounding box which contains all agents that adhere to a given knowledge source. The structures of these boxes and their subsequent expansions and contractions can serve to highlight the nature of each knowledge source.

Boxes that contract over successive steps indicate an exploitative knowledge source, such as the Situational knowledge source. These knowledge sources will tend to focus on a known best example and explore in its immediate vicinity for any possible improvement. Boxes that expand over successive steps or trend toward more encompassing sizes typically represent the explorative knowledge sources, such as the Topographical knowledge source. These knowledge sources tend to send out agents to possibly high-scoring predicted spots based on calculations made with known data.

While explorative search suffers from covering massive amounts of ground with limited agents, exploitative suffers from a blindness brought on from agents that only focus on the immediate. With agents sharing information between knowledge sources, however, both types of knowledge source will benefit.

When the CAT system has finished running its generations across the two landscapes, it is possible to view the results of each generation's top scoring results. In Figure 2.13 these results are depicted, with each line indicating the results of one of the knowledge sources. The static landscape's generations display a steady maintenance of the discovered maximum in the landscape, while the dynamic landscape's generations show the dramatic drop-off each time a dynamic update of the landscape occurs.

Earlier it was mentioned that the homogeneous distribution of agents during the initialization phase of the runs gave a wide breadth of knowledge to the knowledge sources to use during each subsequent step. This could account for rapid early acquisition of a maximum. However, the dynamic landscape's violent landscape changes, which can result in clusters of agents suddenly being on a low-scoring point in the landscape in unfamiliar terrain, show a more dramatic difference between the scores of the agents immediately after the shift, and several steps later when the maximum is reclaimed.

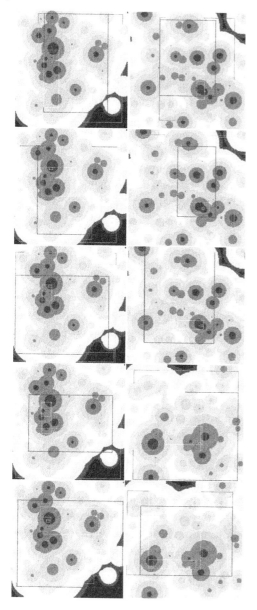

Figure 2.12 Five steps of the static (left) and dynamic (right) bounding boxes.

Also due to the chaotic nature of the 3.5 value of A of the dynamic landscape's updates, note that the overall possible maximum changes not only its position but also its magnitude with the shifts. This explains the low yet stable fitness values achieved during different points in the dynamic landscape, where plateaus occur in the data.

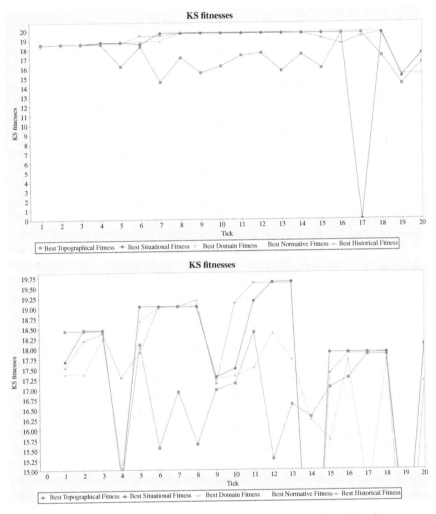

Figure 2.13 The KS fitnesses for the static (above) and dynamic (below) landscapes.

In addition, as noted in the discussion of bounding boxes, the exploitative and explorative aspects of the knowledge sources can be discerned from their adherence to a found maximum when viewed by the knowledge source fitnesses. Those exploitative knowledge sources, such as Situational and Historical, will tend to achieve a high fitness and then stay at that level. The explorative knowledges source on the other hand, such as Topographical and Domain, will tend to stay away from the maximum as they seek out more information.

In Figure 2.14, we can see the areas of each bounding box produced by each knowledge source. It can be seen in this visualization that the two most exploitative knowledge sources, situational and historical, regularly have the smallest

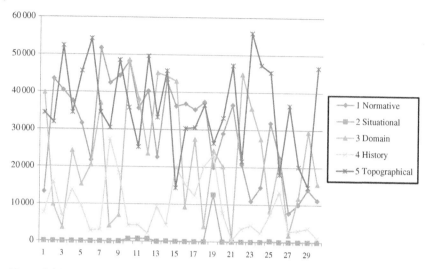

Figure 2.14 The span of each Knowledge Source's bounding boxes.

areas of coverage, while the two most explorative knowledge sources, normative and topographical, cover the largest areas. The domain knowledge source straddles the line between these two methodologies of exploration and exploitation, expanding and contracting itself as data come in, focusing on a transitional region between the more extreme knowledge sources.

Using this resulting information, it is possible to not only find the solution to a given problem but also to illustrate the in-depth means by which the solution was found, and how each knowledge source contributed toward a given goal. It is due to this shared responsibility of the knowledge sources to both maintain acquired knowledge and push for the acquisition of new knowledge that the system maintains the balance between all of the knowledge sources as they each assert their influence over the collected individuals of the simulation.

CAT Sample Runs: Other Problems

In addition to the ConesWorld system, the CAT System's optimization abilities can be used on a number of other optimization problems. As the ConesWorld system had two possible input variables with a single output across a relatively small dataset, it was possible to create a three-dimensional visualization of the data to watch as the system located these optimal values. In these examples, a larger number of variables with wider ranges and finer variations exist, meaning that a visualization of this information in the method previous seen in ConesWorld would quickly become incomprehensible, as the system would attempt to generate images with more than three dimensions.

Despite being unable to visualize the data range, it is still possible to visualize the means in which the knowledge sources deal with the data they encounter. The additional optimization problems observed by the system include the designs of a Tension Spring, a Welded Beam, and a Pressure Vessel. Each problem sought to minimize the dimensions of a given structure to save on material and space, while still remaining within the constraints rendered necessary by factors, such as precision (for the shaping and rendering of parts) and safety (to reduce the likeliness of critical failure).

The Tension Spring example involves the minimized design of the spring as visualized in Figure 2.15. The four variables that describe the spring itself relate to the diameter of the wire (d), the diameter of the coil (D), and the number of coils in the spring (N). The mass of the spring can be equated as follows:

$$f(x) = (N + 2) * D * (d^2)$$

where

$0.05 " d" 2.0$

$0.25 " D" 1.3$

$2.0 " N" 15.0$

It can be seen in Figure 2.16 that each knowledge source yields new discoveries, which are then capitalized on by the other knowledge sources. The topographical fitness, the highly explorative knowledge source which searches across bold predictions, leads the system to higher bounds in the fifth generation, after which the situational knowledge source focuses on this latest achievement. While the other, more explorative knowledge sources continue to explore, the

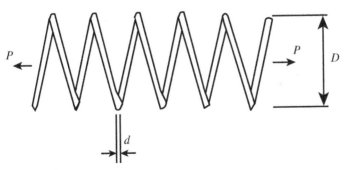

Figure 2.15   The tension spring [1]. *Source:* Reproduced with permission of Elsevier.

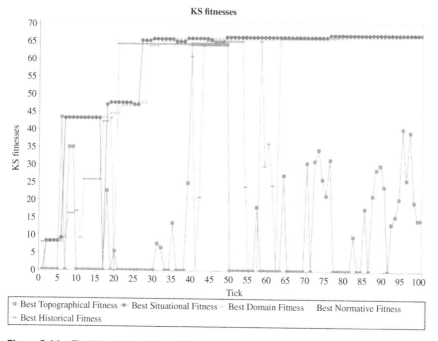

Figure 2.16 The Knowledge Source fitnesses of the tension spring problem.

exploitative knowledge sources continue to refine, examining only those small variations. Notice that at approximately generation 75, while the explorative knowledge sources had dropped off in terms of new discoveries, the highly exploitative situational knowledge discovered a minor improvement to the arrangement of variables in the design of the tension spring.

This concludes our discussion of the basic conesworld system. In chapters 3 through 5 that follow the system will be used as a vehicle to experiment with varying Cultural Algorithm configurations. The focus of these chapters will be on mechanisms by which knowledge is distributed throughout the population. These mechanisms will include majority voting (wisdom of the crowd, auctions, and games.

Reference

1 Mahdavi, M., Fesanghary, M., and Damangir, E. (2007). An improved harmony search algorithm for solving optimization problems. *Applied Mathematics and Computation* 188 (2): 1567–1579.

3

Social Learning in Cultural Algorithms with Auctions

Robert G. Reynolds[1,2] and Leonard Kinnaird-Heether[1]

[1] *Department of Computer Science, Wayne State University, Detroit, MI, USA*
[2] *The Museum of Anthropological Archaeology, University of Michigan-Ann Arbor, Ann Arbor, MI, USA*

Introduction

Recently a number of socially motivated algorithms for problem solving have been proposed that include Particle Swarm and Ant Colony Optimization algorithms among others [1, 2]. These approaches are population-based problem solvers. The Cultural Algorithm is an approach to social evolution that employs a Belief Space or collection of Knowledge Sources that can be used to direct the problem-solving activities of individuals in the population [3]. The knowledge sources compete or cooperate to influence individuals in the network. As such, the knowledge sources represent different meta-heuristics to guide the solution process. Likewise, performance of the individuals can impact the content of the knowledge sources. Cultural Algorithms have been shown to be particularly useful in the solution of data-intensive problem solving. The Cultural Algorithm itself is therefore a hyper-heuristic framework that controls the selection of different approaches to solving a problem (see Figure 3.1).

These approaches reside in the Belief Space in the form of Knowledge Sources. The problem-specific knowledge sources can be associated with basic default categories called knowledge source classes. When a Cultural Algorithm configuration is developed for a given set of problems, the designer identifies the basic knowledge sources for each class and how they are interconnected in the Belief Space. Next, the designer specifies a given influence function that determines how the basic heuristics can be combined to Influence the decisions made by individuals in the population. The Influence Function has two distinct steps. The Direct Influence step and the Knowledge Distribution step. Together they determine how the various meta-heuristics are spread among the population of individuals in the population.

This work was supported by NSF grant #1744367.

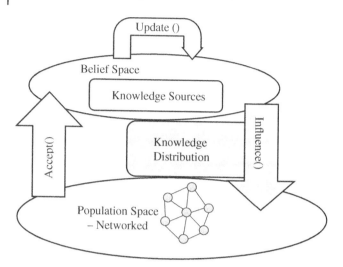

Figure 3.1 The cultural algorithm framework.

Next, the population can be modified by the Selection of individuals in the network for modification based on their performance. As a result, a new network of individuals can be generated by dropping old arcs and individuals while adding new ones. That is why the network is called the Social Fabric since it is woven by the experience of the population over time. The networked population is then Evaluated in a given performance environment. Then, the experience of the population is distilled through the Acceptance function and used to Update the knowledge sources in the Belief Space either statistically or through other symbolic learning mechanisms.

Previous work [4, 5] demonstrated that the structure of the two-step influence function described above impacts the solution of a problem by controlling the spread of problem-solving knowledge through the population. At each time step, knowledge sources directly select individuals to influence in step 1. In addition, an individual knows the direct influence for each of a subset of its neighbors. This information can be used to distribute knowledge sources throughout the population using a knowledge distribution mechanism in step 2. Figure 3.2 gives a spectrum of knowledge distribution functions that range from random on the upper left counterclockwise to game-based mechanisms on the right. As information about the problem and its solution becomes more detailed, the range of viable approaches moves counterclockwise from a random distribution. Similarly, previous work [6] has shown that auctions are an effective means of distributing knowledge within the Cultural Algorithm through the networks that comprise the social fabric when sufficient information is available.

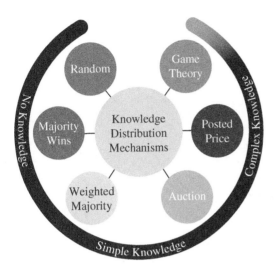

Figure 3.2 Spectrum of knowledge distribution mechanisms.

In this paper, the implementation of additional auction methodologies as a means of distributing knowledge within the Cultural Algorithm is presented. Using this mechanism along with other components and associated metrics, we detail the development of a Cultural Engine. The Cultural Engine represents a means with which to affect the operation of the Cultural Algorithm in situ, by providing a user with a feedback/control loop. This offers the user a higher level of fine tuning than was previously available in the closed system. This opens up the possibility of further control using human-in-the-loop or similar AI-based constructs.

Cultural Algorithms

The Cultural Algorithm is a hyperheuristic framework in which to perform socially motivated learning activities. A schematic view of the Cultural Algorithm and associated pseudocode is given in Figure 3.3 [7].

The key to the Cultural Algorithm is that culture is the aggregation of individual behavior. The knowledge concerning the performance of each of the individuals is collected into the Belief Space by the Acceptance function. That knowledge is then used to Update each of the five basic categories of knowledge sources or containers as shown in Figure 3.4. The update process can vary from a basic statistical aggregation activity to a symbolic learning or inference activity. The

```
Begin
    t = 0;
    initialize Bt, Pt
    repeat
        evaluate Pt {obj()}
        update(Bt, accept(Pt))
        generate(Pt, influence(Bt))
        t = t + 1
        select Pt from Pt -1
    until (termination condition achieved)
End
```

Figure 3.3   Cultural algorithm pseudocode.

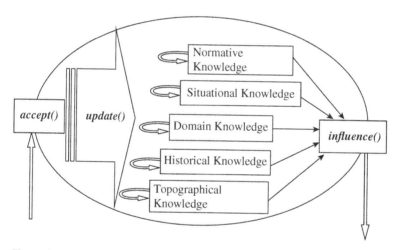

Figure 3.4   Updating the five knowledge source categories.

specific knowledge sources housed in each container category can be networked together within and between categories.

The basic Knowledge Source (KS) categories or containers are as follows. Normative knowledge recalls what is deemed to be an acceptable range of values for the solution to a given problem, and uses this to guide the search for that solution. Situational knowledge is a record of important events, in the form of solutions that were particularly successful or unsuccessful. Domain knowledge uses specific information about the domain of the problem to influence the search. Historical knowledge keeps a temporal record of the search activity. Topographical knowledge is spatial information about the topography of the search space or landscape.

Each KS category can be viewed as one way of influencing an individual or generating a new set of behaviors, and thus each KS provides a different way or meta-heuristic for solving a problem. The Cultural Algorithm framework is designed as a vehicle for the selection and distribution of these KSs throughout a networked population. The network is called the Social Fabric since the connections between individuals can be strengthened and diminished over generations.

These methods are brought together by the influence function. The current influence function used here is called the Social Fabric Influence function, SFI. This is illustrated in Figure 3.5. It consists of two stages. First, each KS has a normalized performance score based on the performance of the individuals that it influenced in recent generations. As such, each KS occupies a portion of a roulette wheel that is proportional to its normalized performance score. For each individual in the population, we spin the wheel and select a KS that can potentially influence it. This is called the direct bidding step.

Once each individual in the population has a direct bidder, that information is communicated to those other individuals who are connected to that individual in the social fabric network. This is step 2 and is called the Knowledge Distribution step. Here, the default is to just communicate the bid to its immediate neighbors, those who can be reached in "one hop." Each individual sums up the weight of its direct bid and those received from its immediate neighbors. The weights derive from their relative performance in the guidance of individuals as reflected by their relative area on the wheel. The KS with the majority of bids wins. If there are ties, then various conflict resolution rules can be invoked to break them. In the prototype described here, the direct bidder wins in the case of a tie.

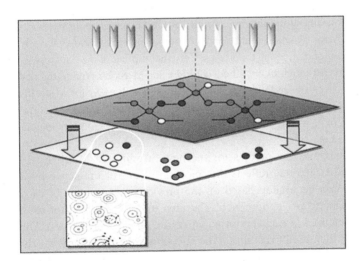

Figure 3.5 The social fabric influence function: each of the knowledge sources competes to influence individuals in the network.

The key to the SFI is that if a KS produces above-average choices, then a KS can disseminate through the population faster and allow the system to focus its search efforts on more desirable places. The current prototype supports six different topologies, some of which have been used in particle swarm optimization. These topologies are LBest, Square, Hexagon, octagon, hexadecagon (sixteengon), and global [6]. The Lbest topology is a ring topology that connects each individual to two others. The Square topology connects each individual to four other neighbors. The Hexagon connects with 6 neighbors, octagon with 8, and hexadecagon with 16 others. Finally, a global topology connects an individual to all others in the population.

Subcultured Multi-Layered, Deep Heterogeneous Networks

Previous iterations of Cultural Algorithms have often used a system where the network topology was fixed and selected prior to the start of a run. This methodology is now termed the homogeneous network approach. Recent research has shown that the use of dynamic networks can facilitate the knowledge discovery process. This discovery leads to the introduction of two new methodologies, heterogeneous networks, and subcultured heterogeneous networks [8]. The focus for this research will be on the latter.

Rather than using a single topology for the agent population, the subcultured system consists of multiple topologies operating concurrently. In addition, the system can learn to associate particular subnetworks with specific knowledge sources. This will facilitate multi-layered or "deep" social learning in that an agent can participate in multiple network layers simultaneously. In subcultured heterogeneous networks or subcultures, the Topology wheel will be divided into n Knowledge Source wheels, where n is the number of competing topologies. Here the number of overlaid topologies is restricted to six although many others could be added as observed in the real world. Each wheel gives the individuals' average fitness of the KSs for a specific topology. After the topology is selected for an individual, they will access the corresponding direct KS by spinning the KS's wheel related to its selected topology as illustrated in Figure 3.6.

Figure 3.6 demonstrates the process for the new Subcultured Multi-layered heterogeneous model. Step one reflects the selection of one of the active fixed topologies for use in a generation based on the previous performance of each topology with a roulette wheel approach. The area under the wheel for each topology is its normalized average performance in the previous generation. The selected topology is then used to condition the selection of one of the KS wheels. Each topology has a separate wheel, shown in step 3, which is used to select a KS that is used to influence each individual based on the past performance of the KSs for the selected topology. Thus, there are six separate KS wheels, one for each

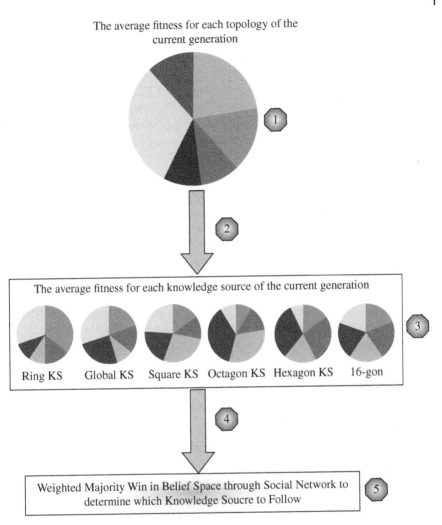

Figure 3.6 Subcultured wheel selection process.

topology that is used for a generation. The wheel is used in step 4 to generate the direct influence for each individual in the population and collect the direct influence KSs for its neighbors. In step five, the distribution mechanism of choice engages its conflict resolution rules to determine the winning KS for each individual as in the heterogeneous model. The individuals are then modified and evaluated. The results are used to update the selection wheels and the process starts again for the next generation.

A Wild Card Mechanism was developed to combat topology dominance in the Subcultures component of Cultural Algorithms. As discussed above, in the

Subculture system, the weighting on the topology wheel is variable and while the topologies are not allowed to fall out and have 0% chance of being selected, they can be marginalized. The Wild Card Mechanism adds a fixed 5% chance to the main topology wheel. If the spin lands on the Wild Card, then a second spin is done on a separate wheel where each topology has a fixed equal chance of winning, as opposed to the variable chance on the main wheel. This allows each topology to maintain participation in the system for the entirety of the run. These can be copied and pasted or removed based on the size needed.

Auction Mechanisms

The Auction distribution mechanism was developed as an addition to the Cultural Algorithm Toolkit (CAT) [9]. The process it follows consists of four main phases once each individual has received its original direct influence. In phase 1, as shown in Figure 3.7, the system calculates the bidding wheels for each of the five KS. This is done by first listing all of the individuals that each KS has influenced, over a given number of generations. The fitness value is recorded for each individual, and these become the value of the bidding tokens that populate a roulette wheel. The total fitness of each KS is also calculated by taking the sum of the

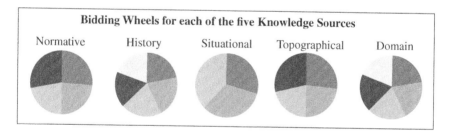

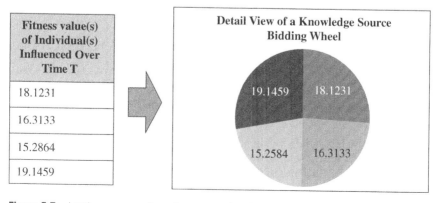

Figure 3.7 Auction process phase 1: constructing the bidding wheels.

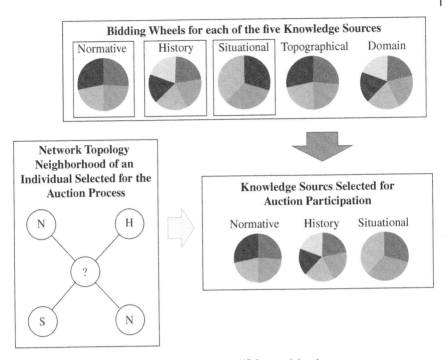

Figure 3.8 Auction process phase 2: selecting KS for participation.

fitness of all individuals that KS influenced. Each token on a given bidding wheel occupies a portion of the wheel equal to its percentage of the total fitness.

Once the bidding wheels have been constructed, the process moves on to the second phase, as shown in Figure 3.8. In this phase, the auction system is called on to determine the influence of a given individual. To hold an auction, the system must first determine which KS is going to participate in the auction. Only a KS that has influence over a neighbor of the disputed individual is allowed to participate in the auction. The system also must determine the number of neighbors of the disputed individual that each KS influences. This value can be used later to allow for multiple spins of the bidding wheel during the bidding process.

In phase 3, as seen in Figure 3.9, the actual auction commences, using the data collected in the previous two phases. The auction mechanism conducts the actual auction and was designed such that it can accommodate many different types of auctions. The auction mechanism requests bids in accordance with the particular auction type and accepts them. The system then collects each KS bid by spinning their corresponding bidding wheel. The system allows that, depending on user preference, a KS can be given multiple spins of their bidding wheel, depending on whether they influence multiple neighbors of the disputed individual. Once the bids are collected, the system submits these bids to the auction mechanism. The mechanism determines if a winning state has been reached for

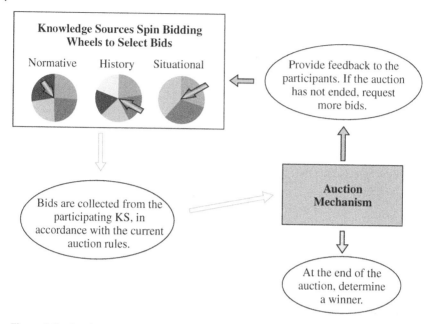

Figure 3.9 Auction process phase 3: conducting the auction.

that individual, and if so declares a winner. If no winner has been determined yet, then the mechanism requests more bids.

When a winner has been determined, the auction system then gives the winner influence rights over the disputed individual, as shown in Figure 3.10, and the process is completed. Optionally, the winning bidding tokens used to purchase influence over the disputed individual can now be rescinded, such that it cannot be used in any further auctions.

The auction mechanism was originally designed with an auction solution meant to emulate the first-price sealed-bid auction [10]. In this case, each KS selected as a bidder spins their associated bidding wheel once to generate a bid, and the KS with the highest generated bid will be declared the winner. In the case of a tie, the winner was chosen randomly between the KS that had submitted an equal value bid.

Two further auction solution types have been added in addition to the first-price sealed-bid (FPS) auction type. The first is a variation on the original first-price sealed-bid solution, with the exception that instead of relying on a random selection to break ties, the solution uses a multiround tiebreaking scheme, lending it the name First-Price Sealed-Bid Multiround (FPM). In the case of a tie, the KS who have submitted an equal value bid is allowed to spin their bidding wheels again and thus submit a new bid. This repeats, in the case of further ties, until one KS submits a singularly higher bid than the other remaining KS and is thus

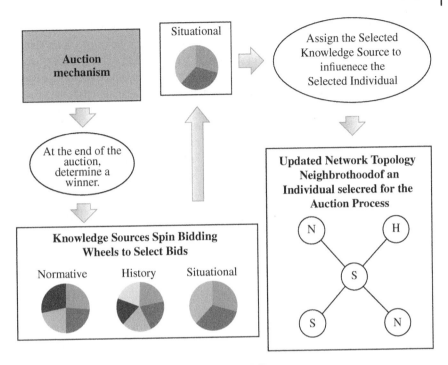

Figure 3.10 Auction process phase 4: assigning influence.

declared the winner. In the case where a multiround situation occurs, only the KS who is declared the ultimate winner will have their associated highest bid taken. All other bid tokens will be returned to the non-winning KS.

The other new auction solution that has been added is designed to emulate the classic English auction. To represent the unordered nature of the bidding process inherent to the English auction, after the participating KSs are defined, an initial bidder is chosen at random. The bidder then spins its bidding wheel to generate a bid. Each additional KS who is involved is then allowed to bid in response until a higher bid is generated. This process repeats until no higher bids are generated, and then the KS with the current highest bid is declared the winner and its corresponding bidding token is rescinded.

The Cultural Engine

The concept of a Cultural Engine has been proposed in previous works, and metrics such as the dispersion coefficient and innovation cost [11] have been developed that can be used to measure the efficiency of the system. By taking these measurements, one can see how the system drives search and identify what components of the system are more effective, given a specific situation or problem. Using this, one can begin to see Cultural Algorithms as a mechanical system, and by using the information taken from the internal measurements, we can begin to find ways to actively engage and alter the running system to drive the search in different directions based on the performance it is achieving at a given point in the search. This can be seen as analogous to how an engine adjusts internal configurations and other things based on data collected from sensors to more efficiently operate.

In the past, Cultural Algorithms has been seen as a closed system in that the general configuration of the system was dictated prior to runtime and maintained throughout the execution of the program. Recent improvements, such as the heterogeneous and Subculture network models, the Wild Card and auction-based distribution mechanisms introduced here, can potentially allow the hyperheuristic system to make rudimentary changes to its internal workings at its discretion, based on the general performance metric. The work described in this paper is designed to act as a template for a system that can alter the internal structure of Cultural Algorithms "on the fly" to more efficiently drive the search. An example of this is shown in Figure 3.11.

By analyzing the system as it performs based on problems of different complexities using different configurations and measuring the diagnostic signals, we can

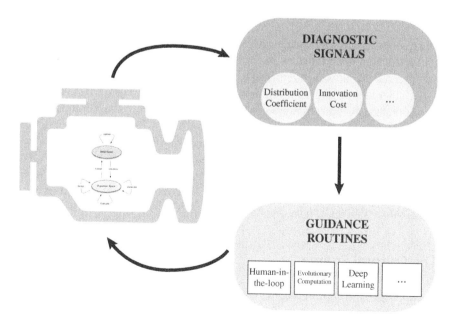

Figure 3.11 The cultural engine.

see what configurations work better in given situations thus giving us a basis for guidance routines that can be implemented in the future. To effectively benchmark what configurations work well under certain conditions, we require benchmarking problems of varying complexities, and for this we will use ConesWorld.

ConesWorld

The implementation of ConesWorld used in this paper was originally developed by De Jong and Morrison [12] to examine the ability of evolutionary problem-solving approaches to solve randomly generated problems of arbitrary complexity. This was proposed as an alternative to the traditional approach of comparing algorithms on a small set of benchmark problems. It was felt that by focusing on a small set of problems, investigators might attempt to sacrifice algorithm generality to produce good results on for specific problems.

The ConesWorld Generator produces a problem landscape using resource cones of different heights and different slopes that are randomly scattered across a multidimensional landscape. This is done in two steps: first a baseline static landscape of resource cones is specified. Then the desired dynamics are applied to adjust the distribution of cones. The base landscape is given by:

$$f\left(\left\langle x_1, x_2, \ldots, x_n \right\rangle\right) = \max_{j=1,k}\left(H_j - R_j \cdot \sqrt{\sum_{i=1}^{n}\left(x_i - C_{j,i}\right)^2} \right)$$

where:

k: the number of cones,
n: the dimensionality,
Hj: height of cone j,
Rj: slope of cone j, and
Cj,i: coordinate of cone j in dimension i.

The values for each cone (Hj, Rj, and Cj,i) are randomly assigned based on the following user-specified ranges:

$Hj \in (H_{base}, H_{base} + H_{range})$
$Rj \in (R_{base}, R_{base} + R_{range})$
$Cj,i \in (-1, 1)$

The max function is used to blend each of these independently specified cones so that if, for example, two cones overlap, the height at a point is the height of the cone with the largest value at that point. An example landscape with $k = 15$, $H_{base} = 1$, $H_{range} = 9$, $R_{base} = 8$, and $R_{range} = 12$ is given in Figure 3.12.

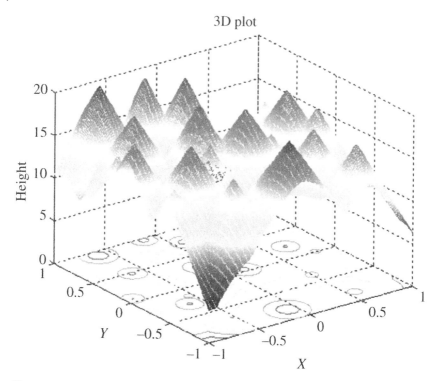

Figure 3.12 An example landscape in two-dimensional space (n = 2) bound by $x \in$ (−1.0, 1.0), $y \in$ (−1.0, 1.0) with k = 15, $H \in$ (1, 10), and $R \in$ (8, 20) [13]. *Source:* Reproduced with permission of John Wiley.

The second step is to specify the dynamics. For each cone j, its parameters (every dimension $C_{j,i}$, height H_j, and slope R_j) can be changed individually and independently. To control the complexity of a landscape, we use the logistics function given as: $Y_i = A \times Y_{i-1} \times (1 - Y_i - 1)$, where A is a constant and Y_i is the value at iteration i.

A bifurcation map of this function is provided in Figure 3.13. This figure shows the values of Y that can be generated by the logistic function, given values of A between 1.0 and 4.0. The particular value of A specifies whether the movement will be in small same-sized steps, large same-sized steps, steps of few different sizes, or chaotically changing step sizes.

This ConesWorld landscape generator function can be specified for any number of dimensions. Each time the generator is called, it produces a randomly generated real-valued surface in which random values for each cone are assigned based on user-specified ranges. By applying the logistic function to the parameter of the cone's generator, we are able to control the complexity of the generated landscape by changing the A-value of the logistics function. Therefore, given that one can generate problem landscapes at different levels of complexity, the relationship

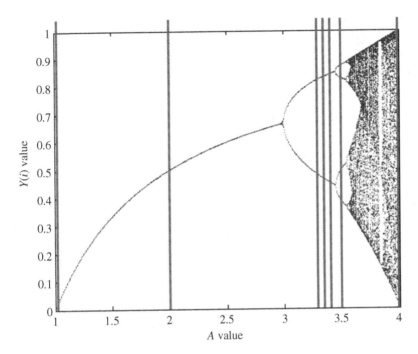

Figure 3.13 Logistic function with characteristic *A* values.

between the social network and different categories of computational problems can be studied. This enables the evaluation of a model in a more flexible and systematic way. From an information theory point of view, the problem environment carrying certain complexity of information could be represented by entropy. The more complex an environment is, the higher its entropy.

We are particularly interested in characteristic points in terms of the complexity in the ConesWorld as shown in Figure 3.13. Here left to right we pick $A = 1.01, 2.0, 3.3$, 3.35, 3.4, 3.5, and 3.99 for our test environment complexity as marked with vertical lines. Langton [14] suggests that as the *A* value relates to entropy of the system, as it increases the system becomes more unpredictable. He demonstrated this in terms of rules needed by a Cellular Automata to solve problems at different points along the curve in Figure 3.13. In particular, he stated that the amount of mutual information that cells in the space needed to know about their neighbors increased as the entropy or amount, A, of information in the landscape increased. Based on that, Langton established several basic computational classes as follows:

Fixed: For problems of low entropy, a fixed set of rules can be given to each cell to allow them to exchange the information needed to solve the problem. In our case this is equivalent to having a fixed set of rules by which information is exchanged.

Periodic: For problems of this nature, the cells need to switch from one set of rules to another depending on the number of bifurcations.

Chaotic: Problems for which the number of bifurcations is so large, the system is inherently chaotic. Thus, there are now many specific rule sets that apply.

Experimental Framework

The experiments detailed in this paper were developed to collect results of the CAT system using multiple different configurations on ConesWorld landscapes of varying complexity. These tests were conducted to determine how combinations of different distribution mechanisms and Wild Card usage perform on problems of a given complexity. By doing this, we gained insight into how to develop the guidance routines that can be used in future research in developing the Cultural Engine.

A test consists of running the CAT system on a given ConesWorld landscape using a specified network topology, for a maximum of 10 000 generations. If the test finds the maximum point in the landscape before the 10 000-generation limit, we say that the solution is found. Otherwise, if no solution has been found, the test stops at 10 000 generations. A test uses 100 individuals and has a window size of 3, meaning that the social fabric influence (SFI) function is applied every 3 turns. The tests were performed on 35 different landscapes, 5 each from 7 different ConesWorld complexities, 1.01, 2.0, 3.3, 3.35, 3.4, 3.5, and 3.99. All three of the auction types, English, First-Price Multiround (FPM,) First-Price Single Round (FPS) were tested, as well as the traditional Weighted Majority Win (WMW) distribution mechanism, which acts as a baseline to previous work.

The mean and standard deviation (in generations) are calculated for all runs, and for only those experiments that ran to completion. The maximum time to completion and how many runs found a solution within the generation limit of 10 000 generations were also recorded.

Results

This section contains the results of tests conducted, delineated by their complexity. For the least complex set of problems, the fixed class, each combination tested could find the solution before the generation limit in every test. Overall the mean time to solution was comparable across the board with the auction-based distribution mechanisms outperforming WMW, FPS with the Wild Card having the best result (Table 3.1).

For the $A = 2.0$ set of fixed problems that contain increased variability in the distribution of cones, only the English and First-Price Multiround auctions could

Table 3.1 Performance comparison for $A = 1.01$.

Auction type	Wild card?	Overall mean	Overall std. dev.	Runs with solution found	Max generations with solution found	Mean with solution found	Std. dev. with solution found
English	FALSE	390.558	735.8965	500	4217	390.558	735.8965
English	TRUE	320.214	636.702	500	4292	320.214	636.702
FPM	FALSE	398.308	784.6721	500	6540	398.308	784.6721
FPM	TRUE	392.908	775.428	500	5149	392.908	775.428
FPS	FALSE	741.678	2241.319	476	7083	274.9223	853.8189
FPS	TRUE	829.052	2352.382	475	9878	346.4232	1075.696
WMW	FALSE	870.5072	2451.356	459	9976	353.4248	1162.682
WMW	TRUE	831.382	2364.79	473	7513	308.0719	911.0545

Table 3.2 Performance comparison for $A = 2.0$.

Auction type	Wild card?	Overall mean	Overall std. dev.	Runs with solution found	Max generations with solution found	Mean with solution found	Std. dev. with solution found
English	FALSE	390.558	735.8965	500	4217	390.558	735.8965
English	TRUE	320.214	636.702	500	4292	320.214	636.702
FPM	FALSE	398.308	784.6721	500	6540	398.308	784.6721
FPM	TRUE	392.908	775.428	500	5149	392.908	775.428
FPS	FALSE	741.678	2241.319	476	7083	274.9223	853.8189
FPS	TRUE	829.052	2352.382	475	9878	346.4232	1075.696
WMW	FALSE	870.5072	2451.356	459	9976	353.4248	1162.682
WMW	TRUE	831.382	2364.79	473	7513	308.0719	911.0545

find the solution before the generation limit in every case. However, the First-Price Single-Round auction without a wild card had the best average time to solution when a solution was found. This is significant because one of the goals of this study is to identify network configurations that are exploitative, even if they are so exploitative that they are sometimes unable to find the solution (Table 3.2).

For the $A = 3.3$, periodic set of problems, the English and First-Price Single-Round auctions were able to find the solution before the generation limit in every test. However, the other methods found the solution in all but one test, so these

Table 3.3 Performance comparison for $A = 3.3$.

Auction type	Wild card?	Overall mean	Overall std. dev.	Runs with solution found	Max generations with solution found	Mean with solution found	Std. dev. with solution found
English	FALSE	220.546	494.1636	500	4462	220.546	494.1636
English	TRUE	239.92	526.7293	500	3754	239.92	526.7293
FPM	FALSE	221.23	481.6861	500	4926	221.23	481.6861
FPM	TRUE	235.854	625.9165	499	3929	216.2886	448.0747
FPS	FALSE	237.144	482.6444	500	4374	237.144	482.6444
FPS	TRUE	259.892	558.1473	500	4155	259.892	558.1473
WMW	FALSE	307.918	797.7059	499	6295	288.497	669.8105
WMW	TRUE	301.212	677.7929	500	5646	301.212	677.7929

are roughly equivalent. Overall, the mean time to solution was again comparable across the board with all of the auction-based distribution mechanisms outperforming WMV, FPM with the Wild Card having the best result (Table 3.3).

For the $A = 3.35$ and $A = 3.4$, the set of problems was again periodic but exhibited more variability in the cone values. For this set, no combination tested found the solution before the generation limit for every test. It is also important to note that not all of the auction methods were able to outperform WMW. The A-values around 3.35 can be difficult for the system to solve because there is a point of divergence at 3.35. This can be seen clearly in the bifurcation graph shown previously in Figure 3.13. This added chaos makes it difficult for the system to find the signal corresponding to the solution. It is suggested that performance of auction methods relates to the nature of the auction, which works well when one knows what one is looking to obtain. However, these chaotic environments are equivalent to going to an auction without any idea of what you are looking to obtain. You may end up with something, but you may not (Table 3.4).

In the $A = 3.5$ result set, the system was unable to find the solution for every test, but when it did find the solution it did it faster than in any of the other complexities across the board. These results are similar to the results from previous work in auctions [6]. Even though $A = 3.5$ is on the more chaotic end of the scale, there is still enough order in the chaos for the system to find a solution with regularity. This is likely because 3.5 is far enough past the divergent chaos around 3.35, but far enough from where the system devolves into complete chaos after 3.99 (Table 3.5).

Table 3.4 Performance comparison for $A = 3.35$.

Auction type	Wild card?	Overall mean	Overall std. dev.	Runs with solution found	Max generations with solution found	Mean with solution found	Std. dev. with solution found
English	FALSE	699.41	1911.805	495	9608	605.4747	1675.656
English	TRUE	552.39	1665.684	495	7783	456.9697	1374.859
FPM	FALSE	425.038	1438.835	498	9892	386.5884	1306.997
FPM	TRUE	509.756	1610.942	496	8549	433.2298	1372.077
FPS	FALSE	671.834	1852.245	496	9543	596.6149	1658.273
FPS	TRUE	707.04	1923.436	494	9764	594.1822	1637.398
WMW	FALSE	748.85	2082.1	488	9757	521.3873	1510.54
WMW	TRUE	878.796	2219.271	490	9953	692.6694	1813.886

Table 3.5 Performance comparison for $A = 3.4$.

Auction type	Wild card?	Overall mean	Overall std. dev.	Runs with solution found	Max generations with solution found	Mean with solution found	Std. dev. with solution found
English	FALSE	874.572	2122.807	488	9933	650.2008	1586.014
English	TRUE	839.998	2137.437	485	9456	556.7299	1424.783
FPM	FALSE	788.822	1965.289	488	9253	562.3422	1347.565
FPM	TRUE	857.24	2039.032	488	8036	632.4426	1466.356
FPS	FALSE	790.108	1889.854	492	9568	640.3699	1491.826
FPS	TRUE	818.896	1987.971	491	9686	650.6253	1564.72
WMW	FALSE	926.252	2276.278	488	9449	703.1516	1797.485
WMW	TRUE	872.912	2151.799	486	9896	610.0206	1513.448

As expected, the auction-based system was able to find the solution with the least regularity on the most chaotic complexity. However, it was often quicker to converge to a solution than other knowledge distribution mechanisms, which is important to note because of the same exploitative reason as mentioned previously (Tables 3.6 and 3.7).

Table 3.6 Performance comparison for *A* = 3.5.

Auction type	Wild card?	Overall mean	Overall std. dev.	Runs with solution found	Max generations with solution found	Mean with solution found	Std. dev. with solution found
English	FALSE	328.232	1435.045	491	6753	150.9674	589.8383
English	TRUE	395.332	1654.563	487	4978	138.9713	527.1431
FPM	FALSE	308.998	1332.149	494	8661	191.3057	799.7413
FPM	TRUE	360.344	1522.661	491	8244	183.668	789.5625
FPS	FALSE	315.74	1460.104	491	9259	138.2485	645.9635
FPS	TRUE	358.39	1508.096	493	9252	221.5091	982.6503
WMW	FALSE	383.38	1611.18	490	9559	187.1429	848.2913
WMW	TRUE	422.3	1768.206	485	8360	126.1134	541.4723

Table 3.7 Performance comparison for *A* = 3.99.

Auction type	Wild card?	Overall mean	Overall std. dev.	Runs with solution found	Max generations with solution found	Mean with solution found	Std. dev. with solution found
English	FALSE	893.854	2342.664	475	9054	414.6358	1083.9
English	TRUE	919.216	2427.15	471	8521	360.1635	924.3749
FPM	FALSE	988.238	2485.376	474	9746	493.9768	1344.894
FPM	TRUE	875.854	2363.936	474	9397	375.4283	1034.07
FPS	FALSE	803.92	2124.815	481	9699	440.7069	1102.0902
FPS	TRUE	1086.24	2562.228	470	9421	517.3362	1256.714
WMW	FALSE	1072.71	2544.678	473	9725	563.1734	1423.9847
WMW	TRUE	1038.44	2566.038	471	9279	486.7304	1315.9156

Conclusions

Cultural Algorithms provide a metaheuristic framework for the application of various solution mechanism represented by Knowledge Sources in the Belief Space to the evolution of complex social networks in the population space. One of the key components in the configuration of a Cultural Algorithm is the knowledge distribution mechanism, and how the influence of a solution approach is spread out among individuals in individual subnetworks, subcultures. In this paper, a specific set of Knowledge distribution mechanisms based on various Auction models are introduced and their performance compared in complex real-valued functional landscapes. While capable of generating solutions to the entire range of problem complexities, from fixed to chaotic, they are best utilized for fixed problems containing low to high variability but begin to lose their edge with increasing periodicity.

It is proposed that auction mechanisms will be most likely found in subcultures where problems associated with that culture have reasonably strong signals that can afford the opportunity to make quick and precise decisions.

References

1 Kennedy, J. and Eberhart, R.C. (1995). Particle swarm optimization. In: *Proceeding of the IEEE International Conference on Neural Networks*, 12–13. Perth, Australia: IEEE Service Center.

2 Dorigo, M., Maniezzo, V., and Colorni, A. (1996). Ant system: optimization by a colony of cooperating agents. *IEEE Transactions on Systems, Man, and Cybernetics* 26 (1): 29–41.

3 Reynolds, R.G. (1978). On modeling the evolution of hunter-gatherer decision-making systems. *Geographical Analysis* 10 (1): 31–46.

4 Kohler, T., Gummerman, G., and Reynolds, R.G. (2005). Virtual archaeology. *Scientific American* 293 (1): 76–84.

5 Reynolds, R.G. and Ali, M.Z. (2008). Computing with the social fabric: the evolution of social intelligence within a cultural framework. *IEEE Computational Intelligence Magazine* 3 (1): 18–30.

6 Reynolds, R.G. and Kinnaird-Heether, L. (2013). Optimization problem solving with auctions in Cultural Algorithms. *Memetic Computing* 5 (2): 83–94.

7 Reynolds, R.G., Ali, M.Z., and Jayyousi, T. (2008). Mining the social fabric of archaic urban centers with cultural algorithms. *Computer* 41 (1): 64–72.

8 Reynolds, R.G., Gawasmeh, Y., and Salaymeh, A. (2015). The impact of subcultures in cultural algorithm problem solving. *2015 IEEE Symposium Series on Computational Intelligence,* Tainan, Taiwan, August 8–September 2, 2015.

9 Che, X., Ali, M.Z., and Reynolds, R.G. (2010). Robust evolution optimization at the edge of chaos: commercialization of cultural algorithms. *2010 IEEE Congress on Evolutionary Computation (CEC)*, pp. 1–8, Shanghai, China, November 10–12.

10 Krishna, V. (2002). *Auction Theory*. Academic Press.

11 Che, X. and Reynolds, R.G. (2014). A social metrics based process model on complex social system. *2014 IEEE Congress on Evolutionary Computation (CEC)*. Beijing, PR-China 6–11 July 2014.

12 Morrison, R. and De Jong, K. (1999). A test problem generator for nonstationary environments. *Proceedings of the 1999 Congress on Evolutionary Computation-CEC99*, pp. 2047–2053. Washington DC, 6–9 July 1999.

13 Reynolds, R.G. and Peng, B. (2005). Knowledge swarms: generating emergent social structure in dynamic environments. *Proceedings of the Agent 2005 Conference on Generative Social Processes, Models, and Mechanisms.*

14 Langton, C. (1992). Life at the edge of chaos. *Artificial Life II* 10: 41–91.

4

Using Common Value Auction in Cultural Algorithm to Enhance Robustness and Resilience of Social Knowledge Distribution Systems

Anas AL-Tirawi and Robert G. Reynolds

Computer Science Department, Wayne State University, Detroit, MI, USA
The Museum of Anthropological Archaeology, University of Michigan-Ann Arbor, Ann Arbor, MI, USA

Cultural Algorithms

Cultural systems provide a framework for human existence. One key observation that can be made is that certain cultures are more sustainable over time than others. Robustness and resilience are key factors behind the sustainability of cultural systems. These two factors are needed, so the system can handle a wide range of inputs/perturbations while maintaining its integrity, structure, and reducing the severity of the impact that these perturbations can have on a system. Robustness is the property of a complex system to withstand the impact of a dynamic change or perturbation in its environment. Like a boxer in the ring, robustness is the quality of a system to endure a series of blows but still continue to function at a certain level or above. Resilience on the other hand is the ability of the system to recover from a major change event such as a knockdown in a boxing match [1].

A cultural system will devote some of its resources to each of these two properties. If too many resources are devoted to robustness in the short term, it may impact its ability to be resilient in the long term and vice versa. So there needs to be a balance between the two in order for a system to be sustainable over the long term.

One key aspect of a Cultural System is how information can be distributed throughout its social networks to support both robustness and resilience. In this paper, the impact that various knowledge distribution mechanisms in a system will have on the systems' robustness and resilience will be assessed. These mechanisms

---

This work was supported by NSF grant #1744367.

include voting schemes, auctions, games, and pure random processes. They will be studied through the lens of a computational model of cultural evolution, Cultural Algorithms.

The Cultural Algorithm (CA) was introduced by Reynolds [2] as a computational model of Cultural Systems and their Evolution. It has been applied to many practical applications since then, one of which is modeling the origins of agriculture in the valley of Oaxaca, Mexico [3]. In addition, CAs have been applied to concept learning [4], decision trees [5], software testing [6], and other activities.

As shown in Figure 4.1, the CA is a knowledge-intensive evolutionary framework. First, the individuals in the population space are evaluated in terms of their performance in a problem space. Next, a subset of individuals is selected via the acceptance function and their performance is uploaded into the Belief Space, which is a network of Knowledge Source (KS). After updating the Belief Space network, the KSs can direct the next generation of individuals in the population space via the influence function. The knowledge sources (KS) utilize a variety of distribution mechanisms to circulate their influences among the individual agents in the population space.

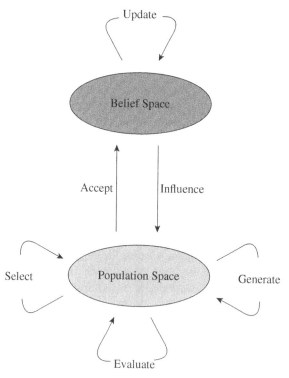

Figure 4.1 Cultural Algorithm framework [2]. *Source:* Reproduced with permission of China heritage.

Previous mechanisms have been utilized by CAs to distribute the influence of the KS over the individuals in the population space. Figure 4.2 shows the different knowledge distribution mechanisms. It is important to note that the amount of information that a distribution algorithm knows about a problem solution, the fidelity, increases from left to right [7].

The first mechanism was called the Marginal Value Approach by Peng [8]. Every individual was controlled or directed by one KS in each generation. Peng in her approach [8] integrated the five KSs in the belief space into a single influence function as shown in Figure 4.3. Peng used a random process based on their relative performance to select a KS to influence an individual. A KS roulette wheel, with proportional areas, based on relative performance, allows for an informed random selection process. However, Peng did not account for the influence among neighbors of a social network.

Next, Ali and Reynolds [10, 11] developed a majority win approach. In their approach, the influence of the neighbors is considered when selecting a KS. The social fabric is the connection between the individuals in a population. A conflict resolution process allows individuals to select the KS by which they are influenced, if their neighbors are influenced by one or more different ones. First, each

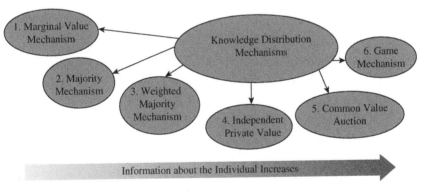

Figure 4.2 The big picture for all Knowledge Distribution Mechanisms that utilize the CA.

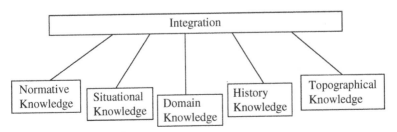

Figure 4.3 Integration of multiple KSs [9]. *Source:* Reproduced with permission of John Wiley.

individual was assigned a direct influence based on the relative performance of the KSs using a roulette wheel as suggested above by Peng. Next, Ali used a conflict resolution strategy based on majority win to calculate the controlling knowledge source for each individual. They summed up the direct influence of the adjacent individuals in the social fabric and those of its current neighborhood. After that, the KS with the majority of the votes won the influence over this individual in that generation of the system.

Another approach is the Weighted Majority Win proposed by Che et al. [7]. Che used the average fitness of each KS to determine how much weight this KS deserves in the vote. The key to determining the weight for each KS is the average fitness value of the individuals that have recently been influenced by the knowledge source in the population. Figure 4.4 gives an example of the weighted voting process. The individual, A0, has information about five competing KSs. They are represented in the figure as follows: S: Situational, D: Domain, H: History, T: Topographical, N: Normative. A0 represents the individual. The number of votes for each KS is given as x. For Situational it is $x3$, or 3 individuals have it as a direct influence. The weight along each arc is the normalized relative performance for each KS.

In Figure 4.4, the winning KS is the Domain KS, even though it does not have the most votes (votes $= 2$). However, (D) does have the greater weight, which is the key factor in the weighted-majority win approach. Che has used many network topologies in his system including LBest, Square, Hexagon, Octagon, Hex-decagon, and Gbest. In addition to that, he has also tested his system on different problem complexity levels [12]. As a result, Che concluded that when the

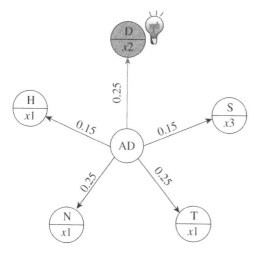

Figure 4.4 Weighted Majority win in belief space through the social network [7]. *Source:* Reproduced with permission of bice.

performance function is of higher fidelity, the weighted approach can spread new information faster through a population than the majority win approach.

When the signal strength of information about the problem becomes even stronger, the auction approach can be effectively employed to find a solution. Kinnaird-Heether and Reynolds [13, 14] embedded auction mechanisms into a CA. The new version was called CAT3. In CAT3, the production of the bidding tokens is the starting point. The process starts by producing bidding tokens and uses them to form bidding wheels for each KS. These tokens are generated by listing all of the individuals who were recently influenced by a KS over a given previous time window, t. The individual's fitness values are the bidding tokens and are normalized so that each previous result takes up a relative proportion of the token bidding wheel. The bid of a KS corresponds to the performance associated with the result of spinning the bidding wheel. Since the KSs do not have specific common knowledge about the location of the individual in the population network, the process must be stochastic based on past performances.

As with the previous mechanisms, the process for a generation starts with the assignment of a knowledge source to each individual as their direct influence. The next step is the selection of the bidders, those KSs who will be participating in the auction, from the KSs list. The KSs compete to influence each individual (x). The algorithm currently only allows the immediate adjacent neighbors of the individual (x) to participate in the auction. The actual auction takes place as shown in Figure 4.5, where the system requests the selected bidders to submit

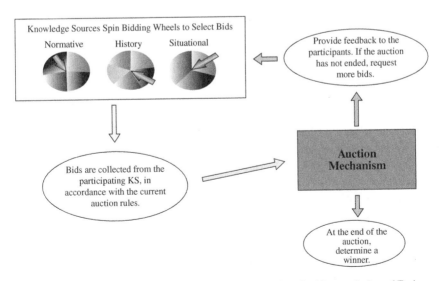

Figure 4.5 Conducting the Auction [13]. *Source:* Reproduced with permission of Taylor and Francis.

their bidding values. Each selected KS will spin its correspondent wheel to get the bidding value. Finally, the auction system will determine the winner and assign the winner KS to influence individual (x). It may take several iterations to do so as shown in Figure 4.5.

In the auction mechanisms above, the bidders did not know anything about the properties of the individuals on which they were making bids. Those properties can be the following: the location in the network; the number of immediate neighbors and the strength of their connections; what knowledge sources have influenced it in the past, among others. In the next section, an approach, the Common Value Auction, is discussed. This approach provides a common set of parameters that are available to all bidders. These parameters can be used to condition the bids made by the participants.

Common Value Auction

The new mechanism, Common Value Auction Toolkit (CAT4) is an extension of CAT3. CAT4 propagates the influence using the Common Value knowledge. The Common Value knowledge is a set of parameters that every KS can know about the individuals in the social network. These include the individual's location in the network and the KS(s) that influenced the individual in the past previous approaches.

The first step is to build the KSs' wheel (one wheel for all KSs) by normalizing the KS average score, where every KS will have a wheel's share that reflects its average (score). Each KS will have a portion of the wheel that reflects the average performance of those individuals who have been influenced by the correspondent KS. Next, the algorithm assigns a direct influencer KS randomly using the roulette wheel approach discussed previously to each individual in the population. This step is the same as that for all other mechanisms discussed so far.

In the second step, each KS constructs a bidding strategy wheel that will be used later to determine their bidding decision on a specific individual. This is done by selecting a subset of recent individual performances directed by that KS over a given past time window. A wheel is constructed such that each score comprises an area that is proportional to its contribution to the total score of the subset for the KS. In addition, a set of rules is selected to determine whether the KS will bid on an individual based on common value knowledge about the location of the individual in the social fabric.

Next, the direct influence for each individual in the population is compared against those of its neighbors, here just the directly adjacent neighbors are used.

If the direct influence of an individual agrees with those of all of its neighbors, its direct influence is then chosen to guide it during that generation. Otherwise, an auction is conducted between those KSs who directly influence that individual and its neighbors.

To do this, the bidding strategy for each of the competing KSs is checked to see if it will bid on that individual based on the common value information. The rule set associated with the KS is checked to see if taken together they support a bid on the current individual. This "expert system" can technically be composed of many rules. For the experiments here, the same rules are used for all KSs. To do so, the following distributing mechanism based on just one subset of common values, the extent to which the individual and its neighbors have been influenced by the KS in past is used:

If KS[j] = has influenced individual (i) in the past m generations or
If KS[j] = is influencing currently the neighbors of individual (i)

Then increase the bidding value by a bonus as shown in the equation below:

$$\text{Bidding value} = \text{KSs' bidding value} + 0.5 \text{ (boost)} \tag{4.1}$$

This is where the Common Value information is used to determine the winner. We simply give an incentive for the KS that influenced the individual in the past and for those KSs that were able to influence the individual's neighbors.

In the fourth step, the influencers that satisfy their bidding rules are then chosen to participate in the auction. The bidding wheel is spun for each to determine their bid. In the experiments conducted here, each KS had a bidding wheel composed of a single average value for the performance of the selected subset to simplify computations at this stage.

In the fifth step, the bidding strategy rules that are satisfied for a KS are then applied to the bid as shown in the rule above to give a final bid for that KS. The bids are then compared with each other and the winner is selected to control the individual for that generation. If there are no bidders, then the direct influencer of the individual is retained. This redistribution process is then repeated for all individuals in the network.

Figure 4.6 presents the big picture of the mechanism. First, the KS roulette wheel is spun to generate the direct influencer for each individual. If one or more of the individual's neighbors possess a different KS, then each decides whether it wishes to bid for that individual using the common value information about the individual. The selection process is governed by a rule-based expert system associated with each KS. The selected KSs then participate in the bidding for the auction as described above.

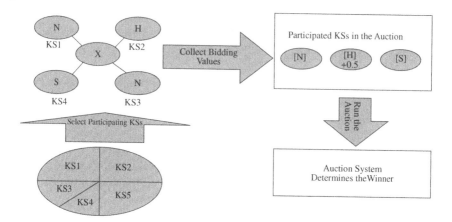

Figure 4.6 Big picture of CAT4 Algorithms.

ConesWorld

To analyze the results and test the performance on the different levels of complexity, a robust problem generator (ConesWorld) was used in both CAT2 and CAT4. The ConesWorld framework was inspired by the work of Morrison and De Jong [15]. This tool has the ability to generate dynamic problem environments over various landscape complexities. A given ConesWorld configuration can be described as follows:

$$f\left(\left\langle x_1, x_2, \ldots, x_n \right\rangle\right) = \max_{j=1,k} \left(H_j - R_j \cdot \sqrt{\sum_{i=1}^{n} \left(x_i - C_{j,i}\right)^2} \right) \qquad (4.2)$$

where K: the number of the cones. H_j: the cone height, R_j: the cone slope, N: the dimensionality, $C_{j,i}$: coordinate of the cone j in dimension i. The values for the cone height, slope, and coordinates can be assigned randomly through the problem generator or logistic function. However, the values would be selected from the ranges below:

$$H_j \in \left(H_{\text{base}}, H_{\text{base}} + H_{\text{range}}\right); \ R_j \in \left(R_{\text{base}}, R_{\text{base}} + R_{\text{range}}\right); \text{ and } C_{j,i} \in \left(-1, 1\right).$$

The Max function here is used to handle the combination of the cones when they overlap. For example, if two cones overlap, the Max function will choose the height of the combined cone to be the height of the highest cone for the two overlapped cones. Figure 4.7 shows what the landscape looks like with the following parameters: $k = 15$, $H_{\text{base}} = 1$, $H_{\text{range}} = 9$, $R_{\text{base}} = 8$, and $R_{\text{range}} = 12$. To determine

3D plot

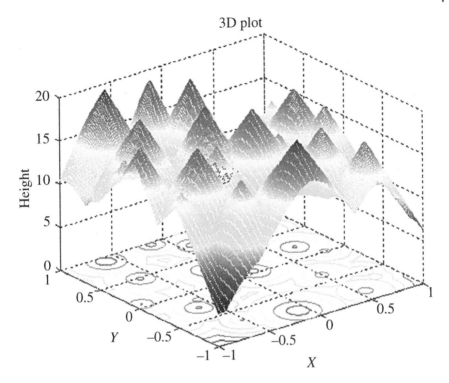

Figure 4.7 An Example Landscape in two-dimensional space (n = 2) bound by $x \in (-1.0, 1.0), y \in (-1.0, 1.0)$ with k = 15, $H \in (1, 20)$, and $R \in (8, 20)$ [8]. *Source:* Reproduced with permission of Nature.

the dynamic changes of the system, Morrison and De Jong used the logistics function below:

$$Y_i = A * Y_i - 1 * \left(1 - Y_i - 1\right) \tag{4.3}$$

A = constant value, Y_i = is value of Y at iteration i.

As the value of A increases, the system generates more complicated behavior. Figure 4.8 shows how Y will change as a result of A for a sequence of landscapes. The x-axis gives the number of generations, the z axis gives the A value, and the Y axis gives the Y-value produced over the given generations for a specific A. The lighter the gray scale for the Y trajectory, the higher the A value that generated it. The grey scale code is in the legend on the right side of the graph. Low values of A produce gradual linear changes, while high values produce wildly oscillating values for Y. In the next section, we discuss the experimental framework of CAT4. Also, we explain how the dynamic environment can affect the learning curve of the whole system and consequently the produced results.

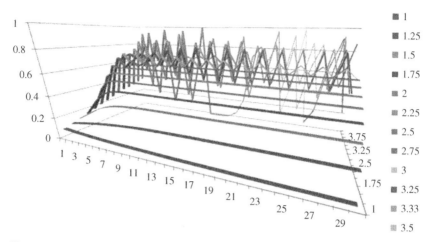

Figure 4.8 The value for Y (on the Y-axis as a function of A (z axis) over the number of generations, x axis. The grey scale code for the A-values is in the legend on the right. The lighter the code the higher the A value..

Dynamic Experimental Framework

In these experiments, the performance of the Common Value Auction was compared with the Weighted Majority algorithm for three complexity levels of $A = \{1.01, 3.35, \text{and } 3.99\}$. These three A-values were selected because they represented a wide spectrum of complexities over which to test CAT4 against. The full list of experimental framework parameters are summarized in Table 4.1. The types of social fabrics are explained here [16].

The key hypothesis to be tested here is whether the Common Value Auction mechanism is able to produce a more sustainable cultural system than the weighted majority voting mechanism. The extent to which this is accomplished will be observed in terms of the two system's relative robustness and resilience over the course of 40,000 generation for each of the 300 runs over the 3 complexity classes.

Robustness will be assessed in terms of the ability of the system to bounce back after each of the 50 landscape shifts for a given run. The standard deviation over the set of 300 runs will provide an indicator of the need for each system to bounce back from a landscape change. Resilience on the other hand will be observed in terms of the extent to which the systems are able to adapt to these landscape shifts by reducing the time needed to achieve the optimum in the next landscape. The systems will then be compared in terms of how the complexity of the environment impacts their relative sustainability as the environmental complexity shifts from static, then to cyclic, and finally to chaotic.

Table 4.1 Experimental framework parameters.

Parameter name	Value
Complexity class	1.01, 3.35, and 3.99
Number of runs per complexity	300
Number of landscapes	50
Maximum number of generation per landscape	800
Number of cones	100
Number of agents	50
Social fabrics	{LBest, Square, Hexagon, Octagon, Sixteengon, Global}
Max fitness value	20
Precision of solution	0.001

Results

The main difference between the two algorithms is that CAT4 uses information about the individuals before the auction starts. The CAT4 algorithm is an informative algorithm that provides crucial information for the bidders about past behavior of the individuals in the population space. This information is used to trigger bidding strategies for each of the knowledge sources. While many different factors can be used to affect bidding strategies, the focus here will be in just a single set of factors, the KS previously used to influence an individual and its neighbors. The goal will be to show that the addition of just this new information can make a substantial difference in the performance of the cultural system.

The first dynamic landscape to be assessed was that produced by $A = 1.0$. As seen in the previous section, that landscape involves a series of small linear shifts in the locations of the cones. Figure 4.9 gives the standard deviation of the two systems over all three environments. For the linear dynamic landscape, both systems took around 85 generations to rebound from a landscape change. So their relative level of robustness is about the same for this environment.

The relative resilience of each of the two systems in the linear landscape is illustrated in Figures 4.10 and 4.11. Both systems are able to significantly reduce the number of generations needed to find the new optimum over time. The CAT4 system was able to produce a correlation of (0.662) between the number of generations needed to solve the changed landscape and landscape number. The corresponding coefficient of determination, the percentage of the total variance,

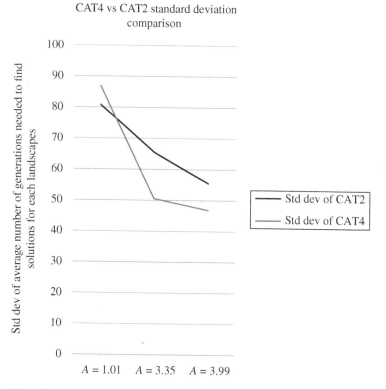

Figure 4.9 CAT4 versus CAT2 standard deviation comparison.

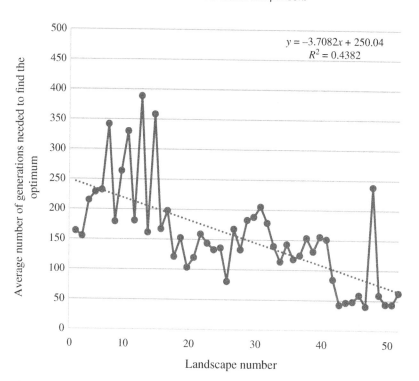

Figure 4.10 CAT4 Regression line over 50 runs for complexity, $A = 1.0$.

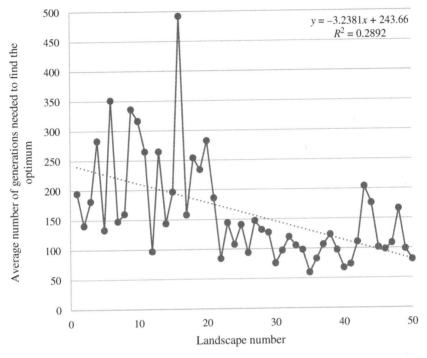

Figure 4.11 CAT2 Regression line over 50 runs for complexity, A = 1.0.

explained by the correlation is (0.43). CAT2 exhibited a coefficient of determination of (0.289). As shown in Table 4.2, the correlations were significantly different from each other at the (0.05) level of significance. So CAT4 was able to do a better job of adapting to the changing linear environment than CAT2.

While CAT4 exhibited a significant level of learning within an environment with linear dynamics, the next question is how it would adapt to an environment in which the changes were nonlinear from landscape to landscape. A nonlinear shift in cone location was produced by the landscape generated for A = 3.35 as shown in Figure 4.8. The relative change in robustness produced by the shift to a nonlinear dynamic for the two systems is given in Figure 4.11. CAT4 exhibited an approximately 15 generation improvement in terms of its response to a perturbation compared to CAT2. That is a significant difference in its ability to rebound from a perturbation in this environment. On the one hand, a nonlinear environment required CAT4 to respond more robustly than before. On the other hand, CAT4 improved on its ability to adjust to the change in landscapes as reflected in an improved correlation coefficient (0.73) and coefficient of determination (54%) as shown in Figures 4.12 and 4.13. The Weighted Majority system

Table 4.2 Comparing CAT4 and CAT2 regression through different A-value complexities.

	A-value	R	CAT4(R2)	CAT2(R2)	Significant F change
Static	1.01	0.662	0.438	0.289	0.000
Periodic	3.35	0.736	0.541	0.170	0.000
Chaotic	3.99	0.384	0.147	0.212	0.006

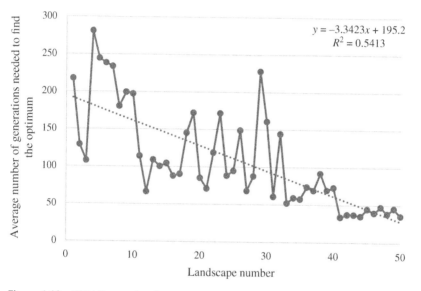

$$y = -3.3423x + 195.2$$
$$R^2 = 0.5413$$

Figure 4.12 CAT4 Regression line over 50 runs for complexity, $A = 3.35$.

exhibited a much lower overall coefficient of determination (0.17). Again, the two systems exhibited a significant difference in adaptability over time, but now in a nonlinear environment as shown in Table 4.2.

Overall when the environment switched from a linear to a non-linear one, the CAT4 mechanism produced a distinctly more robust and resilient behavior than CAT2. The next question is how the two systems would adapt to an extremely "chaotic" environment that was characterized by the superposition of numerous nonlinear patterns of behavior? Since the generating process was deterministic in nature, all of the information needed to provide a perfect prediction of the environment's dynamics is there, it is just a matter of extracting all of the intertwined threads.

As demonstrated in Figures 4.14 and 4.15, the resilience of the CAT4 system is still significantly greater than that for CAT2. In terms of robustness, the difference in the number of additional generations needed to respond to a perturbation is now 10. That is down from 15 before, but still a significant difference in system robustness.

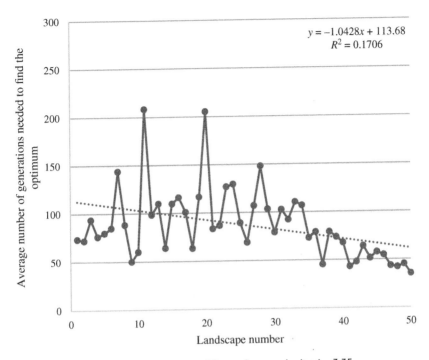

Figure 4.13   CAT2 Regression line over 50 runs for complexity, A = 3.35.

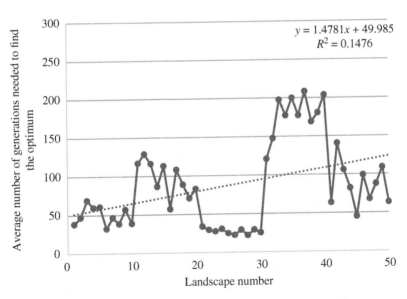

Figure 4.14   CAT4 Regression line over 50 runs for complexity, A = 3.99.

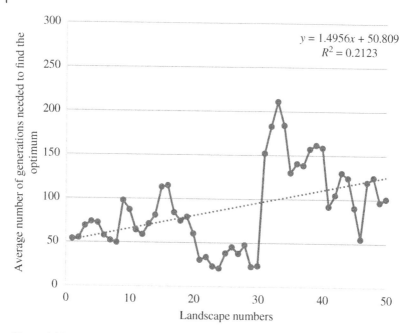

Figure 4.15 CAT2 Regression line over 50 runs for complexity, $A = 3.99$.

In such a chaotic environment, learning is less of an issue than survivability. As shown in Table 4.2, the two systems now exhibit a much lower level of resilience. The coefficient of determination for CAT2 is now significantly greater than that for CAT4, but notice that the relation between the number of generations needed to solve the problem is now increasing with increased landscape number. The rate of increase is now higher for CAT2 than CAT4 which means that its performance is more susceptible to degradation in this environment. While both system's behavior is now clearly nonlinear, the regression line provides a general indicator of the additional stress that is placed on each system over time.

In the first two environments, the systems were not only able to survive the perturbations but adapt to them. This produced a strong sense of sustainability. Of the two, CAT4 was more able to exploit the nonlinear environment. In the chaotic environment, the theme was less on adaptability but survivability over time. Both systems displayed symptoms of stress over time.

However, CAT4 contained only a small sample of knowledge about the social fabric within which the agents were embedded. How would its behavior be affected by the addition of new information? What new information would be most effective in terms of guiding its performance, especially as the environments grow more chaotic over time?

Conclusions and Future Work

In society, there are many ways to collect and distribute problem-solving knowledge. Such mechanisms include games, auctions, and various voting mechanisms. Previous work has focused on Independent value auctions. KSs did not have knowledge about the individuals on who they were bidding and did not have consistent bidding strategies. In this paper, Common Value Auctions were presented. This framework provided common knowledge to all KSs about each individual and supported rule-based systems that were used by those individual KS bidding strategies.

The experimental results suggest that adding the common value auction to the CAs can enhance the robustness and the resilience of the algorithm relative to the commonly used Weighted Majority vote distribution mechanism. The differences in resilience were significant across a wide range of dynamic environments tested, from linear to chaotic. The results effectively demonstrate the impact that knowledge about social networks can have on the sustainability of a Cultural system.

However, it was clear that as the environment of the Cultural Algorithm became increasingly chaotic, there was a shift from the need to sustain the culture through adaptations to that of survival. The presence of additional knowledge in CAT helped in that regard. The question remains what type of information about social networks will be particularly useful in guiding complex social systems into even more complex global environments. That is the focus of future work.

References

1 Husdal, J. (2004). *Robustness and flexibility as option to reduce uncertainty and risk.* Molde, Norway: Molde University College.

2 Reynolds, R.G. (1979). *An Adaptive Computer Model of the Evolution of Agriculture.* Ann arbor, PhD Thesis. MI: University of Michigan.

3 Jayyousi, T.W. (2012). Bringing to life an ancient urban center at Monte Albán, Mexico: exploiting the synergy between the micro, meso, and macro levels in a complex system. PhD Thesis. Wayne State University, Detroit, MI.

4 Sverdlik, W., Reynolds, R.G., and Zannoni, E. (1992). HYBAL: a self-tuning algorithm for concept learning in highly autonomous systems. *Proceedings of the Third Annual Conference of AI, Simulation, and Planning in High Autonomy Systems "Integrating Perception, Planning and Action"*, Perth, Australia, pp. 15–22.

5 Al-Shehri, H.A. (1997). Evolution-based decision tree optimization using cultural algorithms. PhD Thesis. Wayne State University, Detroit, MI.

6 Reynolds, R.G. and Ostrowski, D. (1999). Knowledge-based software testing agent using evolutionary learning with cultural algorithms. *Proceedings of the IEEE Congress on Evolutionary Computation*, Washington, DC, USA (6–9 July 1999).

7 Che, X., Ali, M.Z., and Reynolds, R.G. (2010). Robust evolution optimization at the edge of chaos: commercialization of culture algorithms. *IEEE Congress on Evolutionary Computation*, Spain.

8 Reynolds, R.G., Peng, B., and Che, X. (2005). Knowledge swarms generating emergent social structure in dynamic environments. *Proceedings of the Agent Conference on Generative Social Processes, Models, and Mechanims*, Chicago, Illinois, USA (13–15 October 2005).

9 Peng, B. (2005). Knowledge swarms in cultural algorithms for dynamic environments. PhD Thesis. Wayne State University, Detroit, MI.

10 Reynolds, R.G. and Ali, M. (2008). Embedding a social fabric component into cultural algorithms toolkit for an enhanced knowledge-driven engineering optimization. *International Journal of Intelligent Computing and Cybernetics (IJICC)* 1 (4): 356–378.

11 Reynolds, R.G. and Ali, M. (2009). The social fabric approach as an approach to knowledge integration in Cultural Algorithms. *IEEE Congress on Evolutionary Computation*, Hong Kong, China (1–6 June 2008).

12 Che, X., Ali, M.Z., and Reynolds, R.G. (2010). Weaving the social fabric: the past, present, and future of optimization problem solving with cultural algorithms. *AAAI Fall Symposium: Complex Adaptive Systems*, Arlington, Virginia, USA (11–13 November 2010).

13 Reynolds, R.G. and Kinnaird-Heether, L. (2013). Optimization problem solving with auctions in Cultural Algorithms. *Memetic Computing* 5: 83–94.

14 Reynolds, R.G. and Kinnaird-Heether, L. (2017). Problem solving using social networks in Cultural Algorithms with auctions. *IEEE Congress on Evolutionary Computation*, Donostia, San Sebastián, Spain (5–8 June 2017).

15 Morrison, R. and DeJong, K. (1999). A test problem generator for nonstationary environments. In: *Evolutionary Computation*, 25–31. Washington, DC.

16 Gawasmeh, Y.A. and Reynolds, R. (2014). A computational basis for the presence of sub-cultures in cultural algoithms. *IEEE Symposium on Swarm Intelligence*, Orlando, FL, USA (9–12 December 2014).

5

Optimizing AI Pipelines

A Game-Theoretic Cultural Algorithms Approach

Faisal Waris and Robert G. Reynolds

Computer Science Department, Wayne State University, Detroit, MI, USA
The Museum of Anthropological Archaeology, University of Michigan-Ann Arbor, Ann Arbor, MI, USA

Introduction

The general trend in the auto industry is the shift of investment and R&D from Original Equipment Manufacturers (OEMs) to suppliers [1]. From being highly vertically integrated, the major automotive OEMs have divested significantly; GM and Ford created Delphi and Visteon, respectively, by divesting of their parts businesses. In part, the reason that Tesla could enter a seemingly capital-intensive industry with relative ease was because it could rely on the existing automotive supplier base for noncore components. Today, OEMs need to collaborate intensively with suppliers to develop new designs and technologies. The challenge for OEMs is the seamless integration of supplied components in the design and manufacture of vehicles.

The integration challenge will increase substantially as suppliers shift from the production of relatively "dumb" parts to "intelligent" subsystems – composed of hardware and complex software – in support of highly automated driving capabilities. All major automotive suppliers (Continental, Delphi, Magna, Bosch, etc.) have automated driving programs in advanced stages of development. It would be in the interest of suppliers to design intelligent subsystems that are highly configurable and tunable. This will facilitate broader applicability and reuse across different OEMs so as to maximize the suppliers' return on their investments.

This work was supported by NSF grant #1744367.

The extraction of optimal system-level performance from the integration of intelligent and highly tunable subsystems in an efficient manner is a major challenge for the industry. Currently, it is a labor-intensive process replete with trial and error and may take months or years to complete manually. The goal of this paper is to explore an approach to reducing parts of this effort through the use of a knowledge intensive, evolutionary optimization framework – Cultural Algorithms (CA) enhanced with a game-theoretic Knowledge Distribution (KD) mechanism.

The CA was designed to solve problems posed within Complex Systems. Complex systems can be described at various levels of detail where problems posed at one level may require the solution of problems posed at other levels. Thus, it can support multilevel problem solving within a complex system guided by the knowledge needed to solve problems at each level. This can be accomplished since the CA employs a knowledge-intensive component called the Belief Space that collects and disseminates varied types of knowledge from/to the networked population of problem-solving agents.

A variety of knowledge distribution mechanisms have been employed to distribute information among agents in the social network including voting schemes and auctions. However, these mechanisms are all inherently competitive in nature. In the pipeline problem, each component needs to make adjustments relative to its performance but also take into account the demands of those components that precede and succeed it in the pipeline. The key is how information can be distributed throughout the network to achieve the system's goals. Here we suggest an approach whereby knowledge is distributed through the social network based on a game-theoretic framework. This mechanism can support both competition and cooperation among knowledge sources.

The outline of this paper is as follows. First, a brief overview of Cultural Algorithms is provided in section "Overview of Cultural Algorithms". The nature of the various knowledge distribution schemes previously used with Cultural Algorithms are then given in section "CA Knowledge Distribution Mechanisms". Section "Primer on Game Theory" briefly introduces the game-theoretic concepts necessary to understand the approach taken here. Section "Game-Theoretic Knowledge Distribution" describes the game-theoretic approach in general, while section "Continuous-Action Iterated Prisoner's Dilemma" provides comprehensive detail of the game-theoretic implementation presented here, CATGAME.

The performance of this new mechanism is first compared against the Weighted Majority Win (WTD) voting mechanism using the Cultural Algorithm Toolkit (CAT) test bed in section "Test Results: Benchmark Problem". Its performance suggests it has statistically significant performance advantages over purely competitive approaches. It is then applied to configure a real-world, computer-vision-based AI pipeline that supports autonomous driving in section "Test Results: Computer Vision Pipeline". The preliminary results suggest that a game-theoretic approach is better at combining the workflow stages of the pipeline so as to improve driving behavior than the traditional competition-based approach. Section "Conclusions" provides our conclusions and directions for future work.

Overview of Cultural Algorithms

Cultural Algorithms, developed by Reynolds [2], is a class of evolutionary computing algorithm, inspired by models of human cultural evolution. CA supports socially motivated learning from networked individuals using a collection of heuristics or Knowledge Sources (KS). As such, it is a hyperheuristic approach that supports the application of different metaheuristics (Knowledge Sources) to the problem-solving activities of individuals in a networked population. It has been applied in a diverse set of domains, e.g. numerical optimization [3], archeology [4], biology [5], and gesture recognition [6] to name a few. As with Ant Colony Optimization [7] (ACO) and Particle Swarm Optimization [8] (PSO), the CA approach employs a socially interacting population of agents.

The CA has two major components, the Population Space and the Belief Space. They are linked by the **Acceptance**, **Update**, and **Influence** functions, as depicted in the architecture diagram in Figure 5.1. Taken together, these three functions constitute the Communication Protocol. Here we view each individual agent in the population as a list of parameters whose values represent a point in the problem hyperspace. The parameters are the encoding of the underlying optimization problem being solved. The **Accept** function selects a variety of agent behaviors for induction into the Belief Space from the Population Space. That information is used to **Update** the network of Knowledge Sources housed there.

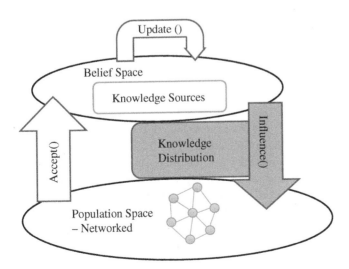

Figure 5.1 Cultural Algorithm framework.

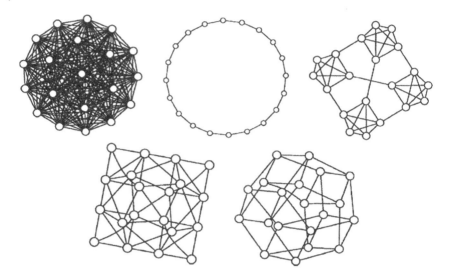

Figure 5.2   Population network topologies.

Knowledge from the Belief Space is then used to **Influence** the next generation, facilitated by the social network structure, the *social fabric* of the population. Some example topologies taken from the Particle Swarm literature are given in Figure 5.2. The **Influence** function first associates KSs in the belief space with individual agents, and this is called the **direct influence**. Then, the agents interact with each other in the social network via the knowledge distribution mechanism. The process is discussed in the next section.

CA Knowledge Distribution Mechanisms

A major component of the **Influence** function is Knowledge Distribution (KD), the mechanism for distributing knowledge or heuristics throughout the networked population [9–11].

The CA framework defines different categories of knowledge, such as Situational, History, Domain, Topographical, and Normative, each of which can be viewed as metaheuristics to guide the problem-solving process. These are referred to as Knowledge Sources (KS). The KD mechanism is the *strategy* for associating KS to the networked population individuals across successive generations. In turn, the KS guide or move the associated individuals in the problem hyperspace, at each generation.

It should be mentioned that KS usage is selective and new types can be integrated if required by the problem domain. Colon [12], for example, augmented CA with a "Contextual" rule-based knowledge representation to determine optimal plans for pediatric nursing care. The reader is referred to other CA papers for the detailed explanation of the commonly used Knowledge Source metaheuristic types [10, 11, 13–15], except for Topographical knowledge. Topographical knowledge in this implementation of the CA framework is inspired by the Brainstorming Optimization (BSO) [16] method and uses k-means clustering instead of decision trees to maintain knowledge of promising regions of the search landscape. (Topographical knowledge maintains information about the promising regions in the search landscape and moves individuals under its Influence toward these regions.)

Figure 5.3 displays the various distribution mechanisms relative to the strength of the environmental signal available in the optimization problem at hand. The left end corresponds to a completely noisy signal. As one moves to the right, the performance signal strength gets increased and noise is reduced. Majority win is a good strategy when there is a signal but some background noise. The voting process filters much of the noise out. As the signal gets stronger, particular knowledge sources may be better at tracking the signal and therefore can begin to carry more weight. Once the signal is strong enough that it is visible to most of them, an auction or bidding mechanism becomes useful to identify the individuals most attracted to the signal. When the signal takes a more precise value, the fixed price solution is possible. Now the agents have a precise set of moves, so they can decide to pay the price or not. At the far right, agents can make specific moves to support cooperation and competition or both.

Only the Weighted Majority Win KD is described here in some detail. It is the most commonly used KD and therefore serves as the benchmark for comparison against the proposed – game-theoretic – approach. The reader is referred to cited literature for details on other mechanisms. Figure 5.4 is a schematic representation of the WTD process at times t and $t+1$. The individual at the center is connected to its neighbors via the social network. Each neighbor is associated with a Knowledge Source represented by letter (H = History, S = Situational, etc.). The relative size of each neighbor's circle represents the relative fitness of their controlling KS in the population. At $t+1$, the center individual is assigned a KS that has the highest weighted sum among its neighbors plus a randomly selected – in proportion to population KS fitness – "direct" influence for the center individual.

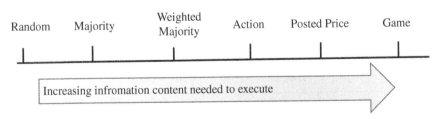

Figure 5.3 Spectrum of Knowledge Distribution mechanisms.

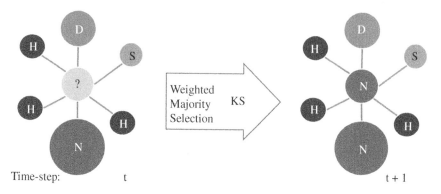

Time-step: t   t + 1

Figure 5.4 Weighted Majority (WTD) Knowledge Distribution.

Primer on Game Theory

Game theory is a well-studied discipline, which is both broad and deep. Any discourse on game theory is beyond the scope of this paper, but the curious reader is pointed to the comprehensive online book by Shoham et al. [17]. This section describes some relevant terms and ideas – just enough to support the approach presented here.

A game can be represented in what is known as "normal" form as a three tuple:

$$\Phi = \left(N, A, u\right),$$

where

- N = set of actors (players),
- A = set of actions available to actors – usually discrete choices but may be continuous [18], and
- u = set of utility functions ($u_1, u_2, ..., u_n$) for each player.
  Often two-player games are represented in matrix form. An example of a payoff matrix for the well-studied, Prisoner's Dilemma game is presented below, where
- $N = \{1, 2\}$,
- $A = \{$Cooperate, Defect$\}$, and
- u = Utilities.

	Player 2: Cooperate	Player 2: Defect
Player 1: Cooperate	1, 1	−1, 2
Player 1: Defect	2, −1	0, 0

Each player is expected to maximize its own utility and thus will take actions accordingly, given the available payoff information. In the Prisoners Dilemma game, rational players are expected to Defect [19]. Note that the available actions may be discrete (e.g. Cooperate/Defect) or continuous (e.g. the degree of cooperation). Also, a game may be played repeatedly leading to very different dynamics. In *Iterated* Prisoner's Dilemma, players can adopt a tit-for-tat strategy leading to higher cooperation, and thus utility for all players.

An important point to note here is that much of game theory is concerned with finding a solution to a posed game as strategies (mix of actions) adopted by the players. Assuming rational players, the action played by an agent should be the best response to the best responses of its peers, determined jointly, i.e. the Nash equilibrium [20]. For many games, finding a solution is a computationally hard problem especially for more than two players. In the proposed framework, each agent is participating in many games concurrently with usually more than two players per game. To clarify, each agent is playing a game against its neighbors which are in turn playing different games with their neighbors. The result is a set of interlinked games. There are no known (computationally tractable) analytical methods for solving such a complex set of interlinked games. To address this situation, we take the view that each agent unilaterally decides to take action based on its and its neighbors' current and prior states, without regard to the actions taken by other agents. We are interested in the emergent properties of the system given bounded rationality decisions of the agents. The system is coaxed into evolving toward a dynamic equilibrium over time through the mechanisms employed.

Game-Theoretic Knowledge Distribution

The minimal terminology given in the previous section is leveraged now to describe the *abstract* structure of the game-theoretic KD mechanism. This mechanism is structured in terms of the following components: *Actor*, *Play*, *Action*, *Payoff*, *Payout*, and *Outcome*.

Actor	**Population individual, linked to other players via network (terms individual, agent, player, and actor are used interchangeably).**
Play function	A function that produces the **Action** or "hand" that a player plays against its neighbors. This function may utilize the current and historic states of all players in addition to other available environmental information.
Payoff function	A function that produces the **Payout** structure – which represents the utility to a player – given its own **Action** and those of its neighbors in the game.
Outcome function	Given the population's collective **Actions** and **Payouts**, this function produces the updated population where each individual is assigned one *primary* and possibly many *secondary* KSs at varying levels of strengths.

```
game = {Play, Payoff, Outcome}

GameKD (Pop, Network, game)
  Actions <- Empty
  Payouts <- Empty

  FOR p in Pop DO                          "play games, collect Actions"
    neighbors <- Network(p)
    Actions[p] <- game.Play (p, neighbors)
  END FOR

  FOR p in Pop DO                          "determine Payouts"
    neighbors □ Network(p)
    pAction <- Actions[p]
    neighborActions □ [FOR j in ns □ Actions[j]]
    Payouts[p] <- game.Payoff(p, pAction, neighborActions)
  END FOR
                                           "distribute knowledge"
  Pop <- game.Outcome(Pop, Payouts, Actions)
  Return Pop
```

Figure 5.5   Pseudocode for a general game mechanism for Knowledge Distribution.

The pseudocode for the game KD mechanism is shown in Figure 5.5. The mechanism is general or abstract and can work with a variety of game types. For this mechanism to work, a *concrete* game must be provided with implementations of Play, Payoff, and Outcome functions as described above. In terms of solving complex problems – e.g. the Computer Vision Pipeline described later – there are two factors of note:

- A game base mechanism provides a better apparatus for utilizing available information in a system, especially when the values of said information may vary over time and knowledge association decisions require the evaluation of trade-offs.
- It provides a platform for experimenting with a variety of KD strategies afforded by the relative ease of devising and injecting concrete games implementing the desired strategy.

The concrete game used for the pipeline problem is described next. It is a continuous action variation of the classic Iterated Prisoner's Dilemma game.

Continuous-Action Iterated Prisoner's Dilemma

Unlike classic IPD (where the available action is a discrete choice – Cooperate/Defect), the IPD variation used here has *Degree of Cooperation* (DoC) as the action. DoC is a continuous value in the range [0, 1].

The determination of the DoC value is explained later in this section in some detail. Here, the elaboration of this decision and its implications are explored. What does it mean to cooperate in this context? Cooperation from x toward its neighbor y is taken to mean x wants to adopt the values and beliefs that y holds – to a degree. Defection consequently implies that x wants to retain its own beliefs and reject its neighbor's beliefs, again to a degree. This is the core idea that is harnessed to control the flow of knowledge in the social network.

Networked individuals have many neighbors. Accommodations are needed for multiple knowledge sources to be combined at varying levels of strengths. This is because an individual will receive different types of knowledge from its neighbors in varying degrees.

To this effect, the knowledge association structure in game KD is a tuple:

$$\left(k_{\mathrm{p}}, \left\{\left(k_{\mathrm{s}}, l\right)\right\}\right) \tag{5.1}$$

$k_{\mathrm{p}}, k_{\mathrm{s}} \in K$, the set of Knowledge Sources
$k_{\mathrm{p}} =$ the primary knowledge source
$k_{\mathrm{s}} =$ a secondary knowledge source, and
$l \in [0, 1]$ level or strength for the secondary KS

In the game-based version of the CA, there is exactly one Primary KS and possibly multiple Secondary KS's. An example of KS association structure for an individual is shown in Table 5.1.

Note that other KD mechanisms (to-date) allow only one ("the winner") KS to be associated with an individual and thus are competitive. By contrast, game KD allows KS to cooperate. The rules governing cooperative behavior will be discussed later in this section.

Given the backdrop of the knowledge association structure, the Play, Payoff, and Outcome functions are defined next for the IPD game. As noted in Figure 5.5, any injected game must be structured as such.

Table 5.1 Example of KS association structure for an individual in Game-based KD.

Knowledge Source	P = Primary S = Secondary	Association strength
Normative	P	$\langle$MAX_VALUE (1.0)$\rangle$
Situational	S	0.4
Domain	S	0.1

Play

Play determines the Action or hand for each player. The IPD Play function first calculates intermediate values – *unnormalized* Cooperation scores – between a player and each of its neighbors:

$$\text{Cooperation}_{x \to y} = \sum_i w_i t_{ixy}^{e_i}$$

where i is the index into the terms given in Table 5.2, x is the individual playing the hand, and y is its neighbor. The weights w_i and exponents e_i are empirically determined for the current iteration of the game. The terms t_{ixy} are described at a high level in Table 5.2. Essentially, each player considers a variety of current and historical factors to arrive at the raw cooperation score.

The component terms can be seen in terms of balancing three forces (see Figure 5.6), namely:

- Global diversity
  - Reflects the systems desire to maintain population and knowledge diversity
  - Explore new ideas and frontiers
  - Foster (not stifle) innovation
- Local specialization
  - Reflects the systems desire to refine and exploit promising domain knowledge for better incremental solutions
  - Stepwise refinement
- Self-interest
  - The individuals desire for self-improvement primarily through learning from social peers
  - Opportunistically acquire knowledge in search of finding better solutions.

DoC is normalized Cooperation:

$$\text{DoC}_{x \to y} = \frac{\text{Cooperation}_{x \to y}}{\sum_y \text{Cooperation}_{x \to y}}$$

$$\text{DoC}_{x \to y} \neq \text{DoC}_{y \to x}$$

$$\text{DoC} \in [0,1]$$

The hand or Action for player x (see Figure 5.7) is the set:

$$\text{Action}_x = \left\{ \text{DoC}_{x \to y} \,\middle|\, y \in Y_x \right\}$$

$$Y_x = \text{neighbors of } x$$

Table 5.2 Component terms of Degree of Cooperation score.

i	Term	Rationale (*x* refers to the player and *y* its neighbor)
1	*Knowledge Source Compatibility*	Both *x* and *y* have associated primary Knowledge Sources. If *x*'s KS is explorative and *y*'s is exploitative, then this term sets a positive value.
2	*Improvement Defection Coefficient*	If *x*'s primary KS is exploitative and *x*'s fitness improved since last generation, then *x* would like to defect – meaning a negative value is assigned to this term.
3	*Low KS Count*	If *y*'s primary KS is getting pushed out (i.e. the count of the KS is very low in the population), then this term gets a positive value.
4	*Attraction*	If *y* has higher fitness than *x*, then *x* is attracted to *y* and would like to adopt *y*'s knowledge sources. This term gets a value proportional to the difference between *x* and *y*'s fitness values.
5	*Stability*	A count is maintained for each individual and is incremented in each generation if the individual retains its primary KS from the previous generation. If the individual gets a different KS, this count is reset to 0.
6	*Diversity*	This score is the relative diversity of *x* and *y*. This term helps to maintain diversity in the population. The absolute diversity between *x* and *y* is the sum of absolute differences between the respective parameter values of *x* and *y*.
7	*Same KS Defection*	If *x* and *y* both have the same primary KS, then this term gets a negative value; otherwise it is 0.

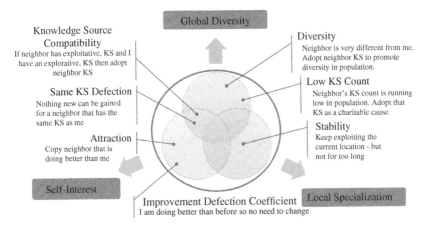

Figure 5.6 Forces guiding cooperation and defection component terms.

DoC is normalized Cooperation:

$$\mathrm{DoC}_{x \to y} = \frac{\mathrm{Cooperation}_{x \to y}}{\sum_y \mathrm{Cooperation}_{x \to y}}$$

$$\mathrm{DoC}_{x \to y} \neq \mathrm{DoC}_{y \to x}$$

$$\mathrm{DoC} \in [0,1]$$

The hand or Action for player x (see Figure 5.6) is the set:

$$\mathrm{Action}_x = \left\{ \mathrm{DoC}_{x \to y} \middle| y \in Y_x \right\}$$

$$Y_x = \text{neighbors of } x$$

Payoff

The Payoff function converts Actions to Payout structures (which are in turn utilized for Knowledge Distribution by Outcome). The IPD Payoff function matches DoC scores for linked players to calculate Mutual DoC

$$\mathrm{Mutual\ DoC}_{xy} = \mathrm{DoC}_{x \to y} + \mathrm{DoC}_{y \to x}$$

$$\mathrm{Mutual\ DoC}_{xy} = \mathrm{Mutual\ DoC}_{yx}$$

$$\mathrm{Mutual\ DoC} \in [0,2]$$

The Payout for individual x is the set of Mutual DoC scores:

$$\mathrm{Payout}_x = \left\{ \mathrm{Mutual\ DoC}_{xy} \middle| y \in Y_x \right\}$$

The general game play is as follows:

- At each time step (generation), each player plays its "hand" (Action).
- The hand for a player is the *set* of DoC scores – one for each of its neighbors (Figure 5.7).
- The scores for mutual neighbors are added together for Mutual DoC.
- Mutual DoC are used as weights for knowledge distribution.
- Each player "receives" Knowledge in proportion to the Mutual DoC from each of its neighbors.

Outcome

The Outcome function uses Payouts (one for each player) to set Knowledge association levels for the corresponding player. This processing is described next.

Let x be some individual for which Outcome determines knowledge association,

$N(x)$ = set of x's neighbors.

$P(x) = \{(x, y, m) | y \in N(x)\}$ is the Payout, where $m \in [0, 2]$ is the Mutual DoC between x and y.

Let $V_{min}, V_{max} \in [0, 2]$, $V_{min} < V_{max}$ be two constants which are used to control the rate of knowledge flow. There are three mutually exclusive cases to consider for x.

Case 1

$P'(x) = \{(x, y, m) | m > V_{min}, y \in N(x)\} \subseteq P(x)$ is a set that filters out payout values where $V_{min} \leq m$, thus eliminating knowledge flow from corresponding neighbors. If $P'(x) = \emptyset$ (empty set), then x retains its primary KS and loses any secondary KS.

Case 2

$P''(x) = \{(x, y, m) | m > V_{max}, y \in N(x) \subseteq P(x)\}$ is a set that only contains elements, where m is above the V_{max} threshold. If $P''(x) \neq \emptyset$, then x gets the primary KS from a randomly selected neighbor in P'' and no secondary KS.

Case 3

$P'''(x) = \{(x, y, m) | V_{min} \leq m \leq V_{max}, y \in N(x)\}$ contains the neighbors of x with intermediate values of m. Here, x retains its primary KS but gets secondary KS from the primary KS of its neighbors with levels proportional to corresponding m values.

Recall that knowledge assignment is of the form:

$A(i) = (k_{pi}, \{(k_{si}, l_i)\})$ for individual i (from Eq. 5.1)

For Case 3, $A(x) = (k_{px}, S(x))$, where k_{px} is the primary KS that x retains and $S(x)$ is as follows:

Let $Y''' $ = set of all y (neighbors) in $P'''(x)$

$$S(x) = \{(k_y, l_y)\}$$

where:

k_y is the primary KS of a $y \in Y'''$

$$l_y = \max\left(\sum \frac{M_y}{2.0}, 1.0\right).$$

$M_y = \{m_y | y \in Y''' \text{ with primary KS } k_y\}$

The constants V_{min}, V_{max} thus can be used to control the rate of knowledge flow. Higher values of V_{min} will dampen knowledge flow whereas lower values of V_{max} will make it more it disruptive by allowing greater primary KS changes. For the test run, the values of V_{min}, V_{max} were empirically determined by a grid search on several types of optimization problems.

After computing the knowledge association levels as described above, the Outcome function does further pruning by applying the following two rules to ensure that any "cooperation" between KS is not detrimental.

Firstly, if the primary KS is exploitative, then all secondary KS are removed. Exploitative KS make small changes to the individual to find a local extremum. By contrast, exploratory KS makes larger changes to explore diverse regions of the landscape. The effect of the primary exploitative KS will be lost if the individual is displaced a large distance subsequently by an explorative KS.

Secondly, any secondary KS that is the same as the primary KS is removed to eliminate redundancy.

Game-based KD mechanisms can effectively operate with greater information content and therefore is suitable for problem solving in Complex Systems such as those described earlier.

Learning Rate Adjustment

In the case of the primary KS being exploitative, a further adjustment may be made to the association strength. The association strength is reduced in each subsequent generation, if the individual retained its primary exploitative KS. The reduction rate can either be linear or geometric but stops at a specified minimum. For example, using a geometric reduction rate of 0.95, the association strength for each subsequent generation is calculated as follows:

Generation	Derivation of association strength	Effective association strength
0	1.0	1.0 (MAX_LEVEL)
1	1.0 * 0.95	0.95
2	1.0 * 0.95 * 0.95	0.9025

The reduction mode and levels are configured at CA initialization. Association strength is analogous to learning rate in other optimization techniques, e.g. stochastic gradient descent [21]. As an individual "lingers" in a region (while under the influence of the same exploitative primary KS), the expected value of the distance it can jump to find extrema is made progressively smaller. If the individual is very close to an extremum, then the chances of finding the true peak (or trough) are better over successive generations due to progressively finer movements of the individual. Note that this "adaptive" association strength works in conjunction with the iterative game; the probability of retaining the same primary KS is higher if the individual improved its fitness from the previous generation. See "Improvement Defection Coefficient" box in Table 5.2 for an explanation.

Test Results: Benchmark Problem

The "ConesWorld" landscape generator inspired by the work of Morrison and De Jong [22] (see Figure 5.8) was used to compare the performance of CATGAME and Weighted Majority Knowledge Distribution mechanisms. The generator is part of the Cultural Algorithm Toolkit, CAT, which is used to generate and compare various Cultural Algorithm configurations. Details of the CAT system can be found in [4]. The CAT system can generate both static and dynamic landscapes by the positioning of cones over a search region. Here, the problem employed was static in nature. The test landscapes generated to evaluate performance, range from simple to complex to chaotic, by controlling the number of cones in the landscape. The basic landscape structure is given by:

$$f\left(\left\langle x_1, x_2, \ldots, x_n \right\rangle\right) = \max_{j=1,k}\left(H_j - R_j \cdot \sqrt{\sum_{i=1}^{n}\left(x_i - C_{j,i}\right)^2} \right)$$

where f returns the height of the landscape surface at the given coordinates $x_1 \ldots x_n$; k is the number of cones; n is the dimensionality; H_j is the height of the cone j; R_j is the radius of cone j; and C_{ij} is the coordinate of cone j in dimension i.

The CATGAME and Weighted Majority mechanisms were compared by measuring their performances on randomly generated landscapes. The landscape cones were generated using random values for height, radius, and location from specified ranges. Furthermore, different population sizes were used to broaden the comparison between the two methods. Cone numbers were 100,

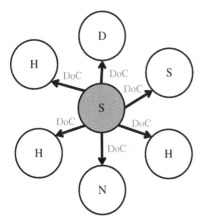

Figure 5.7 The "hand" played by each player in IPD is set of the Degree of Cooperation scores – one for each neighbor (note: node labels represent **primary** knowledge types, e.g. H = Historical, D = Domain, etc., associated with individual [center] and neighbors).

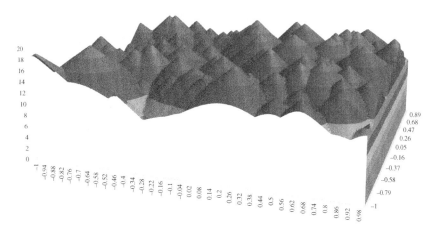

Figure 5.8 ConesWorld Landscape.

500, and 1000. Population sizes were 100, 250, and 1000 individuals. A fixed topology, hexagonal social network, was used for both mechanisms (each individual was linked to six others). The choice of a 6-degree network reflects the need to have enough variety in games for effective knowledge flow. Limited experimentation showed that CATGAME does not perform as well with low-degree networks. For each cone size-population size combination (3 * 3 = 9), 50 landscapes were randomly generated.

The Morrison and De Jong generator can produce real-valued problem landscapes – essentially nonlinear and nondifferentiable functions – of arbitrary complexity and thus serves as a convenient mechanism for benchmarking evolutionary optimization algorithms. For the test problems, two-dimensional landscapes were used with cone heights in the interval [5, 20] and widths in [10, 40]. While future research will focus on higher dimensional and real-world problems, the 2D test landscapes provided key insights into CATGAME performance through easier visualization of algorithm performance.

The CATGAME and Weighted Majority mechanisms were then run on each generated landscape (9 * 50 = 450 landscapes). The mean-number-of-generations-till-solution-found were recorded for each combination. The performance results are shown in Table 5.3. CATGAME performs better than WTD on all landscapes, yielding faster convergence to solution. Additionally, CATGAME is more predictable as indicated by the comparatively lower standard deviation scores. Statistical t-tests of the difference between two sample means were significant at $p = 0.05$, for all landscapes.

One of the goals for game KD is better balancing of the KS distribution of the population. The attainment of this goal is visually reflected in Figure 5.9, where

Table 5.3 Mean generations to solution: CATGAME versus WTD Majority.

Cones	Population size	CAT-GAME mean	WTD mean	CAT-GAME std. dev.	WTD std. dev.	*t*-Test, *p* < 0.05
100	100	137	1008	199	1026	Y
100	250	71	542	135	897	Y
100	1k	32	212	46	603	Y
500	100	571	1743	852	1012	Y
500	250	313	951	642	1070	Y
500	1k	120	736	308	1001	Y
1k	100	924	1692	943	1033	Y
1k	250	515	1232	852	1123	Y
1k	1k	325	912	734	1085	Y

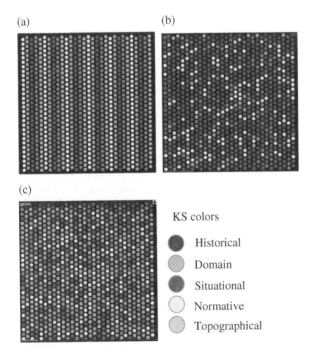

(a)   (b)   (c)

KS colors

● Historical
◐ Domain
● Situational
○ Normative
◔ Topographical

Figure 5.9 KS distribution in a hexagonally networked population (a) initial, (b) after WTD run, and (c) after CATGAME run.

each dot is a population individual connected via a hexagonal network structure to other individuals. Image (a) shows the KS assignments at the start of the run, where the KS are distributed evenly across the population. Image (b) is the KS distribution for WTD and (c) for CATGAME at the end of the respective runs to solve the same ConesWorld problem configuration.

The Knowledge Sources can be generically classified as exploratory (Topographic, Domain, and Normative) and exploitative (Situational and Historical). Notice that in the Majority Win distribution scenario, an overwhelming majority of individuals are controlled by Historical knowledge along with situational knowledge. Both of these are exploitative knowledge sources. In the population network produced by the Game Theoretic knowledge distribution mechanism that emphasizes cooperation and competition, the knowledge sources used there are much more diverse. They contain both exploratory and exploitative knowledge sources. That configuration will be more flexible in response to changes in the problem landscape.

Also interesting is the change in KS distributions over generations as depicted by the following YouTube™ videos:

- WTD – https://youtu.be/QmdVJrzka9c
- CATGAME – https://youtu.be/dPeXhOfNqms

For WTD, one KS tends to dominate. The crowded-out KS are reinserted at random which leads to oscillations in the KS distribution over generations. By contrast, in CATGAME, the change in KS distribution is smoother with a seemingly dynamic equilibrium state being reached and maintained by the system.

The Computer Vision Pipeline problem requires that the configuration of each component be compatible with its predecessors and successors in the pipeline. Therefore, a knowledge distribution scheme for each component that allows it to adjust to demands of its neighbors in the pipeline is essential for effective performance. Based on the experimental studies presented here, it appears that the Game-Theoretic approach will be more successful when applied to a real-world vision pipeline problem. Whether this is in fact is the case will be described in the following section.

Test Results: Computer Vision Pipeline

The performance of CA configured with game-based KD (CATGAME) was compared with that using Weighted Majority Win KD (WTD) – all other parameters being the same – on a computer vision pipeline. While relatively simple, the pipeline mimics the type of perceptual processing done in real autonomous vehicles and thus is a suitable test problem. It is implemented here using the OpenCV toolkit (opencv.org). The pipeline accepts an image of the road ahead from a camera mounted on the front of the vehicle and produces another image where the lane marks are identified and marked with solid lines. The key computer vision problem is to identify the left and right lane boundaries as line segments in image space as illustrated in Figure 5.10.

The pipeline steps are as follows:

- Image masking (Figure 5.11).
- Color range thresholding to pick pixels that are likely lane markers.
- Edge detection (Figure 5.11), using Canny algorithm [23].
- Requires conversion to grayscale first.
- Hough Transform [24] for lines detection.
- Identification of left and right lane lines
  (lines that fall within allowable slope ranges).
- Draw overlay lines.

There are several (hyper or tunable) parameters that control the performance of the pipeline over different types of road surfaces, shadows, and lighting conditions:

- Color range for allowable lane marking colors
- Canny thresholds and aperture values
- Hough threshold and line parameters
- Allowable slope ranges for left and right lane lines

Altogether, there are 15 distinct parameters that need to be jointly optimized. This is a complex problem where the choices of parameter values have a cascading effect on downstream processing in the pipeline. In other words, the pipeline cannot be globally optimized by tuning each component individually and then assembling the pipeline. For example, whether a particular value of Canny

Figure 5.10   Sample processed image (base image: Udacity).

Image mask   Edge detection

Figure 5.11   Image processing, masking, and edge detection.

Figure 5.12   Before and after optimization (base image: Udacity).

aperture parameter is good or bad cannot be known until the entire pipeline is processed and the final image rendered. Selection of the aperture affects edge detection, which in turn affects line detection by the Hough method and so on.

To set up the optimization problem, (human) best-guess values of the tunable parameters were first selected, and the pipeline executed on an input sample of 60 images representing differing conditions. The processed images were then studied by a human expert for errors and misalignments. A labeled training dataset was created with "correct" (as determined by a human) line segment end points for each set of lane markings, for each image.

The CA was then executed to find the parameter values that minimize the sum of the squared error (SSE) distance between the human-determined and the pipelined-determined line segment end points. As an example, see Figure 5.12 for the before and after optimization versions of the same processed image for a difficult section of the road with dark patches.

The CA was run 15 times each for CATGAME and WTD, distribution mechanisms on the computer vision test problem, and the lowest SSE values achieved noted. A population size of 50 with hexagonal network was used. Each run was capped at 2500 generations. The results are summarized in Table 5.4. One tailed t-test is significant at $p < 0.002$.

Table 5.4 CATGAME versus WTD on Computer Vision Problem.

	CAT-GAME mean	WTD mean	CAT-GAME std. dev.	WTD std. dev.	t-Test
SSE after 15 runs	1240	1819	418	462	$p < 0.002$

The CATGAME distribution function using the IPD game significantly outperformed the WTD in terms of overall accuracy and standard deviation. The SSE values of the CATGAME mechanism were approximately 40% less than that of the WTD approach. Likewise, the standard deviation of CATGAME was approximately 10% less than that of the WTD. This suggests two things. First, that the signal strength was strong enough to support the CATGAME approach. Second, that the CATGAME approach was able to exploit the many non-linearities present among the problem variables.

Conclusions

Production-level AI applications in autonomous vehicles will be composed of intelligent and highly configurable subsystems sourced from a variety of suppliers. OEMs are faced with a laborious integration challenge. Can this burden be alleviated with the application of evolutionary optimization methods? To answer this question, the CA framework was tested on a simple but representative problem. The CA is suited for problem solving in complex systems; here, its capability was further enhanced with game-theoretic knowledge distribution to meet foreseeably harder challenges in this arena. Test results show that: (i) evolutionary optimization algorithms in general and the CA in particular are suitable candidates for meeting the presented challenges, and (ii) game-based approaches show a promise and need to be further studied and exploited. Future research will focus on more complex, real-world problems and explore different game types for knowledge distribution in relation to the type and complexities of the problems.

An interesting area for future research is the study of network dynamics and community formation in response to the complexity of problems to be solved. Another research area of interest is multiagent optimization, rooted in the work of John Tsitsiklis [25]. In such configurations, agents cooperate over a network to work toward global optima while acting locally with limited domain knowledge. Conceivably, agents could be assigned to operate on each of the components in the pipeline and exchange information periodically to minimize the global cost function described earlier.

References

1 McKinsey & Company (2012), Evolution of component costs, penetration, and value creation potential through 2020 the future of the North American automotive supplier. mckinsey.com. (accessed 18 June 2018).

2 Reynolds, R.G. (1978). On modeling the evolution of hunter-gatherer decision-making systems. *Geographical Analysis* 10 (1): 31–46.

3 Ali, M.Z., Suganthan, P.N., Reynolds, R.G., and Al-Badarneh, A.F. (2016). Leveraged neighborhood restructuring in cultural algorithms for solving real-world numerical optimization problems. *IEEE Transactions on Evolutionary Computation* 20 (2): 218–231.

4 Jayyousi, T.W. and Reynolds, R.G. (2014). Extracting urban occupational plans using cultural algorithms [application notes]. *IEEE Computational Intelligence Magazine* 9 (3): 66–87.

5 Judeh, T., T. Jayyousi, L. Acharya, et al. (2014), GSCA: reconstructing biological pathway topologies using a cultural algorithms approach. *IEEE Congress on Evolutionary Computation*, Beijing (6–11 July 2014).

6 Waris, F. and Reynolds, R. G. (2015). Using cultural algorithms to improve wearable device gesture recognition performance. *IEEE Symposium Series on Computational Intelligence*, Cape Town (7–10 December 2015).

7 Dorigo, M., Maniezzo, V., and Colorni, A. (1996). Ant system: optimization by a colony of cooperating agents. *IEEE Transactions on Systems, Man, and Cybernetics* 26 (1), no. 1083–4419: 29–41.

8 Kennedy, J. and Eberhart, R.C. (1995). Particle swarm optimization. *Proceeding of the IEEE International Conference on Neural Networks*, Perth, Australia (27 November–1 December 1995).

9 Peng, B. (2005). Knowledge swarms in cultural algorithms for dynamic environments. PhD thesis. Wayne State University.

10 Che, X. (2009). Weaving the social fabric: optimization problem solving in cultural algorithms using the cultural engine. PhD Thesis. Wayne State University.

11 Reynolds, R.G. and Kinnaird-Heether, L. (2013). Optimization problem solving with auctions in Cultural Algorithms. *Memetic Computing* 5 (2): 83–94.

12 Colon, D.L. (2012). Ubiquitous learning laboratory for pediatric nursing: a cultural algorithm approach. MS Thesis. Wayne State University.

13 Reynolds, R.G. and Saleem, S.M. (2005). The impact of environmental dynamics on cultural emergence. *Perspectives on Adaptions in Natural and Artificial Systems*: 253–280.

14 Ali, M. (2008). Using cultural algorithms to solve optimization problems with a social fabric approach. PhD Thesis. Wayne State University.

15 Reynolds, R.G., Gawasmeh, Y.A., and Salaymeh, A. (2015). The impact of subcultures in cultural algorithm problem solving. *2015 IEEE Symposium Series on Computational Intelligence*, pp. 1876–1884.

16 Shi, Y. (2011). An optimization algorithm based on brainstorming process. *International Journal of Swarm Intelligence* 2 (4): 35–62.

17 Shoham, Y. and Leyton-Brown, K. (2009). *Multiagent Systems: Algorithmic, Game-Theoretic, and Logical Foundations (Book)*. Cambridge University Press.

18 Veelen, M.V. and Spreij, P. (2009). Evolution in games with a continuous action space. *Economic Theory* 39: 355–376.

19 Axelrod, R. and Hamilton, W.D. (1981). The evolution of cooperation. *Science, New Series* 211 (4489): 1390–1396.

20 Nash, J. (1950). Equilibrium points in n-person games. *Proceedings of the National Academy of Sciences* 36 (1): 48–49.

21 Duchi, J., Hazan, E., and Singer, Y. (2011). Adaptive subgradient methods for online learning and stochastic optimization. *Journal of Machine Learning Research* 12: 2121–2159.

22 Morrison, R. and De Jong, K. (1999). A test problem generator for nonstationary environments. *Proceedings of the 1999 Congress on Evolutionary Computation*, Washington, DC (6–9 July 1999).

23 Canny, J. (1986). A computational approach to edge detection. *IEEE Trans. Pattern Analysis and Machine Intelligence* 8 (6): 679–698.

24 Hough, P.V.C. (1959). Machine analysis of bubble chamber pictures. *Proceedings, 2nd International Conference on High-Energy Accelerators and Instrumentation*, HEACC 1959, CERN, Geneva, Switzerland (14–19 September 1959).

25 Tsitsiklis, J. (1984). Problems in decentralized decision making and computation. PhD thesis. Department of Electrical Engineering and Computer Science, Massachusetts Institute of Technology.

6

Cultural Algorithms for Social Network Analysis

Case Studies in Team Formation

Kalyani Selvarajah[1], Ziad Kobti[1], and Mehdi Kargar[2]

[1] School of Computer Science, University of Windsor, Windsor, ON, Canada
[2] Ted Rogers School of Management, Ryerson University, Toronto, ON, Canada

Introduction

Social networks are supported online in various ways such as Facebook, Twitter, Instagram but these can also be a kind of social structure that human beings have been assembling for the variety of reasons. Because the pattern of social structure is treated as a network, it grabbed the name "Social networks." It has so much hidden and powerful information that makes us see the world in an entirely new way. Social networks are intricate things of beauty and do not follow either random or regular pattern. Social Network Analysis (SNA) can be simply defined as an in-depth analysis of social network structure, dynamic nature, multirelational aspects, the pattern of relationship with social actors, and the available data along with them.

Since the social networks used to represent the large scale of social structure and the underlying networks in the real world can be very complicated, researchers usually called it a complex system. Moreover, these are ubiquitous and can be created from various fields, such as coauthor network, Twitter friendship, LinkedIn profile, and protein-to-protein networks. Therefore, the demand for contribution to the fundamental research of complex SNA has become high. Investigating complex social networks is more challenging, and study of complex social networks is limited in the literature because of unexpected challenges in the ownership of the real data.

Cultural Algorithms: Tools to Model Complex Dynamic Social Systems, First Edition.
Edited by Robert G. Reynolds.
© 2021 John Wiley & Sons, Inc. Published 2021 by John Wiley & Sons, Inc.
Companion website: www.wiley.com/go/CAT

Application of Social Network

In recent years, SNA has been used in various disciplines such as business, academics, politics, economics, law enforcement, sports, health care, and daily life activities that are highly related to real-world problems. SNA is most commonly applied to help to improve the effectiveness and efficiency of decision-making processes and deals with different issues. Several of them are very popular in SNA research: Team formation, Link prediction, leadership detection, Community detection, Migration Between Communities, Sentiment Analysis, Collaborative Recommendation, Influence Analysis, and Fraud Detection. This chapter will discuss the Team Formation Problem (TFP) in SNA.

Forming Successful Teams

Today, it is essential to have some collective thoughts and creative ideas for productive results in various fields, such as educational, health-care, industrial, and human resource management settings. As specialization in every field increases, there is a need for an expert in specific skills. Therefore, bringing these experts together as a team for a collaborative working environment would be a great idea for the effective result. However, what guarantee do we have that the combination of these individuals who may or may not know each other would actually succeed? The links connecting these individuals are very critical. Are these connections between them that we have made for the right team with the right people? And, will they make a huge difference in the outcomes of the result?

In the complex social system of billions of connected components, forming a group of experts while maximizing their social compatibility is a great challenge for researchers. The challenges have increased with both the size and the structural changes of the online network with the giant growth of the Internet. Many expert networks exist in our professional world. For example, LinkedIn is an employment-based service network, GitHub is for the code repository hosting service, Stack Overflow is for community-based question answering, and Google Scholar and DBLP are the research-based author websites.

The team formation problem has been employed by the researchers from various disciplines for a long time. Earlier, researchers from psychology and sociology tried to understand what controls the individual and social behaviors of members of a team have. Then, because human nature is unpredictable, the mathematicians and statisticians tried to approach this problem in the dynamic environment. Zzkarian and Kusiak [1] designed a conceptual framework for the selection of multifunctional teams. Although the general idea of these studies is highly connected with social sciences, social scientists have not designed any effective model to solve TFP. Therefore, the problem of forming successful teams needs a model to evaluate the team performance, to define the rules to setup the members of the teams, and to predict the team of experts who would work together in future. Therefore, the researchers from computer science showed interest in designing the computational model for TFP. Authors of [2–4] tried to solve TFP with various techniques, such as branch-and-cut, simulated annealing, and genetic algorithms. But, they did not consider the relationship among them such as the social structure. The performance of a team depends not only on the capacities of individuals but also on how these individuals communicate with each other is also very important. Therefore, Lappas et al. [5] incorporated social networks with TFP to discover the team of experts for the first time in SNA and considered communication cost as measuring the parameter to form the effective team. Inspired by his work, authors of [6–9] have extended it by including additional parameters, such as skill level, personnel cost, and workload. Some of them defined the communication cost in various ways such as using the sum of distance, diameter distance, and Steiner distance. A later section will define the basic idea of those parameters.

This chapter will discuss the computational models which we designed and our future directions for TFP. In addition to that, we will further elaborate the primary differences of our models with other existing models, the domain of research, and chosen approach to solve the problem. Our study mainly focuses on two primary fields: health-care networks and coauthor networks. For the first time in this research, we deploy knowledge-based evolutionary optimization algorithms called Cultural Algorithms (CA) to discover successful teams.

Formulating TFP

Let $A = \{a_1, a_2, a_3, ..., a_n\}$ specifies a set of n experts, and $K = \{k_1, k_2, ..., k_m\}$ specifies a set of m skills. Each expert a_i has a set of skills, specified as $S(a_i)$, and $S(a_i) \subseteq K$. If $k_j \in S(a_i)$, then expert a_i possesses skill k_j. A subset of experts $A' \subseteq A$ have skill k_j if at least one of them possesses k_j. For each skill k_j, the set of all experts that possesses skill k_j is specified as $A(k_j) = \{a_1 \mid k_j \in S(a_i)\}$. A project $P = \{k_1, k_2, ..., k_s\}$ is composed of a set of s skills that are required to be completed by some experts. A subset of experts $A'' \subseteq A$ is able to project P if $\forall k_j \in P \, \exists \, a_i \in A'', k_j \in S(a_i)$.

Definition: (Team of Experts)
Given a set of experts A and a project P that needs a set of skills $\{k_1, k_2, ..., k_s\}$, a *team of experts* for P is a set of s skill-expert pairs: $\{\langle k_1, a_{k_1} \rangle, \langle k_2, a_{k_2} \rangle, ..., \langle k_s, a_{k_s} \rangle\}$, where a_{k_j} is an expert who possesses skill k_j, for $j = \{1, 2, ..., s\}$. This means expert a_{k_j} is responsible for skill k_j.

Each skill has to be completed by an expert. However, one expert may be assigned to more than one skill. Many possible teams may satisfy each project P. However, we aim to discover the efficient teams that can be evaluated using the following parameters.

Communication Cost

The experts in A are connected to each other. This network can be related to the fundamental definition of social network. Therefore, it can be modeled as an undirected graph G, where each expert is represented as a node. Each expert possesses a set of skills that decide their expertise based on education, experience, or training. If two experts have past collaboration, they are connected to each other in the social network with a named edge. The edge weight can be resolved based on their number of past collaboration between two experts. If the two experts collaborated more in the past, their edge weight would be small.

The distance between two experts a_i and a_j specified as dist(a_i, a_j) is equal to the sum of the weights on the shortest path between them in the input graph G. If a_i and a_j are not connected in graph G (i.e., there is no path between a_i and a_j in G), the distance between them is set to ∞. Our research considers two variations of communication cost functions.

Definition: (Sum of Distances)
Given a graph G and a team of experts $\left\{ \left\langle k_1, a_{k_1} \right\rangle, \left\langle k_2, a_{k_2} \right\rangle, \ldots, \left\langle k_s, a_{k_s} \right\rangle \right\}$, *the sum of distances* of the team is the sum of weights on the shortest path between a_{k_i} and a_{k_j}, and defined as

$$\text{SumDistance} = \sum_{i=1}^{s} \sum_{j=i+1}^{s} \text{dist}\left(a_{k_i}, a_{k_j} \right)$$

where $\text{dist}\left(a_{k_i}, a_{k_j} \right)$ is the distance between a_{k_i} and a_{k_j} in G.

Definition: (Diameter)
Given a graph G and a team of experts $\left\{ \left\langle k_1, a_{k_1} \right\rangle, \left\langle k_2, a_{k_2} \right\rangle, \ldots, \left\langle k_s, a_{k_s} \right\rangle \right\}$, the *diameter* of this team is the largest shortest distance between any two experts a_{ki} and a_{kj} for $1 \leq i \leq j \leq s$.

Minimizing the diameter or the sum of distances of team T is proven to be NP-hard in [5, 8], and they proposed greedy algorithms to find the best approximate teams which minimize these functions.

Personnel Cost

In the real-world project setting such as in any organization or freelancer work, individuals need to be paid for their work. We label it as personnel cost and can decide the value based on their expert level and the responsibility they have on the project. In some cases, the government pays for some services such as health care in Canada. In this case, our research considers personnel cost as contact cost, which means the maximum time he/she is available for service.

Definition: (Sum of Personnel Cost)
Given a graph G and a team of experts $\{\langle k_1, a_{k_1} \rangle, \langle k_2, a_{k_2} \rangle, ..., \langle k_s, a_{k_s} \rangle\}$, the sum of *personnel cost* of this team T is defined as

$$\text{SumPersonnelCost} = \sum_{i=1}^{s} pc\left(a_{k_i}\right)$$

where $pc\left(a_{k_i}\right)$ is the cost of expert a_{ki}.

Distance Cost

A few investigators believe that the significance of proximity in skill-based production will, in the long run, vanish with the improvement of technologies. However, the geographical proximity is proven to be important [10] in some disciplines, such as coauthorship, health service, and educational setting. For instance, the care providers in health services need to reach the patient. So, the distance between care provider and patient should be reachable. The distance can be measured for each expert based on the project location and must be minimum.

Definition: (Distance Cost)
Given a graph G and a team of experts $\{\langle k_1, a_{k_1} \rangle, \langle k_2, a_{k_2} \rangle, ..., \langle k_s, a_{k_s} \rangle\}$, the sum of *geographical distance cost* of this team T is defined as

$$\text{DistanceCost} = \sum_{i=1}^{s} dc\left(a_{k_i}\right)$$

where $dc\left(a_{k_i}\right)$ is the cost of expert a_{ki}

Workload Balance

The workload takes an essential role in group formation. A person can only handle a certain number of tasks at a given time. It can be distributed based on their expert level or experience of handling the task. The balanced task assignment problem is proven to be NP-hard [11].

Why Artificial Intelligence?

Since the social network is considered as a complex system, it has been treated far more in comprehensive and careful way in computer science. Since complexity requires the number of basic operations to execute a specific algorithm, heuristic optimization would be suitable and reduces the computational "cost" in problem solving. The nature of the problem environment is to find the suitable experts as a team for the projects from the complex expert network system. Thus, we can have multiple possible teams of individuals who satisfy the required skill and need to choose the best possible outcome.

At this point, we can treat the problem of finding the best solution similar to the rational agent approach in Artificial Intelligence (AI), because it has to search through the large solution space to provide the best result. The search algorithms in AI are most significant. The classical search algorithms, inspired by evolutionary biology can be designed with simplified assumptions than other search algorithms to guide the search process and are mostly closer to the real world [12]. In our research, cultural algorithms, which are based on the principle of genetic inheritance and cultural evolution, have been used as the classical (or local) search algorithms.

Cultural Algorithms

Evolutionary computation is inspired from biological evolution and helps to solve complex computational problems. The Cultural Algorithm (CA) [13] is an extension of Evolutionary Computation and inspired by the fundamental of cultural evolution. It allows societies to adapt to their changing environments at rates that exceed that of biological evolution.

The CA is a dual-phase evolutionary system and maintains a population space and a belief space as shown in Figure 6.1. The population space is used to represent a biological evolution based on Darwinian principles, and individuals represent candidate solutions, are mostly distinct, and their quality can be determined by the cost function in the problem domain. The belief space is to represent the cultural evolution and treated as a knowledge repository, which records various type of knowledge based on the nature of the problem. It contains five knowledge components: situational, normative, domain, history, and topographical. In our research, we used at least situational and normative knowledge.

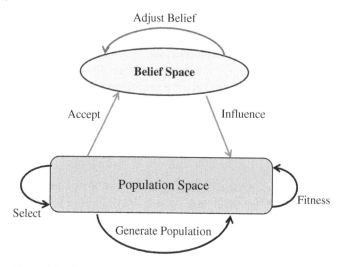

Figure 6.1 Cultural Algorithm Framework.

Forming Teams in Coauthorship Network

Because of availability and the simplicity of collecting information through bibliographic databases, scientific collaborations are examined on coauthorship data, which play an especially essential role to investigate the shared social structure of science. Coauthorship networks can be considered as a personal network in which the vertices are authors, and an edge connects two authors if they work together on one or more publications. Figure 6.2 shows the personal network of Dr. Ziad Kobti from DBLP dataset from 2003 to 2018 and provides the information to understand easily, such as the number of authors who work with him and who have more publications with him.

Our research focuses on the problem of forming a team of experts from a given experts' network to work on specific project/paper. In this context, a project/paper is composed of a set of skills, where each skill should be covered by one expert in a team to complete it. The success of a task relies on how well the experts on the team communicate and collaborate with each other.

To discuss the benefit of evaluating the communication cost in TFP, we consider an example of experts' network presented in Figure 6.3. This network has seven experts with their skill. The edge weight is the communication cost between experts. Smaller values between the experts means they have more past collaboration, and therefore, the chances of having the collaboration in the future are high and would perform well as a team for a project. Therefore, if a project requires

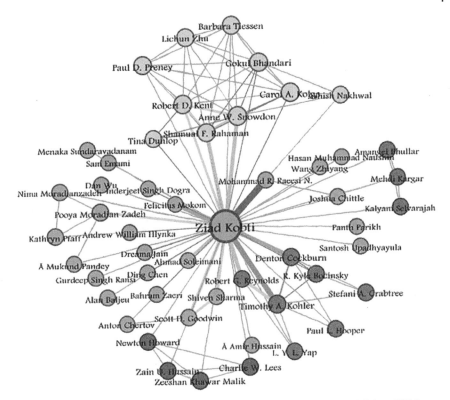

Figure 6.2 Coauthorship Social Network: Personal network of Dr. Ziad Kobti on DBLP dataset.

experts who have the skills of artificial intelligence (AI), databases (DB), and Machine Learning (ML). Teams A, B, and C are possible solutions for this problem. To find the best team among them, we consider the total communication cost of each team which is 30, 27, and 6 respectively. As we need to choose the team with less communication cost, Team C would be the better solution.

Our research employs CA on TFP for a computational model. The following section will elaborate on the idea behind the formation problem for an expert's network.

Individual Representation

A team (individual) represents a candidate solution to the problem and consists of an array structure with *s* cells, which is the number of the required skills to complete a project. For example, as shown in Figure 6.4, if a project needs four skills,

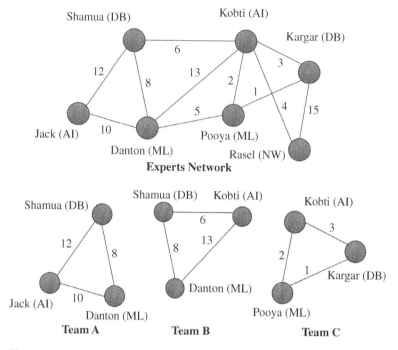

Figure 6.3 The experts' network and three possible teams for the project/paper, which requires the skills of AI, DB, and ML.

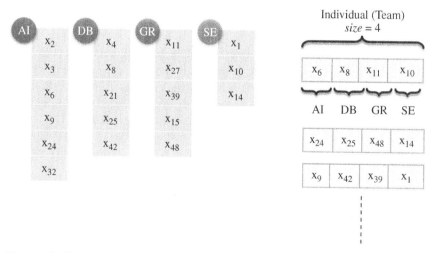

Figure 6.4 The representation of teams for the project/paper, which requires the skills of AI, DB, ML, and SE.

the size of the array, s is equal to 4. The element of each cell is selected from the set of experts who possess that skill. Therefore, for each cell representing a required skill k_j, a value is filled by an expert, a_i, where $k_j \in S(a_i)$.

Fitness Function

In the coauthorship network setting, we use the weighted graph to provide the number of frequent collaborations of experts in the past as communication cost. We use both the sum of distance and the diameter as the fitness function to evaluate how close a given solution is to the optimum solution of the desired problem.

The shortest path between many pairs of nodes needs to be evaluated frequently since a number of individuals will be generated in each iteration and we need to decide their eligibility for next generation. However, computing the shortest path is very slow, while precomputing the shortest path distance between all pairs of nodes takes too much space. It takes $O(N^2)$ for a graph with N nodes and quickly runs out of memory for very large graphs. Therefore, we use an efficient indexing method called 2-hop cover [14]. It returns the value of the shortest path between any pair of nodes in graphs with hundreds and thousands of nodes almost instantly.

Belief Space

The belief space in our research is defined as the transpose matrix of the selected population, which is composed of top best-selected teams. Let a selected team be defined as $\mathrm{SI}_j = \left[a_{k_1}^j, a_{k_2}^j, \ldots, a_{k_s}^j \right]$, where $k_i \in P$, and $a_{k_i}^j \in A(k_i)$. Now, let the selected population in each iteration with the size of t be defined as follows:

$$\mathrm{SP} = \begin{bmatrix} \mathrm{SI}_1 \\ \mathrm{SI}_2 \\ \vdots \\ \mathrm{SI}_t \end{bmatrix} = \begin{bmatrix} a_{k_1}^1, a_{k_2}^1, \ldots, a_{k_s}^1 \\ a_{k_1}^2, a_{k_2}^2, \ldots, a_{k_s}^2 \\ \vdots \\ a_{k_1}^t, a_{k_2}^t, \ldots, a_{k_s}^t \end{bmatrix} \quad \mathrm{BS} = \begin{bmatrix} a_{k_1}^1, a_{k_1}^2, \ldots, a_{k_1}^t \\ a_{k_2}^1, a_{k_2}^2, \ldots, a_{k_2}^t \\ \vdots \\ a_{k_s}^1, a_{k_s}^2, \ldots, a_{k_s}^t \end{bmatrix}$$

The optimal solution can be created by choosing the elements of the best teams. In the next iteration, the algorithm generates the new teams based on this belief space and not from the actual set of experts for each skill, $S(k_j)$. This approach produces teams with lower communication costs and reduces the size of the search space.

Dataset and Observations

We generate the input graph from the DBLP[1] dataset. The graph contains 200k nodes and 1.16M edges. The DBLP is the coauthorship social network. In this case, the experts are authors of the papers. If two authors publish papers together, they are connected through an edge in the graph. The expertise of an author is extracted from the titles of their papers. We generate two more subgraphs of the main graph with 100k and 50k nodes for this research. The observation for 50k, 100k, and 200k equal-weighted graphs based on the number of required skills has been represented in Figure 6.5, which compares the CA with various algorithms, such as Genetic Algorithms, Greedy Algorithms, Random Method, and Exact Algorithms. As a result, the CA discovers the teams with near to the optimal solution. Since the problem is NP-hard, the exhaustive search takes a very long time. We are able to run the project with four to ten skills due to the lack of memory. The obtained results from the same fitness function on 50k graphs with logarithmic and semantic weights also are shown in Figure 6.6, respectively.

Skill Frequency

The skill frequency is the number of experts who possess that skill. For example, if the required skill is "Artificial Intelligence" and the frequency is 150, then it means there exist 150 experts in the network with the skill in "Artificial Intelligence." We study the effect of different skill frequency on the performance of algorithms. By setting the skill frequency to the minimum and maximum value, we can select multiple teams of experts within the given frequency range for various projects/paper.

As shown in Figure 6.7, the runtimes of GA and CA have fewer changes when the frequency of required skills increases, which contrasts with the greedy algorithm. By increasing the frequency of skills, the runtime of the greedy algorithm rises dramatically.

Forming Teams in Health-care Network

The complexity of health system's frameworks pose fundamentally the same difficulties for the investigation to the ones produced by social networks. In recent years, geriatric populations are proliferating around the world, and the risk of chronic diseases, social isolation, and depression increases along with other

---

1 http://dblp.uni-trier.de/xml

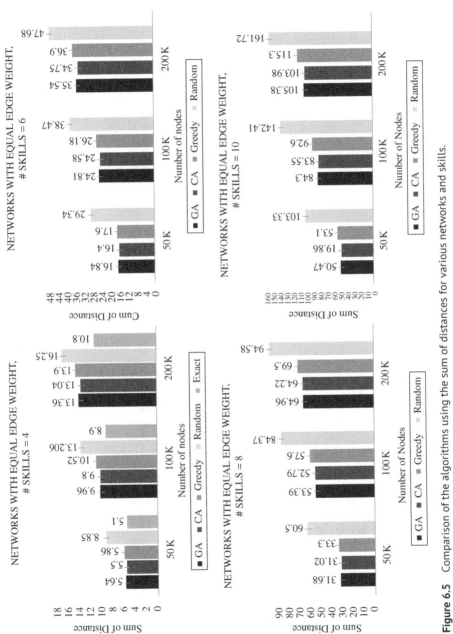

Figure 6.5 Comparison of the algorithms using the sum of distances for various networks and skills.

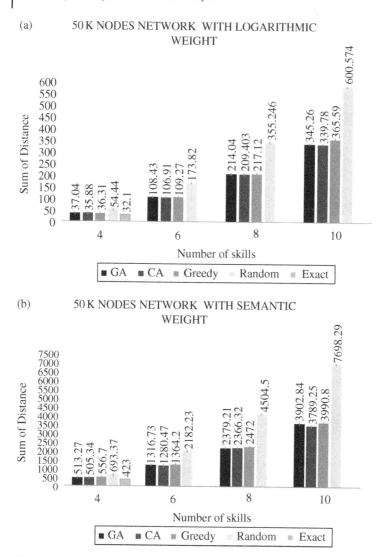

(a) 50 K NODES NETWORK WITH LOGARITHMIC WEIGHT

(b) 50 K NODES NETWORK WITH SEMANTIC WEIGHT

Figure 6.6 Comparison of the algorithms on 50k nodes network with different weight methods: (a) logarithmic edge weight and (b) semantic edge weight.

health-related problems. Some studies have shown that improving health and overall well-being of seniors can be achieved by enhancing their social support networks and choices to make critical decisions and direct their care. Person-centric and community-oriented palliative care systems are in the center of attention due to the need of support for aging and other related challenges. Palliative care is a type of health care, which focuses on improving the quality of

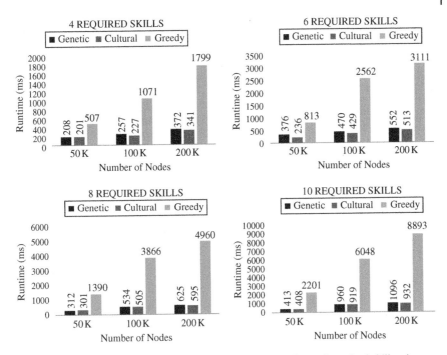

Figure 6.7 Runtimes of the algorithms with different numbers of required skills when the frequency of skills varies. The input graph contains 200k nodes.

life of individuals who are living with life-threatening illnesses, primarily with the chronic diseases, such as cancer, cardiac disease, and Alzheimer. The main goal of our research is to provide various support services to help patients to live an active life and dignity while considering the patients' prognosis.

This care system analyses a team approach to address the needs of patients and their families. In fact, a multidisciplinary team of health-care professionals, volunteers, family members, and friends needs to work together to achieve a primary goal of providing the optimal care services for a patient. This team forms a social circle of care for the patient as shown in Figure 6.8.

Generally, a palliative care network includes two groups of individuals:patients who are typically not able to do some of their ordinary routine tasks, and care providers who are ready to offer a wide range of services to the patients, to cover their disabilities and support them with leading a healthy life. However, each care provider can provide a limited number of capabilities and the special type of services, while only having the capacity to support a limited number of patients. On the other hand, there are several barriers, such as geographical distance, communication costs, time availability, which make this process more complicated, and the problem is NP-hard.

Figure 6.8 Social circle of Palliative care.

We assume that care providers are experts for providing a limited number of services, and the patients who have a profile which shows his/her capabilities and disabilities need those services. Capability here means the ability to do a task. Setting up the social circle of care for each patient in an optimum manner can be seen as a TFP in social networks. In fact, based on the structure of the network and the relationship among the social actors in the network as shown in Figure 6.9, the best team of care can be discovered. The framework visualizes the sample palliative care network, which connects all care providers and patients in the society. We have designed a framework to analyze various networks that the user has. The back-end of this work uses python and d3.js for visualization. However, in reality, care providers are not distributed in an efficient way among patients. Therefore, forming efficient teams is significant, because the success of the care system depends on their performance, especially on how well the team members communicate and collaborate with each other and how quickly they can be available for offering the required services.

Network Details and Diagram

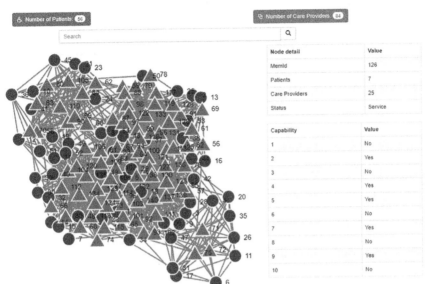

Node detail	Value
MemId	126
Patients	7
Care Providers	25
Status	Service

Capability	Value
1	No
2	Yes
3	No
4	Yes
5	Yes
6	No
7	Yes
8	No
9	Yes
10	No

Figure 6.9 Palliative Care Social Network: The framework is to visualize the palliative care social network.

The whole care network can be mapped to a weighted graph to consider the distance, communication, and contact costs. Hence, the problem can be defined as discovering the best teams of care providers for the patients in the palliative care network by offering his/her required capabilities in the most cost-effective way. In addition to that, at a system level, the challenge is to identify the optimal configuration of teams that will support as many patients as possible.

As the problem is an NP-hard problem, the authors are proposing an evolutionary model based on the Cultural Algorithm to tackle it.

Individual Representation

The team (individual) represents a candidate solution to the problem and consists of an array structure with s cells, which is the number of the required services to to be provided to patients in the palliative care network. For example, as shown in Figure 6.10, assume our network has eight nodes where the number of care providers is 5 and number of patients is 3. If $P1$ (patient) needs 2 services, $P2$ needs 4 services, and $P3$ needs 3 services, the size of the array, s, is equal to 9. The element of each cell is selected from the set of care providers (experts) who

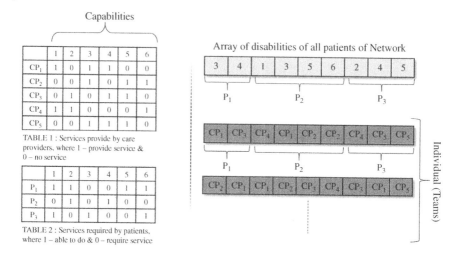

Figure 6.10 The representation of teams for the whole patients of a palliative care network, which has five care providers and three patients.

provide that service. Therefore, for each cell representing a required service k_j, a value is filled by an expert, a_i, where $k_j \in S(a_i)$.

Fitness Function

In the palliative care network setting, we use the weighted graph communication cost, contact cost, and geographical proximity, which already were defined in the previous section. The fitness function has been formulated by combining all three cost values as below while considering the workload balance.

$$\text{Fitness} = \lambda C_{\text{cost}} + \beta\left(1 - T_{\text{cost}}\right) + \gamma$$

where $\lambda + \beta + \gamma = 1$, λ, β, γ are balance factors and C_{cost} is communication cost, T_{cost} is contact cost, and D_{cost} is distance cost.

Given a team T of care providers for all patients in the palliative care network: $\left\{\left\langle \text{RC}^{p_1}, \text{S}^{cp_1} \right\rangle, \left\langle \text{RC}^{p_2}, \text{S}^{cp_2} \right\rangle, ..., \left\langle \text{RC}^{p_n}, \text{S}^{cp_m} \right\rangle\right\}$, where $\{p_1, p_2, ..., p_n\}$ are n number of patients and $\{cp_1, cp_2, ..., cp_m\}$ are m number of care providers. For the communication cost in this study, we consider only the sum of distance function. Moreover, our network is limited in size because the care providers should be within the range of distance required to reach the patients. Therefore, we use the Dijkstra algorithm to evaluate the shortest path distance. We are then able to calculate the sum of distance instantly.

The belief space in this research work is also defined similarly as in the work of coauthorship network setting.

Dataset and Observation

Since the health-care data are confidential, we tested our research work on synthetic social networks. The networks are generated based on LFR benchmark[2] for generating social networks with the default setting. We consider four various sizes of networks with 25, 50, 75, and 100 nodes and test with different ratios of patients and care providers. We try to answer the following challenging questions:

- What would be the ratio between patients and care providers to support as many patients as possible?
- For that ratio, at least how many services a care provider needs to provide?
- Based upon both above questions, what is the optimal individual which includes teams for all patients in the palliative care social network.

In our testing model, we assumed 10 capabilities are most significant for palliative care patients. To answer the questions 1 and 2, we checked various ratios with the different number of services from Care Providers (CP) as shown in Table 6.1.

Moreover, we check the most efficient teams by evaluating the fitness values from various algorithms to compare the fitness values obtained from our Cultural Algorithm as shown in Figure 6.11. We use genetic algorithms and a random method for comparison.

Additional information about this work can be found in the 2018 IEEE International Conference on Innovations in Intelligent Systems and Applications [15].

Table 6.1 The result of the various ratio of patient to care provider and what can a Care Provider (CP) provide the number of services.

	Number of service from a CP			
Patient: CP	**3**	**4**	**5**	**6**
25–75	Yes	Yes	Yes	Yes
30–70	Yes	Yes	Yes	Yes
50–50	No	Yes	Yes	Yes
60–40	No	No	No	Yes
75–25	No	No	No	No

---

2 https://sites.google.com/site/andrealancichinetti/files

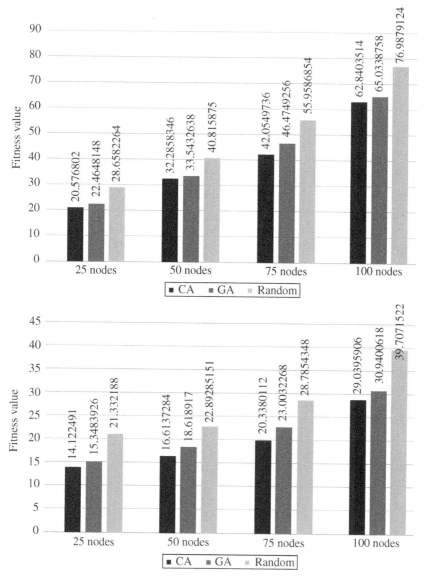

Figure 6.11 Comparing result of CA with various other algorithms for finding efficient teams for Palliative care.

Summary and Conclusion

A social network has much hidden and powerful information useful for the current world. Doing an investigation on social network rigorously will make us see the world in a completely different way. Although research in SNA have been conducted for many years, it became the popular research during the last decade since the social network started to influence various disciplines for different applications. Among all diverse applications, our center of focus is on the team formation problem.

Since the collaborative work of experts from their specialized field can provide more productive results in various fields, such as business, academic, sports, and health care, forming a successful team of experts becomes more significant. Therefore, our research is primarily focussed on TFP in different environments. In this chapter, we discuss two domains of research: forming teams in coauthorship networks and health-care networks.

Forming the efficient teams of experts from a complex network is proven to be the NP-hard problem because to find the optimal solution, we need to balance other influencing factors, such as communication cost, geographical proximity, personnel cost/contact cost, and workload balance. Therefore, we approach this problem with fewer simplifying assumptions than other search algorithms in order to guide the search process and employ Cultural Algorithms, which is inspired by biological evolution and cultural evolution to solve with less computation cost.

With the observation from two different setups in coauthorship dataset (DBLP) and palliative care dataset (synthetic network), CA performed well to discover efficient teams when compared with other algorithms. In the future, our research direction will be closer to dynamic networks in the real-world environment.

References

1 Zzkarian, A. and Kusiak, A. (1999). Forming teams: an analytical approach. *IIE Transactions* 31 (1): 85–97.

2 Chen, S.-J. and Lin, L. (2004). Modeling team member characteristics for the formation of a multifunctional team in concurrent engineering. *IEEE Transactions on Engineering Management* 51 (2): 111–124.

3 Fitzpatrick, E.L. and Askin, R.G. (2005). Forming effective worker teams with multi-functional skill requirements. *Computers & Industrial Engineering* 48 (3): 593–608.

4 Baykasoglu, A., Dereli, T., and Das, S. (2007). Project team selection using fuzzy optimization approach. *Cybernetics and Systems: An International Journal* 38 (2): 155–185.

5 Lappas, T., Liu, K., and Terzi, E. (2009). Finding a team of experts in social networks. *Proceedings of the 15th ACM SIGKDD International Conference on Knowledge Discovery and Data Mining* (28 June 2009), pp. 467–476.

6 Li, C.-T. and Shan, M.-K. (2010). Team formation for generalized tasks in expertise social networks. *2010 IEEE Second International Conference on Social Computing (SocialCom)* (20 August), pp. 9–16.

7 Dorn, C. and Dustdar, S. (25 October 2010). Composing near-optimal expert teams: a trade-off between skills and connectivity. In: *OTM Confederated International Conferences on the Move to Meaningful Internet Systems*, 472–489. Berlin, Heidelberg: Springer.

8 Kargar, M. and An, A. (2011). Discovering top-k teams of experts with/without a leader in social networks. In: *OTM Confederated International Conferences*, 472–489. Berlin, Heidelberg: Springer.

9 Gajewar, A. and Das Sarma, A. (2012). Multi-skill collaborative teams based on densest subgraphs. In: *Proceedings of the 2012 SIAM International Conference on Data Mining*, 165–176. Society for Industrial and Applied Mathematics.

10 Sonn, J.W. and Storper, M. (2008). The increasing importance of geographical proximity in knowledge production: an analysis of US patent citations, 1975–1997. *Environment and Planning A* 40 (5): 1020–1039.

11 Anagnostopoulos, A., Becchetti, L., Castillo, C. et al. (2012). Online team formation in social networks. *Proceedings of the 21st International Conference on World Wide Web* (16 April 2012), pp. 839–848.

12 Russell, S.J. and Norvig, P. (2016). *Artificial Intelligence: A Modern Approach*. Malaysia: Pearson Education Limited.

13 Reynolds, R.G. (1994). An introduction to cultural algorithms. *Proceedings of the Third Annual Conference on Evolutionary Programming* (24 February 1994), pp. 131–139.

14 Cohen, E., Halperin, E., Kaplan, H., and Zwick, U. (2003). Reachability and distance queries via 2-hop labels. *SIAM Journal on Computing* 32 (5): 1338–1355.

15 Selvarajah, K., Zadeh, P.M., Kobti, Z. et al. (2018, July). Team formation in community-based palliative care. In: *2018 Innovations in Intelligent Systems and Applications (INISTA)*, 1–7. IEEE.

7

Evolving Emergent Team Strategies in Robotic Soccer using Enhanced Cultural Algorithms

Mostafa Z. Ali[1], Mohammad I. Daoud[2], Rami Alazrai[2], and Robert G. Reynolds[3]

[1] *Department of Computer Information Systems, Jordan University of Science and Technology, Irbid, Jordan*
[2] *Department of Computer Engineering, German Jordanian University, Amman, Jordan*
[3] *Department of Computer Science Wayne State University, Detroit, MI, USA and Museum of Anthropological Archaeology, University of Michigan-Ann Arbor, Ann Arbor, MI, USA*

Introduction

Recently, soccer simulation became an attractive domain for applying learning concepts and strategies in the Artificial Intelligence field [1–6]. The soccer simulation system fosters research in various fields. Researchers from such different disciplines use different types of techniques and strategies, integrated, enhanced, and adapted to provide a competitive and interesting play. In such research, the target is to provide at least near-optimal evolved behaviors and policies for the agents and the team, during the gameplay.

One of the most famous competitions in such research is RoboCup [7–9], an international robotics competition, and the leading competition in the field. It constitutes many leagues: simulation league (2D and 3D), small size, middle size, standard size, and humanoid. This paper uses a 2D simulation platform as training for the 2D simulation league in RoboCup, for a nice introduction to the field. Furthermore, the 2D soccer simulation league offers an imperative experimental platform, which is a multiagent stochastic domain that is fully distributed, with continuous state, observation, and action space. AI researchers have been using this platform to pursue research in a wide variety of domains, including cooperation, coordination, and negotiation in real-time multiagent systems.

In distributed AI, the study of collaboration and coordination of a team of agents in multiagent systems (MASs) is one of the greatest challenges and research

Cultural Algorithms: Tools to Model Complex Dynamic Social Systems, First Edition.
Edited by Robert G. Reynolds.
© 2021 John Wiley & Sons, Inc. Published 2021 by John Wiley & Sons, Inc.
Companion website: www.wiley.com/go/CAT

directions. Teaching the robots to play soccer is one of the fields where researchers have thoroughly studied new strategies for different skills and tactics, such as how to shoot, intercept, and pass the ball, as well as how to handle it when surrounded with different types of agents with different roles [7-12].

The environment of the 2D soccer simulation is highly unpredictable and dynamic. Hence, it is very hard to generate an effective team strategy that is based on trained actions. Different works were introduced in this domain [13-19]. The Monte Carlo method was presented by Fang in [13] to develop a defensive strategy for the entire team. Researchers in [14] found a better way to dribble the ball and evolved a way around the opponent's defense, using a reinforcement learning method. Other researchers used the Markov decision process to handle the proximal dribble issue during gameplay [15]. A value strategy to improve the success rate of the passing action was presented by Zhang in [16]. On the other hand, anticipating the shooting action of the ball from opponent players was accomplished using inductive logic programming [17]. In a different type of research, the researchers used a BP neural network and mathematical analysis to improve the probability of interception success [18]. In [19], the researchers predicted the distance that the ball will cover when the agent successfully intercepts it using a Support Vector Regression method. Given that cooperation and the overall strategy of the team in a multiagent system is a challenge that is yet to be handled more efficiently, this problem continues to provoke significant interest [19].

The Cultural Algorithm (CA) has been used previously to examine such type of evolutionary computation models to evolve the cooperation within cultures of humans [20-22]. These researches investigated the extent to which conceptions of resource sharing and collaboration can emerge between groups of agents. The aim of this study is to modify and configure the CA to control the evolution of team strategies. This work develops a controller behavior and generates controllers that are able to govern the behavior of the whole team (a set of four autonomous robot soccer players) to play effectively using evolved skills and cooperative strategies. A discussion of the specific technical issues (implementation of basic agent actions and managing the communication between the agents) is beyond the scope of this work. Testing such targets will be based on an open-source simulation system that is used to evaluate the skills and proposed plans of the controlled team of robots.

The rest of the paper is organized as follows: a brief introduction to this research area and a motivation on the current work are given in section "Introduction." Then in section "Related Work," we discuss the current techniques from the literature that were used to tackle similar type of problems. In section "The 2D Soccer Simulation Test bed," an overview of the current test bed simulator in which our team of robots will have their skills and behavior evolved, which is a system with simplicity to serve as a tutorial for Cultural Algorithms and its application to dynamic systems. The methodology, includes a brief introduction to the canonical Cultural Algorithms. The encoding for this problem and the modification of the basic components of Cultural

Algorithm to suite such a problem are given in section "Evolution of Team Strategies via Cultural Algorithm." In section "Experiments and Analysis of Results," we describe the conducted experiments within this framework. Conclusions and future work will be given in section "Conclusion."

Related Work

As was previously mentioned, different researches investigated the use of evolutionary algorithms (EAs) to simulate the evolution of collaboration and cooperation in human cultures [20–22]. The goal of this work is to identify the limitations in information exchange and cooperation between individuals in a multiagent system, which greatly affects the progress and success of the work of all these agents as a team.

Evolutionary Algorithms were used in other types of dynamic environments such as RoboCup [23, 24]. This competition is considered an organization for multidisciplinary research and is held every year. It can carry different implementations that support leagues that are composed of agents with different capabilities and scope [25, 26].

Researchers in [27] developed an evolutionary algorithm to manipulate location parameters of agents on the field, represented as regions in the pitch. The work is based on a Genetic Algorithm (GA). The chromosomes in their representation contain the information for the individual's team, in a manner that makes tactical information accessible to all players in the team. The algorithm was able to always find a good solution. On the other hand, the algorithm consumes too many generations before they were able to obtain a fitness ranking at a satisfactory level where the performance of the team is acceptable.

The representation of the pertinent behaviors was extracted using a methodology that is based on a plan definition language as proposed in [28]. Such technique promoted the reuse of such pertinent behaviors in future scenarios. In their work, the authors studied behaviors, starting from set pieces and enhanced scoring, in addition to enhancing their possession of the ball, during gameplay. Conclusions of their work helped them in inferring expressive rules. Such expressive rules helped in influencing the development of rules from scratch.

A standard GA to learn team strategies and set events – set plays that are concluded as a consequence of a specific scenario – was used in [29]. The algorithm helped in optimizing the behavior of all robotic agents in the game. The concluded rules were able to generate better performing strategies, when comparing to the base team. Other researchers also investigated how to learn set plays as can be seen in [30, 31]. Interaction nets were used in [31] to learn team strategies and an optimal role assignment with a behavior that is similar to the cooperation between agents, according to guidelines of the RoboCup competition.

The 2D Soccer Simulation Test Bed

Prototyping Environment Motivation

This section describes the 2D soccer simulator and its main features that are common to all contestant teams and prototypes across all the known leagues. This simulator is not the first of its kind for testing theoretical research in the 2D soccer simulation league. The first prototype of this kind was attempted using the RoboCup simulator. This simulator is a rich environment for testing the development and formation of teams and appropriate skills. However, this richness imposes extra constraints that made it less desirable for our research. As an example of the imposed constraints that made it less desirable is that the simulated robot players are not capable of recognizing their teammates on the field. Hence, dealing with perception is the appropriate thing that these robots find themselves forced to face in such as environment. As the focus of this research is on tactics and theories, spending most of the time on object recognition and perception handling is considered out of scope. The test bed simulator used in this research can be thought of as a first step toward the RoboCup simulator, to improve theories and basic to intermediate skills of team formation, and advancements in evolving offensive and defensive plays. Moreover, it will help in avoiding noise in the test data at this stage of development. Hence, this will facilitate the isolation of tested behaviors in the system that is meant to be a tutorial on using CA for such complex dynamic environements.

Simulator Overview

The playing area of this simulator is a rectangular area that is enclosed by walls from all sides, in a manner similar to indoor soccer, as can be seen in Figure 7.1. In this rectangular area, representing the pitch, and at the end of the field from each of the two sides, there is a goal area for each of the two teams. The game consists of two opposing teams. Each of the teams contains one goalie and four field players. The game starts with a kick-off and continues until a goal is scored by either of the two teams. At this point, the game resumes at the center of the field with a kick-off again. The technical description of the simulator is not relevant at this stage and hence will not be discussed here. More information can be found in [32].

Teams

Formed teams are very important to this research as they form the basic construct for implemented behaviors and tested formations and skills. The following features are the basic ones and they are implemented for both teams in the game.

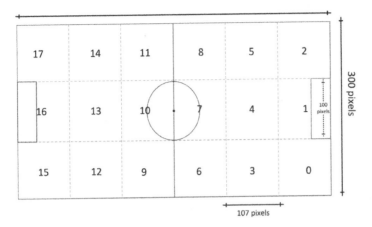

Figure 7.1 2D soccer simulation test bed.

For each of the two teams, the basic implementation has two attackers and two defenders and a goalie. This configuration dictates that there will be a right attacker, left attacker, right defender, and left defender. The basic heuristic in the game is implemented using finite state machines (FSMs) and steering behaviors. The players have steering behaviors that are available to them, such as:

- Separation: steering the player away from other agents.
- Pursuit: the player deals with the target as a moving object (such as a moving player) and steers to its direction.
- Seek: moving toward the target without adjusting the robot's speed.
- Arrive: same as the seek behavior but with the difference that the robot slows down as it arrives at the target.
- Interpose: steer the robot toward the midpoint between two objects.

The FSM that is utilized by field players (main constructs of formations and skills evolved in this research) and used in the game is self-explanatory, as can be seen in Figure 7.2. The *ReceiveBall* state guides the robot to either pursuit the ball or arrive at the ball's target. This is determined by either some related factors (such as the presence of an opponent robot in the threatening radius) or is performed at random. *ReturToHomeRegion* will direct all players to return to their predefined home regions on the field. *KickBall* is a state that will be entered by the player whenever it attempts to pass the ball to its teammate or when they shoot at the opponent's goal. The *GlobalPlayerState* is responsible for message routing. These messages are connected to the implemented states, as can be inferred from the messages' names. Such messages include *Msg_PassToMe*, *Msg_SupportAttacker*, *Msg_GoHome*,

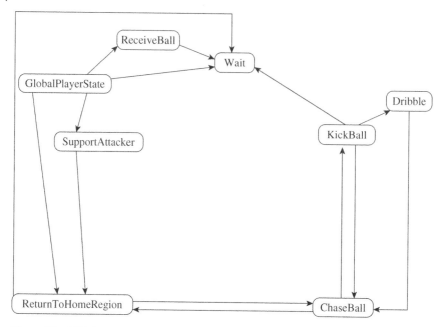

Figure 7.2 FSM for any player in the simulator.

Msg_Wait, and *Msg_ReceiveBall*. A message usually determines the next state that the robot will go into during gameplay.

Evolution of Team Strategies via Cultural Algorithm

Basic Engine of CA

Cultural Algorithm is a class of computational models derived from the cultural evolution process in nature [33]. The pseudocode for the canonical CA is given in Figure 7.3.

$P(t)$ and $B(t)$ are the population and Belief spaces at time t. The first step of the algorithm is to initialize the belief and population spaces, after which the evolution loop starts. The evolution continues for a certain number of generations until the termination condition is true. The communication topologies ($F_{obj}()$, $F_{acc}()$, and $F_{inf}()$) will form a dual inheritance framework for both spaces. At the end of each generation, the function $F_{obj}()$ is used to evaluate each individual in the population. At this point, the fitness scores for all the individuals will be ready, and the function $F_{acc}()$ will select the individuals that will be used to update $B(t)$. Next, the function $F_{update}()$ will be used to add the experiences of the accepted individuals to $B(t)$.

```
Begin
    t = 0;
    initialize B(t), P(t)
    while (!termination condition)
        evaluate P(t)        { F_obj() }
        update B(t), F_acc(P^t))
        evolve (P(t), influence(B(t))
        t = t + 1;
        select P(t) from P(t-1)
    end
End
```

Figure 7.3 Pseudocode of basic CA.

The function $F_{inf}()$ will then use the generated knowledge to affect the selection of the individuals for the next generation.

Knowledge Sources in CA

The Belief Space in a Cultural Algorithm consists of five knowledge sources. The knowledge sources include: Situational, Normative, Domain, Topographic, and Historic. A brief description of each of these knowledge sources is given below:

Situational knowledge provides illustrative cases of exemplar individuals and is used to interpret the experiences of individuals. This will help the individuals to imitate the exemplars in the population.

Normative knowledge offers promising ranges for the parameters at all times. Such ranges for the variables can be thought of as the basics for the behaviors of individuals and are used to guide the adjustments of such individuals [34].

Domain knowledge directs future search based on information from the problem domain. As an example, knowledge about all the regions in the field, where to move to players when the team loses possession of the ball, and where to move them when the team regains possession of the ball will be useful for reasoning during the game.

Topographic knowledge utilizes area-based functional landscape patterns [35]. It uses spatial characteristics of the landscape and produces a division in the form of cells for the landscape. Each of these produced cells keeps track of the best individual in its region. This process emulates the cell-best.

Historic knowledge archives important scenarios and events by observing all events in the game. As an example of these events that it records, it records any change in the functional landscape and can be used to reason about future moves.

The five knowledge sources were added to the CA engine at different times. These knowledge sources are used to add different problem-solving capabilities to the CA framework. As any problem can be expressed as a subset of these knowledge sources, such set is considered to be complete [34, 35]. When these knowledge sources are interlaced together, their interaction results in interesting behaviors in the soccer simulator.

Evolution of Team Strategies

This study starts by producing and evolving a set of rules that will control the responses, which depend on the current state of play, of the agents in our controlled team, at every instant in the game. The agent uses its basic sensors, as defined above, to communicate with the basic engine of the game to be informed about the ongoing state of the game. In a manner that depends on the current state, the agent executes new actions that might in turn change the state of the agent itself. Hence, modifying the team strategy is a result of the sum of behaviors of all the controlled agents.

As the definition of precise strategies for each player is intricate, costly, and necessitates a profound knowledge of the needed behavior of each of the players in the team, it results in a predictable behavior. To avoid the aforementioned issues, the same evolved controller (except the goalkeeper who has a different implementation) will be used to manage all the agents. Using just one type of controller to devise the team strategy will make the process much simpler. However, not all the agents will be executing the same action at a certain point in time as that depends on the reached state and perceived input for each of the agents, during the game.

Modified Cultural Algorithm

Encoding
The first step is to study the chromosome representation that is needed to evolve the strategies. The population space in Cultural Algorithm will contain a number of individuals. Each individual represents a team strategy, which is a mutual set of actions that each of the agents will have to perform after perceiving the environment at a certain point in time. This greatly depends on the information obtained via the agent's visual range, which is different from agent to agent at any moment. Such information is structured as parameters that can take different values from specified ranges [36]. Therefore, an agent in the population space is represented as a vector A of n components, where n is the number of the different cases that agent can be in, and $A[i]$ is the component that represents the action to be

performed in a specific state. Hence, if we have k parameters, and parameter m_i ($0 \leq i \leq k - 1$) can have n_i possible values (labeled 0 to n_{i-1}), then the component:

$$A\left[\sum_{i=1}^{k}\left(a_{k-i} \times \left(\prod_{j=1}^{i-1}n_{k-j}\right)\right)\right],$$

This describes the action that must be executed when parameters m_0, m_1, ..., m_{k-1} have the values a_0, a_1, ..., a_{k-1}, respectively. The management of the large number of parameters, as those provided by the game engine, is a complex task. To reduce such complexity, and to match the plan of evolving our controller, the following related and manageable set of parameters have been considered in the experiments:

- Can kick the ball (B_{kick}): Checks if the player can kick the ball. This parameter has two values: (i) cannot kick the ball, (ii) can kick the ball.
- Ball possession ($B_{possession}$): Checks if the agent is in possession of the ball. These parameters can have one of four values. (i) the agent possesses the ball, 1. (ii) a teammate possesses the ball, (iii) a rival player possesses the ball, (iv) it is not known.
- Position of player in the pitch (P_p): These parameters determine the position of the agent in the field. With the help of supporting spots that are calculated next to each goal area, this parameter can assume one of three possible values. (i) closer to the area surrounding its goal area, (ii) closer to the region surrounding the rival goal area, (iii) not defined.
- Potential situation (P_s): This parameter can assume one of two values. (i) if the player is supported by more teammates (candidate supporting players) than rival players, (ii) otherwise.

Therefore, inspecting the encoding of the individual in the population, one finds that it consists of 48 genes. This number represents the combination of all possible outcomes from such parameter values (before filtering it for logical combinations). Moreover, the proximity of the ball ($B_{position}$) to the goal areas was studied as a new parameter that can be added to the previous primary set. This parameter can take one of three values. (i) the ball is close to the goal area, (ii) the ball is close to the rival goal area, (iii) not defined. Experiments that used this additional parameter had to be dealing with a chromosome of length 144. On the other hand, filtering such combinations for logical settings reduced the resulting complexity. This filter had to be applied as some combinations make no sense. An example of such excluded combinations by this filter is when $P_p = 1$ and $B_{position} = 2$ with $B_{kick} = 1$. Such knowledge leads to a simplified representation.

Each component of the vector encoding a candidate solution contains an action. For this study, the adopted actions that match this game engine can be stated as follows:

ReturnToHomeRegion: Each player can either be in their designated home region (which might change based on the adopted strategy), which is the position at the kickoff time or is placed in the target_position which represents the potential positions for those defenders or forwards, depending on the strategic plan, or reaction to the upcoming events during the game.

Chase_Ball: If the ball is visible, the agent will try to seek the ball's immediate position, in an attempt to get within kicking range. As soon as the agent enters this state, its seek behavior will also be activated as follows:

```
void Chase_Ball::Enter(Player* player)
{
        player->player_steering()->player_seek();
}
```

The next expected state after this action is executed is to change state to the Ball_kick, if it is within kicking range. Otherwise, the player will continue to chase the ball, assuming it is the closest to the ball.

Dribble_ball: Moving the ball around in the form of a series of dashes and small kicks. At this state, the agent will be able to, while controlling the ball, move agilely around the rival agent or it will be able to rotate on the spot.

Ball_kick: Attempt shooting the ball in the direction of the opponent's goal. This involves informing the rest of team who the controlling player is, as follows:

```
void Dribble_ball::Enter(Player* player){
        player->Team()->set_controlling_agent(player);
}
```

Executing the main logic of this action involves inspecting to see if the position of the ball is between the agent and the agents downfield. Although this is undesirable, it is necessary to check and see if it is needed to turn the player, while maintaining control of the ball, and move the ball as far as possible from its own home goal. It achieves this via turning a series of dribbles in a direction of $\pi/4$ degrees away from the agent's facing course, as follows:

```
Vector2D direction = player->Heading();
double angle = QuarterPi *
-1 * player->Team()->HomeGoal()->Facing().Sign
(player->Heading());
Vec2DRotateAroundOrigin(direction, angle);
const double KickingForce = 0.8;
player->Ball()->Kick(direction, KickingForce);
```

Support_attacker: When the team is the controlling team, the playerBase class inspects all the team members to see who is closest to the best calculated supporting spot (which is calculated every few time steps), around the rival goal region. This includes finding who to pass the ball to, whether the closest member or the farthest team member.

Receive_ball: The player who has just made the pass sends a message, through the defined router of messages in the game, to the receiving player. The message contains an extra information field about the target position of the ball so that the steering target of the receiving agent can also be set, appropriately. Hence, this receiving agent will be able to move to position to intercept the ball. This Receive_ball state can be presumed by only one agent at a time to properly update the pointers, in case they are sought by the other team members if needed.

```
if ((player->InRivalRegion() ||
RandFloat() < Prm.Chance_Using_ArriveType_
ReceiveBehavior) &&
!player->Team()->Opponent_Within_Radius(player->Pos(),
PassThreatRadius))
{
player->Steering()->ArriveOn(); //steer towards the
target position of ball
}
else
{
player->player_steering()->Pursuit_On(); //pursue the
ball
}
```

Executing this state requires the agent to move into position and wait or if the ball comes within a specified distance of if the agent's team loses control of the ball, then the agent will have to chase the ball.

Wait: The agent will execute this state, waiting at the location it was positioned at, given by its steering behavior target. When the agent finds itself as the closest player to the ball in the team, then it will exit this state to chase the ball. Moreover, if it finds itself upfield of a teammate controlling the ball, then it will message the teammate through the router to see if it is possible to pass the ball. The teammate will answer only if it is safe to pass the ball, and hence the agent will exit its wait state.

```
if ( player->Team()->In_Control() &&
(!player->control_the_ball()) &&
player->upfield() )
```

```
{
        player->Team()->Pass_Request(player);
        return;
}
if (player->Pitch()->GameOn())
{
if (player->closest_member_to_ball() &amp;&amp;
        player->Team()->Receiving_player() == NULL
&amp;&amp;
                !player->Pitch()->GoalKeeper_got_ball())
                {
                player->ModifyState(player, Chase_
Ball::Instance());
                        return;
                }
}
```

One can find that the search space as a representation of the different number of strategies that can be generated by the different combination of values of the used actions, is 7^{144}, if we carry on with the second representation, and 7^{48} if we consider the first representation (with the addition of the proximity of the ball ($B_{position}$) to the goal areas). The example in Table 7.1 shows a sample from the encoding knowledge of length 48. This should serve as a strategy that makes the teammates play best and locate the best position and/or move that should determine the subtarget for the next time step. As the resulting search space will be vast, this problem is an impracticable for the traditional methods, while it will be an ideal choice for an algorithm like Cultural Algorithms.

Fitness Function

This function is very crucial to the evaluation of the adequacy of the team strategy in question. If we assume that the population of Cultural Algorithms is P^t at time step t, then evaluating the fitness of individual X_i^t is a result of the

Table 7.1 Performance of the algorithm against all other teams.

Game description (30 × 1.0E + 03)	Wins	Losses	Draw	Avg. goals	Avg. opponent's goals
Experiment 1 (CA vs. Default)	30	0	0	10.1341	4.1009
Experiment 2 (CA vs. EP)	26	1	3	7.2624	3.3432
Experiment 3 (CA vs. Defense)	18	4	8	6.2936	2.3662
Experiment 4 (CA vs. GA)	20	3	7	13.6671	7.2096

simulation of the match between the implanted opponent strategy and that strategy encoded in X_i^t. The fitness function uses the statistical data and tallies (like goals scored, winning team, etc.) that we collect at the end of the match. The computational cost will be high if we collect more statistical data. Therefore, for evaluating the fitness of X_i^t and the opponent strategy, the following data were collected:

Goals scored (gs_i): in the opponent's goal

Goals received (gr_i): in the modified team's goal

Possession of the ball (pb_i): average time the team was able to possess the ball during the match

Attacks on rival's area (ar_i): average time the team was able to keep the ball in the opponent's area

Ball distance (d_i): average distance between the ball and the team players.

Then, the fitness function in CA is defined as follows:

$$\text{Fit}\left(X_i^t\right) = f_1\left(d_i, pb_i, ar_i\right) + f_2\left(gs_i, gr_i\right)$$

where,

$$f_1\left(d_i, pb_i, ar_i\right) = c_1 \cdot d_1 + c_2 \cdot pb_i + c_3 \cdot ar_i$$

and

$$f_2\left(gs_i, gr_i\right) = \begin{cases} 0, gs_i = 0 \\ c_4 \cdot \left(\left(gs_i - gr_i\right) + 1\right), & gs_i \geq gr_i \\ \left(c_4 - 1\right)/\left(gr_i - gs_i\right), & \text{o.w.} \end{cases}$$

where $c_1 = 0.02$, $c_2 = 0.2$, and $c_3 = 1.2$. On the other hand, c_4 is set to 50 so that the function returns multiples of 50 in the case of a victory or a draw, hence increasing the importance of the higher difference of goals. While in the case of a defeat, the importance is given to the minor difference of goals ($gr_i - gs_i$). The first component of the fitness function (f_1) emphasizes evolving strategies where individuals know the basics of how to play soccer well. At the beginning, the population is randomly initialized and hence will play with just the basic steering behavior skills defined in the game. The first three weight constants (c_1, c_2, and c_3) will emphasize strategies where the ball will mainly stay the larger portion of time in the opponent's second half of the pitch. The second part of the fitness function (f_2) will reward strategies that evolve toward better arrangement of plays. Those will be the strategies that are able to beat the opponent team.

The fitness function of this dynamic environment is non-deterministic as it is being affected by some random operators that are used by the game engine, to make it as realistic as possible. This is another reason for not using exact solution techniques, when they exist, and is another incentive for using CA for handling such a complicated problem.

The operators used in CA are single point crossover and binary tournament for parent selection. Moreover, CA uses elitism for the replacement policy. The mutation is performed by selecting that mutation point and randomly mutating the action to any other action. The performance of the influence function is evaluated at any point in time as:

$$E\left[KS_k\right] = \frac{\sum_{i=1}^{N_k} f\left(X_i\right)}{N_k}$$

where KS_k is the kth knowledge source, $f(X_i)$ is the fitness of the ith individual, and N_k is the number of followers of knowledge source k.

Enhancing the Defense

Some of the developed skills and their related parameters will help the controlled team reduce the number of received goals by the opponent team. Defensive plans are considered more important than the offensive plans. Even if the team has basic offensive tactics but a strong defense, this will help to increase the rank of the team against its opponent. Defense is one of the two team states. When the team enters this state it will have to know where to place every player and what state every player should be made at. The controlled team was trained to know how to steer the closest player to the position between the opponent player possessing the ball and his supporting teammate. This is a simple, yet very effective, strategy as it will force the opponent player in possession of the ball to continue on his own toward the goal of the controlled team, or shoot the ball from the position when it finds that it cannot pass the ball to its supporting robot player. This will help in reducing the opportunity to receive goals from the opponent team. Such a plan is illustrated in Figure 7.4.

A vital thing here is to train the robot when to anticipate to interpose itself between the player in possession of the ball and its teammate with its state Support_attacker that is waiting to receive the pass.

Experiments and Analysis of Results

An intensive study was carried out for testing the best values for the sensitive parameters. The number of generations for the evolution was selected to be $1.0E+03$; the tested mutation rates μ were 0.1, 0.01, and 0.05; the size of the individual (144 and 48, as mentioned before); and length of the offspring (1, 2, 3, and 4).

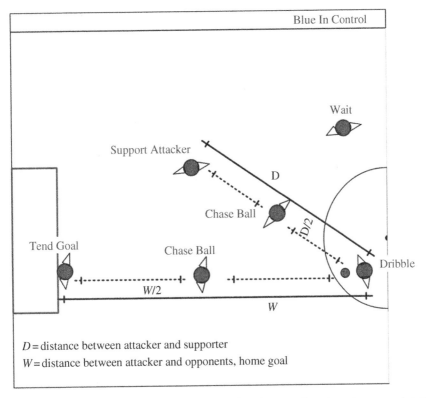

Figure 7.4 Enhanced defense through interposing the opposing player in possession of the ball and his supporting player.

After sufficient tests, the population size N is considered to be 40 and the crossover rate was set to 0.85. The population was randomly initialized at all times. We used 30 runs/test instances. Different tests were carried out where the first target was to beat a manually implemented opponent, and then the resulting winning strategy is to be implemented in the objective function. This will be used as the new opponent and so on. A large set of experiments will result from such parameter testing and hence some of these will be illustrated next. This is computationally expensive. However, it is necessary to understand the nature of such simulated soccer environment in which the robots compete using evolved skills as an introduction for the RoboCup simulator at a later stage. It is worth mentioning that most of the statistical data and results have been presented in graphical format for ease of discussion and a richer content.

Figure 7.5 shows the average fitness over 30 runs for one test instance. The evolutionary process shows a common behavior in all the tests. The team strategies that

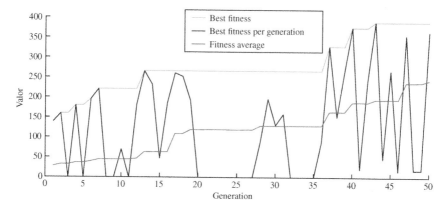

Figure 7.5 Average results for fitness value/generations.

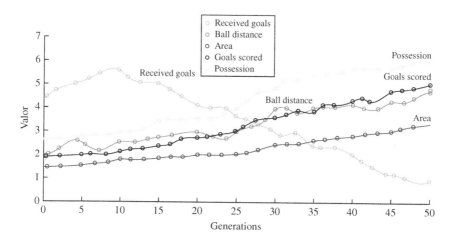

Figure 7.6 Evolution of values defining the fitness function.

were encoded as individuals in the population performed with the basic steering behavior and play skills that were coded in the game engine. However, they evolve faster within a few generations, where we are evolving the best actions to be taken from what the agents start with and how they cooperate with their team.

Figure 7.6 shows, for the same test instance, the evolution of the data values that are part of the fitness function defined in CA and are used to define it. As can be seen, there is an improvement in the amount of time spent in the opponents area (area) along with ball control (ball distance). Moreover, the number of scored goals compared to the received ones has clearly increased with time.

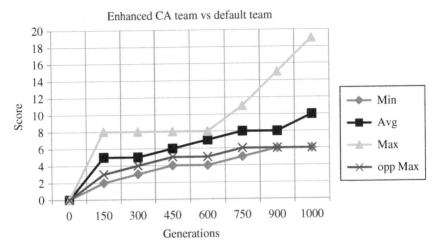

Figure 7.7 The average, maximum, and minimum number of goals that were recorded in 30 runs, each of 1.0E+03 generations long for a game between CA team and the default team.

Experiment 1. Enhanced CA Team Against the Default Team

It is evident from this experiment that the controlled team via enhanced CA evolved a better set of skills as it clearly increased the number of scored goals compared with the default team. As can be seen in Figure 7.7, these results were tallied over 30 runs, each of which were run for 1.0E+03 generations. By giving enough time for the evolution of the controlled team, it is clear from the worst, average, and best curves that the CA-enhanced team has a better score compared with the default team with the basic skills. This is due to the idea that the CA-enhanced team was able to enhance its offensive skills by selecting the most appropriate states, regions, and timed moves. Moreover, it was able to enhance its defense skills by selecting the appropriate time and position to interpose itself between the opponent player and its supporting teammate. All calculations were based on the calculated supporting spots in the goal region of the opponent. As can be seen in the figure, the curve for the opponent's maximum score was kept between the curve for minimum values and the curve of the average values of the enhanced team. The curve of the maximum score shows a great improvement when compared with the curve of the maximum values of that of the opponent.

Experiment 2. Enhanced CA Team Against the Team with a Strong Offense

In this experiment, the controlled team played against another team with enhanced offense skills. That team was hardcoded with rules and skills from some

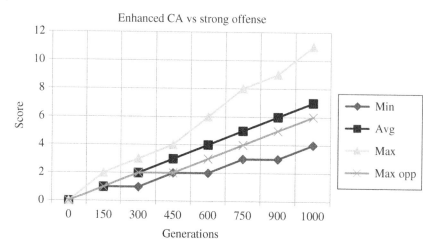

Figure 7.8   The average, maximum, and minimum number of goals that were recorded in 30 runs, each of 1.0E+03 generations long for a game between CA team and the EP team.

of the scripts that we obtained from the enhanced CA team in the other experiments. As can be seen in Figure 7.8, although the score was less in general for all types of curves that were sketched for the enhanced CA team, it was able to adapt and enhance skills to a better level. These skills were able to strengthen the defense and find a better cooperation through enhancing the main elements of the fitness functions, such as possess the ball more than the opponent team and find better regions through which the pass to a supporting player is safer. The maximum number of goals the enhanced team was able to obtain at the end of the evolution was 11, compared to 19 when playing against the default team in experiment 1.

Experiment 3. Enhanced CA Team Against the Team with Enhanced Defense

In this experiment, the enhanced CA team played against a team with hardcoded rules to place an interposing player between the player who possesses the ball of the enhanced CA team and his supporting robot. This made it difficult for the enhanced CA team to score goals. As was the case with experiment 2, and despite the lower score as can be seen in Figure 7.9, the enhanced CA team was able to evolve its skills to support the possessing player with other strategies like rotating back until there is a better supporting player. This better supporting player will work side-by-side with the attacker who possesses the ball to open a safe wing through which it can approach closer to the goal. The team had to learn all the distances and the mechanism of applying such a strategy.

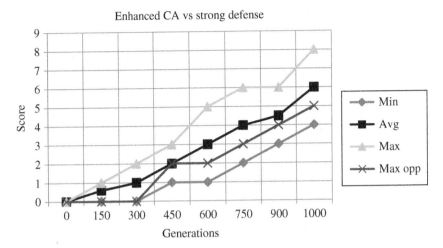

Figure 7.9 The average, maximum, and minimum number of goals that were recorded in 30 runs, each of 1.0E + 03 generations long for a game between CA team and the strong defense team.

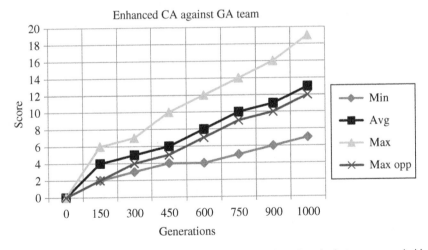

Figure 7.10 The average, maximum, and minimum number of goals that were recorded in 30 runs, each of 1.0E + 03 generations long for a game between CA team and the GA team.

Experiment 4. Enhanced CA Team Against the GA Team

This experiment shows how the enhanced CA team played against a GA team that used tournament selection. As shown in Figure 7.10, the curve showing the scores of the GA team over all the generations exhibits a performance that is better than the minimum curve of the enhanced CA team. On the other hand, the curve of the

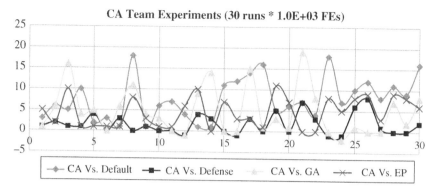

Figure 7.11 Difference in scoring between the different pairs of experiments.

Table 7.2 Sample encoding for an arbitrary individual.

$P_sB_{kick}P_p$	$B_{possession}$			
	Player	Teammate	Opponent	Unknown
111	1	5	3	2
112	4	4	2	5
113	4	1	3	3
121	4	2	4	6
122	6	3	4	4

GA team lies between the minimum scores and the average scores of the enhanced CA team. The enhanced CA team was able to score as high as 19 goals when playing against the GA team which was able to score 12 goals at the end of the evolution.

The results of the 30 runs for the previous experiments are shown in Figure 7.11. In this figure, a peak or the trough of a wave above the X-axis means that there is a positive difference to the favor of the enhanced CA team. While a part of the curve below the X-axis means a negative difference in favor of the opponent team. Small amplitudes mean that the difference, if it exists, is a small one. A summary of the statistics for all the experiments is given in Table 7.2.

Conclusion

The modified Cultural Algorithm with an EP component as a population space, was able to adapt the skills and emergent behavior strategies of the robot players, when compared with other types of strategies. The fitness function has been composed in a manner that captures the basic metrics that affect the score of each team. This fitness function is guided by two heterogeneous components. The first component guides the basic learning of soccer strategies, while the other component attempts to find winning strategies. This modified version of the CA recorded ranges of the robot player behaviors in the belief space. The algorithm was able to evolve a set of challenging offensive and defensive skills in terms of moves, states, regions, and distances in order to make better and organized moves. Such skills were evolved by having the enhanced algorithm play against opponents with different types of skills and tactics, to assess them. This work could be used to generate opponents in soccer simulators based on the human player's measured skills. The play domain could include other types of parameters that are useful for enhancing the rank of the system during gameplay. Such parameters and situations will be the content of future work.

References

1 Wang, C., Chen, X., Zhao, X., and Ju, S. (2004). Design and implementation of a general decision-making model in Robocup simulation. *International Journal of Advanced Robotic Systems* 1 (3): 207–212.

2 Dashti, H., Aghaeepour, N., Asadi, S. et al. (2006). Dynamic positioning based on voronoi cells (Dpvc). In: *Robocup 2005: Robot Soccer World Cup*, 9e, vol. 4020 (eds. A. Bredenfeld, A. Jacoff, I. Noda and Y. Takahashi), 219–229. Heidelberg, Germany: SBH.

3 Almeida, F., Abreu, P.H., Lau, N., and Reis, L.P. (2013). An automatic approach to extract goal plans from Soccer simulated matches. *Soft Computing* 17 (5): 835–848.

4 Niemueller, T., Reuter, S., Ferrein, A. et al. (2015). Evaluation of the RoboCup Logistics League and derived criteria for future competitions. In: *RoboCup 2015: Robot World Cup XIX. RoboCup 2015. Lecture Notes in Computer Science*, vol. 9513 (eds. L. Almeida, J. Ji, G. Steinbauer and S. Luke), 31–43. Cham: Springer.

5 Adachi, Y., Ito, M., and Naruse, T. (2017). Classifying the strategies of an opponent team based on a sequence of actions in the RoboCup SSL. In: *RoboCup 2016: Robot World Cup XX. RoboCup 2016. Lecture Notes in Computer Science*, vol. 9776 (eds. S. Behnke, R. Sheh, S. Sarıel and D. Lee), 109–120. Cham: Springer.

6 Farazi, H., Allgeuer, P., Ficht, G., and Brandenburger, A. (2017). RoboCup 2016 humanoid TeenSize winner NimbRo: robust visual perception and Soccer behaviors. In: *RoboCup 2016: Robot World Cup XX. RoboCup 2016. Lecture Notes in Computer Science*, vol. 9776 (eds. S. Behnke, R. Sheh, S. Sarıel and D. Lee), 478–489. Cham: Springer.

7 Kyrylov, V., Greber, M., and Bergman, D. (2005). Multi-criteria optimization of ball passing in simulated Soccer. *Journal of Multi-Criteria Decision Analysis* 13: 103–113.

8   Mota, L., Reis, L.P., and Lau, N. (2011). Multi-robot coordination using setplays in the middle-size and simulation leagues. *Mechatronics* 21 (2): 434–444.

9   Abreu, P.H., Silva, D.C., Mendes-Moreira, J. et al. (2013). Using multivariate adaptive regression splines in the construction of simulated Soccer team's behavior models. *International Journal of Computational Intelligence Systems* 6 (5): 893–910.

10 Abreu, P.H., Moura, J., Silva, D.C. et al. (2012). Performance analysis in Soccer: a cartesian coordinates based approach using Robocup data. *Soft Computing* 16 (1): 47–61.

11 Cooksey, P., Mendoza, J.P., and Veloso, M. (2017). Opponent-aware ball-manipulation skills for an autonomous Soccer robot. In: *RoboCup 2016: Robot World Cup XX. RoboCup 2016. Lecture Notes in Computer Science*, vol. 9776 (eds. S. Behnke, R. Sheh, S. Sariel and D. Lee), 84–96. Cham: Springer.

12 Speck, D., Barros, P., Weber, C., and Wermter, S. (2017). Ball localization for Robocup Soccer using convolutional neural networks. In: *RoboCup 2016: Robot World Cup XX. RoboCup 2016. Lecture Notes in Computer Science*, vol. 9776 (eds. S. Behnke, R. Sheh, S. Sariel and D. Lee), 19–30. Cham: Springer.

13 Bao-fu, F., Bing-rong, H., Bao, D.-q. et al. (2007). A multi-agent defensive strategy based on the Monte Carlo method. *Journal of Harbin Institute of Technology* 39 (s1): 77–80.

14 Tavafi, A., Majidi, N., Shaghelani, M. et al. (2013). Optimization for agent path finding in Soccer 2D simulation. *Communications in Computer and Information Science* 296: 109–114.

15 Ke, S. and Xiao-ping, C. (2011). Action-driven Markov decision process and the application in RoboCup. *Journal of Chinese Computer Systems* 32 (3): 511–515.

16 Zhang, X.-b., Liu, Y.-c., and Chen, L. (2011). Robocup passing strategy based on the passing evaluation function. *Journal of Anhui University of Technology (Natural Science)* 28 (2): 171–174.

17 Illobre, A., Gonzalez, J., Otero, R. et al. (2011). Learning action descriptions of opponent behavior in the Robocup 2D simulation environment. *Inductive Logic Programming Lecture Notes in Computer Science* 6489: 105–113.

18 Jian-Huai, C., Mao-Qing, L., and Wu, S.-X. (2010). Collaboration interception strategy of multi robots in RoboCupSoccer. *Computer Engineering and Applications* 46 (16): 1–5.

19 Yang, L., Wang, H., Baofu, F. et al. (2007). Application of the method of support vector regression in RoboCup. *Journal of Hefei University of Technology (Natural Science)* 30 (10): 1258–1260.

20 Reynolds, R.G. (1979). An adaptive computer model of the evolution of agriculture for hunter-gatherers in the valley of Oaxaca, Mexico. PhD dissertation. Department of Computer Science, University of Michigan Ann Arbor, MI.

21 Reynolds, R.G. (1978). On modeling the evolution of hunter-gatherer decision-making systems. *Geographical Analysis* 10 (1): 31–46.

22 Reynolds, R.G., Whallon, R., Ali, M.Z., and Zadegan, B.M. (2006). Agent-based modeling of early cultural evolution. *IEEE Congress on Evolutionary Computation*: 1135–1142.

23 Jin, X. and Reynolds, R.G. (1999). Using knowledge-based evolutionary computation to solve nonlinear constraint optimization problems: a cultural algorithm approach. In: *IEEE Congress on Evolutionary Computation (CEC 99)*, vol. 3, 1672–1678. Washington, DC: IEEE.

24 Kvasnicka, V., Pospíchal, J., and Tino, P. (2000). *Evolucné Algoritmy*. Slovakia, Bratislava: STU.

25 Lau, N., Lopes, L.S., and Corrente, G.A. (2008). Cambada: information sharing and team coordination. In: *Proceedings of Eighth Conference on Autonomous Robot Systems and Competitions*, 27–32. Aveiro, Portugal: Universidade de Aveiro.

26 Lekavy, M. (2005). Optimising multiagent cooperation using evolutionary algorithm. In: *Proceedings of Student Research Conference in Informatics and Information Technologies (IIT. SRC 2005)* (ed. M. Bielikova), 49–56. Slovakia, Bratislava: Faculty of IIT, STU.

27 Mota, L., Lau, N., and Reis, L.P. (2010). Co-ordination in Robocup's 2d simulation league: ssetplays as flexible, multi-robot plans. *IEEE Conference on Robotics Automation and Mechatronics (IEEE RAM)*, Singapore (28–30 June 2010), pp. 362–367.

28 Hannebauer, M., Wendler, J., and Pagello, E. (eds.) (2001). *Balancing Reactivity and Social Deliberation in Mas – from Robocup to Real-World Applications*, vol. 2103. Heidelberg, Germany: SBH.

29 De Raadt, M., Prokopenko, M., and Butler, M. (2003). Evolving tactical formations on the RoboCup field. In: *Electronic Proceedings of the Workshop on Adaptability in Multi-Agent Systems at The First RoboCup Australian Open*, Sydney, Australia (January 2003), pp. 170–175.

30 Stone, P., Sutton, R., and Kuhlmann, G. (2005). Reinforcement learning for Robocup-Soccer keepaway. *Adaptive Behavior* 13 (3): 165–188.

31 Zweigle, O., Lafrenz, R., Buchheim, T. et al. (2006). Cooperative agent behavior based on special interaction nets. *Intelligent Autonomous Systems* IAS-9: 651–659.

32 Buckland, M. (2005). *Programming Game Ai by Example*. Plano, Texas: Worldware Publishing Inc.

33 Reynolds, R.G. (1994). An introduction to cultural algorithms. *Proceedings of Third Annual Conference on Evolutionary Programming*, San Diego, CA, pp. 131–139.

34 Ali, M.Z. and Reynolds, R.G. (2009). An intelligent social fabric influence component in cultural algorithms for knowledge learning in dynamic environments, web intelligence and intelligent agent technology. *IEEE/WIC/ACM International Conference on Web Intelligence and Intelligent Agent Technology (WI-IAT '09)*, vol. 2, Milan, Italy, 15–18 September 2009, pp. 161–168.

35 Chung, C. and Reynolds, R.G. (1998). CAEP: an evolution-based tool for real-valued function optimization using cultural algorithms. *International Journal on Artificial Intelligence Tools* 7 (3): 239–291.

36 Fernandez, A.J., Cotta, C., and Ceballos, R.C. (2008). Generating emergent team strategies in football simulation videogames via genetic algorithms. *Game-on 2008: 9th International Conference on Intelligent Games and Simulation*, UPV, Valencia, Spain, pp. 120–125.

8

The Use of Cultural Algorithms to Learn the Impact of Climate on Local Fishing Behavior in Cerro Azul, Peru

Khalid Kattan[1], Robert G. Reynolds[1,2], and Samuel Dustin Stanley[1]

[1] Computer Science Department, Wayne State University, Detroit, MI, USA
[2] Museum of Anthropological Archaeology, University of Michigan, Ann Arbor, MI, USA

Introduction

Evolutionary computation is a subfield of Artificial Intelligence, which is based on Darwinian principles of evolution. Evolutionary computation is often applied to the solution of complex computational problems especially global optimization problems. Several Evolutionary Computation systems have been proposed, and one of them is the Cultural Algorithms [1, 2].

The Cultural Algorithm (CA) is a class of computational models imitating the cultural evolution process in nature. CA has three major components: a population space, a belief space, and a protocol that describes how knowledge is exchanged between the first two components. The population space can support any population-based computational model, such as Genetic Algorithms [3] and Evolutionary Programming.

An Overview of the Cerro Azul Fishing Dataset

Introduction

The data we analyze are from 1980s, while the historic site is more than 500 years prior. Dr. Joyce Marcus spent 1982–1986 excavating in Cerro Azul, Peru. Due to arid weather, architecture, fishing nets, and fish from 1100 AD to 1470 AD were

This work was supported by NSF grant #1744367.

all well preserved. Dr. Marcus explored early "community self-sufficiency" and "community specialization" during Incan times. The Kingdom of Huarco contained two localities [4]. The coast proper was ruled by the Kingdom of Huarco, and the piedmont was ruled by Kingdom of Lunahuana. Both sites were later defeated by the Incas in 1470. As in any society, the diet will typically differ based on a person's social status. From bone remains found in different housing compounds, Marcus observed that different fish were eaten by different levels of society, such as the diets of the elites' versus that of the commoners'. While modern fishermen use equipment that allows them to catch a wider variety of species, the catches can be destined for local consumption or exported commercially to larger cities, such as Lima. As a result, the movements of certain catches that are targeted for commercial sale are more likely to be tracked than others, and fishermen may want to take more risks or more effort to find them. These factors will be key to the model developed later.

Wirth states that, "Each city, like every other object in nature, is, in a sense, unique" [5]. However, according to Blanton, "culture change in the direction of increased scale and complexity can occur in varied ways. I suggest that the cultural ecologists should do as others have and view this variety as a source of stimulation for theory-building." As Jayoussi presented in his PhD thesis [6], a complex system can be viewed at different levels of granularity relative to the questions that we wish to ask about it. Similarly, we also implement the several levels of analysis here: the entire three year period of the survey; monthly, weekly; and daily. In this research, we investigate the potential for applying multiobjective cultural algorithm models of fishing patterns at the weekly and daily scales by applying suitable tools from Artificial Intelligence and Data Science to the existing archaeological data from a prehistoric fishing center, Cerro Azul. We begin by describing the basic structure of the Database system developed to support model development from the raw data in the following section.

An Overview of the Database Content as a Complex System

Drs. Joyce Marcus and Maria Rostworowski led a team of researchers from The University of Michigan from 1982 through 1986 to excavate five seasons of research at ancient nearby site of Cerro Azul. Later, in the last three years of their project, they began recording the catch of every boat that returned to the Capitanian del Puerto with the cooperation of the local government. In addition, further data on fishing were collected from Peru's Instituto del Mar [4], and Marcus refers to the fishermen as "Artisanal" Fishermen in the sense that they are small scale and independent entities that can provide for both local consumption and export. The dataset consists of 6013 records. Each record has the following properties:

1) Relates to exactly one fishing trip.
2) Contains fish from only one site location (main source).
3) Contains fish belonging to only one species (main catch).
4) Fishermen always departed from the home site (Cerro Azul).

The fishing activity around Cerro Azul is a complex system that has many different parts that interact with each other. We can view the different levels as Macro, Meso, and Micro in terms of their temporal scale. The three basic phases of ENSO constitute the Macro scale. The Meso scale is represented by the monthly statistics. The micro level corresponds to the days of the week for a given week. These form the basic structure of the Cerro Azul database constructed here. In the next section, we discuss the three different levels in detail.

The basic organization of the database reflects the most-coarse grained temporal measurement used here, which is based on the ENSO phases summarized below. ENSO, the El Niño Southern Oscillation, consists of three phases: El Niño, La Niña, and back to normal. El Niño is the first phase of change from the normal weather pattern. It is the warming phase of the ENSO. El Niño means "The Little child, referring to baby Jesus," and this term was originally applied to the lighter warming effect that happens around Christmas time. The El Niño not only affects temperature but also rainfall. The next phase, La Niña, is the cooling phase, with increased upwelling. La Niña is Spanish for "Little Girl." Sometimes there will be more than one La Niña during the same ENSO. The final phase of the ENSO is the "back to normal." At this point the weather has returned to pre-El Niño conditions along with the food chains. Using ENSO's cycles, our dataset of fishing trips is divided into these three different temporal phases at the Macro level: Phase I, Phase II, and Phase III respectively.

Table 8.1 gives the Peru Fishing Database Dictionary listing the data variables and their possible values. It shows that there are 6013 Identifiers, one for each fishing trip. We used Catches and Sites name and abbreviation for each species and site in the data analysis and the model. The fishermen caught 48 different catch types by travelling to 29 different sites. The number of Individual Catch trips range from 1 to 6013 catches and the Total Weight of Fishing Expedition's catch range from 0.2 to 1000 kg. Meanwhile, the number of days for each fishing trip varies between one and seven days. The desirability of each catch based on modern preferences is given below:

3 = Highly desirable (targeted)
2 = Desirable (okay), and
1 = Fall back (opportunistic)

"Highly desirable" catches are targeted by fishermen as the most commercially desired fish. "Desirable" fish are still commercial in nature, but will attract less of

Table 8.1 Data dictionary for the Peru database.

Field Name	Description	Values	Comments
ID	Unique identifier	(1–6013)	Fishing trip ID
Catch	Catch name	48 different catch types	
Site	Site name	29 different sites	
Count	Number of individual catch	(1–6000)	
Weight	Total weight of Fishing Expedition in kilograms	(0.2–1000)	
Depart Date	Departure date of Fishing Expedition	(02/29/1984–07/27/1986)	
Return date	Return date of Fishing Expedition	(03/01/1984–07/28/1986)	
Trip duration (Length)	Number of days for Fishing Expedition	(1–7)	
Round trip distance From CA	Round trip distance from CA (Extended) in kilometers	(0–198)	Round trip dist. in kms
Phase	Phase of Return date Fishing Expedition	(1–3)	1 = Residual El Niño, 2 = La Niña, 3 = Back To Normal
Return day of week	Day of the week for Fishing Expedition return	(1–7)	1 = Monday, 2 = Tuesday, ..., 6 = Friday, 7 = Saturday
Number of DOW using RtnDate	Number of days of the week (using Return Date) that occurred in that month	(4, 5)	Number of M, T, W, R, F, S, S in month
Site Loc North to South	Ordering all site locations from North to South		Numbers are used for sorting purposes only and do not represent distances
Site Relative to CA	Site Location relative to CA (Extended) Includes Faro and La Centinela	(1–3)	1 = North of CA, 2 = Cerro Azul, 3 = South of CA

Species category	Classification of catch	(1–6)	1 = Cartilaginous, 2 = Bony, 3 = Crustacean, 4 = Mammal, 5 = Penguin, 6 = Turtle
Comments	Changes or notes to data	Count updated, sites combined	
Depart Year	Fishing Expedition – Depart Year	(1984–1986)	
Depart Month	Fishing Expedition – Depart Month	(1–12)	
Depart Day	Fishing Expedition – Depart Day	(1–31)	
Return Year	Fishing Expedition – Return Year	(1984–1986)	
Return Month	Fishing Expedition – Return Month	(1–12)	
Return Day	Fishing Expedition – Return Day	(1–31)	
Desirability	Desirability of species (decision by Fishermen)	(1–3)	3 = Highly Desirable, 2 = Desirable, 1 = Fall Back
Indicator Fish	species that signify climate change	True or false	Sensitive to temperature

a return. The "Fall Back" classification corresponds to more ubiquitous but less commercial catches – ones that reflect the result of fishing rather than the catch that was produced. Risk-wise, it is better to come back with something rather than nothing from a subsistence point of view.

In addition, there are six classifications of catches that reflect generic differences in species:

1 = Cartilaginous,
2 = Bony,
3 = Crustacean,
4 = Mammal,
5 = Penguin, and
6 = Turtle.

Data Mining at the Macro, Meso, and Micro Levels

Cerro Azul can be Viewed as a Complex System

The fishing activity around Cerro Azul is a complex system that has many different parts that interact with each other. We can view the different levels as Macro, Meso, and Micro in terms of their temporal scale. The three basic phases of ENSO constitute the Macro scale. The Meso scale is represented by the monthly statistics. The micro level corresponds to the days of the week for a given week. These form the basic structure of the Cerro Azul database constructed here.

The Three Levels of Data Analysis

The collected data were analyzed at three different temporal and spatial scales as given below.

1) Macro – This scale provides analytics that summarize behavior over the entire period of observation. We consider the data in all three phases: Residual El Niño, La Niña, and Back to Normal.
2) Meso – This scale corresponds to monthly patterns of behavior. We look for patterns that might represent something **unique to a month or a sequence of months.**
3) Micro – This scale provides statistics about fishing behavior on a daily basis. We look for patterns that might signify differences based on the day of the week.

Each of the different levels of analysis can reveal patterns that can be useful in the interpretation of results on the other scales. We might be able to observe some species that are present during all three phases so we will need to look at a very coarse grained view. Additionally, we may notice some learning or information sharing between fishermen if we observe at the daily or fine-grained view. Finally, we might notice some patterns that show species that correlate with each other; for example, one species moves to another location, then a week later another species moves to the same location. This requires a Meso or "somewhere in the middle" view. In Figure 8.1, we present sample data based on the different levels of data analysis.

The analysis of these results will be used to constrain the multiobjective model and its behavior. The results support the importance of both catch quality (PAYOUT) on the one hand and the investment of resources in terms of number of trips and overall distance travelled on the other hand (SUSTAINABILITY). One of the key themes is the LEARNING CURVE, where the CATCH COUNTS can increase over time during the week relative to certain targeted species. There are indications that there is a priority in terms of what catch to pursue first. Another interesting pattern can be seen with fall back catches, which mimic trends in targeted catches since as the number of desirable catches starts to dwindle, the deficit can be made up by Fall Back categories. The goals of catch quality and trip investment will be key to the multiobjective model that we develop. To prepare for the computational demands of a multiobjective approach, we will employ an extension of the Cultural Algorithm, CAPSO [7], which will be described in the section that follows.

Cultural Algorithms and Multiobjective Optimization

Introduction

Multiobjective Cultural Algorithms will be used to validate our agent-based model of artisanal fishing. If the goals in our model are conflicting, then we should expect that an optimal decision represents a trade-off between them. This will result in a hyperbolic model or Pareto front. Computation of the Pareto Front from a set of examples is an NP-Hard problem. We will use the Cultural Algorithm to do that for us. This hyperbolic model then can be compared to a best fit linear model to determine which best describes the simulation results. CAPSO is a Cultural Algorithm Particle Swarm Optimizer. It uses collected domain knowledge to implement a parallel recursive search of the problem space using multiple swarms of agents [7].

Introduction to the Cultural Algorithm

In the 1970s, a class of evolution programming models was developed by Dr. Robert Reynolds called Cultural Algorithms. Dr. Reynolds drew an analogy between group learning, the Darwinian natural selection process and the process of

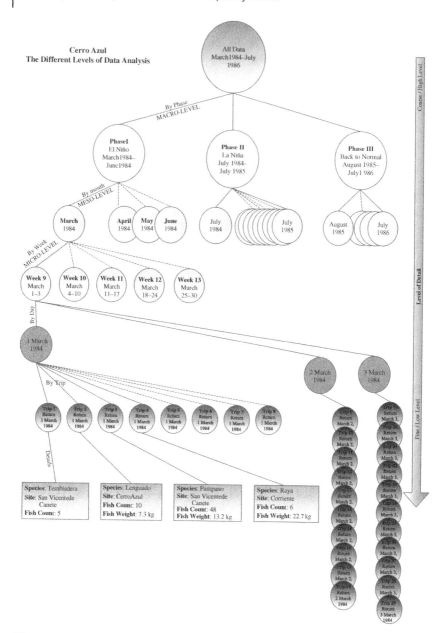

Figure 8.1   The Three Levels of Data Analysis.

group knowledge distribution in order to fashion the Cultural Algorithms model. Cultural Algorithms can provide a flexible framework within which to study the emergence of organizational complexity in a multiagent system. The Cultural Algorithm is a computational model simulating the cultural evolution process in nature.

A Cultural Algorithm has three major components: population space, belief space, and communication protocol that define how knowledge is exchanged between the first two components. The population space is defined as a set of solutions to the problem. These individuals are connected by a social fabric over which information can be passed. The belief space can be defined as the collection of experiential and domain knowledge, which can be influenced by individuals within the population space according to their varying degrees of success. The belief space also has the ability to influence following generations of individuals within the population space.

The following is a general statement of a generic cultural algorithm:

1) The algorithm begins by initializing the Population and Belief Space.
2) Individuals in the Population Space are first evaluated and ranked through a fitness function.
3) An acceptance function, Accept (), is used to determine which individuals within Population Space will be allowed to update the Belief Space.
4) Experiences of those accepted individuals are then recorded in the Belief Space through the function Update ().
5) Knowledge from the Belief Space is used to influence the selection of individuals for the next generation of the population through the Influence () function. Operators are applied to the population members based on a given knowledge source.
6) Steps 2 through 5 are the evolution loop which is repeated until the termination condition is satisfied (Figure 8.2).

Figure 8.2 Basic Pseudocode for Cultural Algorithm [2]. *Source:* Reproduced with permission of China heritage.

```
Begin
t = 0
InitPop(t)      // init population
InitBelief(t)   // init belief space
Repeat
EvaluatePop(t)
Update(Belief(t), Accept(Pop(t)))
Generate(Pop(t), Influence(Belief(t)))
t++
Select Pop(t) from Pop(t – 1)
Until (termination condition)
End
```

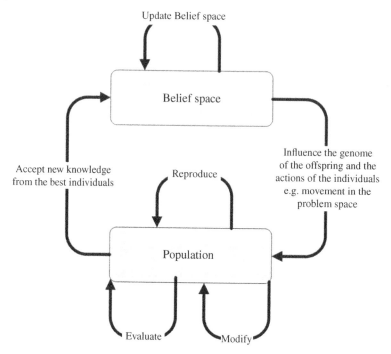

Figure 8.3 Schemata of Cultural Algorithms.

The two feedback paths of information, one through the Accept () and Influence () functions, and the other through individual knowledge and the Evaluate function create a system of dual inheritance of both the population and the belief spaces. The Cultural Algorithm repeats this process for each generation until the prespecified termination condition is met. In this way, the population component and the Belief Space interact with, and support each other, in a similar mode to the evolution of human culture. A visualization of this process can be found in Figure 8.3.

CAPSO, Cultural Algorithm, and Particle Swarm Optimizer

The CAPSO system is a hybrid system composed of Particle Swarm and Vector Genetic Algorithm components operating under the control of a Cultural Algorithm framework. The guiding principle in its design is to keep each as vanilla as possible to facilitate their interaction and support explicit parallelism in the search process. A brief description of the CAPSO functionality will now be presented.

The Main function recursively calls SearchInSpace to generate a new swarm thread. The basic population unit here is a swarm of individuals. A swarm population is associated with that thread via a call to PopSpaceAlg. PopSpaceAlg is in charge of updating the swarm associated with the thread. Each new swarm is given a number of generations to add a new point to the Pareto front, maxGensWoImprov. If it has not by then, it is removed and control is returned to its parent. If it is productive over a maxRepeatsBeforeDivide, it is divided into a number of new subspaces, newSubspace.

In PopSpaceAlg, agents are awarded points for the number of agents currently in the Situational Knowledge that it Pareto dominates in one or more dimensions. The sum of those points for an agent is its objective function value. The VegaMethod (Vector Evaluated Genetic Algorithm) is called then to select the elite points from the swarm.

CASteps is then called and accepts a certain number of points, elite, into the Belief Space to update it. It then applies the knowledge sources to selectively modify the remaining ones based on their relative performance as expressed in a Relative Roulette Wheel. The process continues recursively until only one thread remains and is unable to generate new points in a certain number of generations. In that case, the system can be restarted with a new random swarm but still using the acquired knowledge from the currently completed run that resides in the Belief Space. The pseudocode for the algorithm is given in (Figure 8.4) [7]. Additional detail about the CAPSO algorithm can be found in Chapter 9.

The Artisanal Fishing Model

Biobjective

A traditional single objective problem is the result of a combination of contributing terms. G1 = P1, P2,..., PN, where N is the number of contributing factors or subgoals that are correlated with each other. In a multiobjective problem, sometimes the goals are conflicting and need to be addressed separately. Here are the two goals. Neither can be completely achieved without some sacrifice with regards to the other.

Goal 1 reflects the need for profitability with regards to the artisanal fishing activity for a given household. If given the opportunity to choose between a catch that can fetch a higher local market value than another, this goal would be in favor of targeting that catch. To the extent that this can be done over a succession of trips for a family, the presumed social unit here, the fishing agent can even reap a profit over time.

Goal 2 relates broadly to the issue of sustainability. That is, the agent needs to invest sufficient resources into a trip to bring back something to sustain the family unit and perpetuate the fishing activity. It reflects the general goal of just being able to get out and fish on a given day. It is expressed as the overall ratio of effort to overall yield regardless of quality. In this case it is quantity over quality.

Goal 1: PAYOUT – Maximum Market Value of the catch produced by a trip for a day. For the departing trips on a day, select the one that will yield maximum desirability. HD (High Desirability) [1, 2, or 3]

CA.Initialize() // Initialize the Belief Space

CA.CreateSituationalKnowInitGuesses(numInitGuesses)

//The Population Space
objfuncs = [objective functions provided by problem/user]
pop = Population.Initialize(locations, velocities)
pFront = ParetoFront.Initialize()

do repeat until termination condition:

Foreach indiv in Pop:
    indiv.position += indiv.velocity

Foreach indiv in Pop:
If no pFront members dominate or equal F(indiv):
pFront.Add(F(indiv))
If F(indiv) dominates an item(s) in pFront:
remove dominated item(s) from pFront

//VEGA method of selecting elites
elite = []
foreach objf in objfuncs:
elite.Add(Pop.Select(top 1/7 of performers according to objf)
elite.Remove(any duplicates)

//GA Method of evolving particle velocities
foreach indiv in pop and not in Elite:
Rnd0 = random.between(0, 1)

Rnd1 = random.between(0, 1)
Rnd2 = random.between(Rnd1, 1)
Rnd3 = random.between(Rnd2, 1)
Rnd4 = random.between(Rnd3, 1)

If rnd0 < rnd1: //both crossover and mutation
Indiv.velocity = Crossover(elite.pickrandom().velocity, indiv.velocity)
Indiv.velocity = Mutation(Indiv.velocity)
Else if rnd0 < rnd2: //(crossover but no mutation)
Indiv.velocity = Crossover(elite.pickrandom().velocity, indiv.velocity)
    Else if rnd0 < rnd3: //(mutation but no crossover)
Indiv.velocity = Mutation(Indiv.velocity)
    Else if rnd0 < rnd4 //(weighted average between part's velocity & an elite's)
Indiv.velocity = vectorWgtAvg(elite.pickrandom().velocity, indiv.velocity)
    Else: #Neither crossover nor mutation

Figure 8.4 CAPSO Pseudocode.

//END PSO Population

CA.Acceptance(elite)

CA.Update()
Foreach indiv in pop but not in elite:
    ks = CA.ChooseKnowledgeSource(sit, norm, or hist)
    targVelocity = CA.Influence(indiv, ks)
    indiv.velocity = vectWgtAvg(indiv.velocity, targVelocity)
    indiv.knowSource = ks

Figure 8.4 (Continued)

Goal 2: MINIMIZE RELATIVE EFFORT (MRE) – minimize the ratio of the effort expended for a catch relative to the overall yield of the catch in pounds regardless of quality.

The Two Formulas of agent goal achievement:

Goal 1: Maximize Payout (HD) = Fish Count * Desirability
Desirability = High Desirability = 3, Medium Desirability = 2, Low Desirability = 1.
Goal 2: Minimize Relative Effort (MRE) = ((RTD/MPG) * RE)/Fish-Weight
RTD = Round Trip Distance in kms from Cerro Azul
MPG = 5 (8 km PG)
Relative Effort (RE) = 1 for Cerro Azul and 3 = for North/South
Fish-Weight = Total weight of entire catch in kilograms

The Agent-Based Model

This sequence of trips for a given phase will be called a tour.

A tour will begin on the first day of the Phase and end on the last day. The parameters used to guide an agent's decision will be:

1) Strategy Goal tuple: The extent to which they wish to follow Goal 1 (profitability) versus Goal 2 (sustainability).
2) Phase: (I, II, III)
3) The days of the week that they will fish (depart out): (Full Week [FW]; No Sundays [NS]; MTW; TFRSAT).
4) DT: The downtime between trips. For our experiments here, we assume that the agent makes just one trip out a day (does not go out fishing again on the same day they returned).

5) Tour Performance: The sum of the PAYOUT for the trips that it selects through the given phase on the given days and the corresponding MRE.

The Trip_Graph Model

A tour is a sequence of trips that are produced by the concatenation of individual trips that follow a particular set of goal priorities for an agent. That is, what would a series of tours look like if individual agents had the same goal priority throughout the phase. A strategy tuple generates a path through a Trip_Graph. The tuple corresponds to the likelihood of selecting a trip on a day based on one or the other goal. Example: (75, 25) means that the likelihood that a profit maximizing trip is selected is 75/100. If there is more than one trip that has the same HD level, a random number generator then picks the goal for that day which is then used to select the trip. Figure 8.5 and Table 8.2 give the results for an and an example tour with a weight of 100% for MRE.

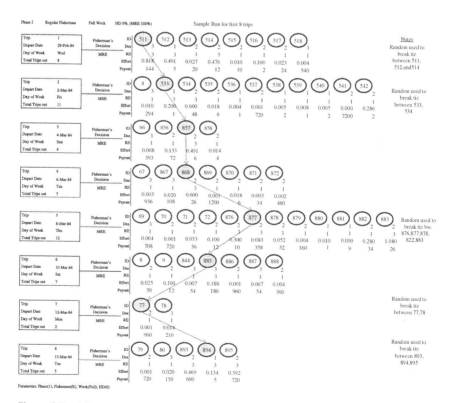

Figure 8.5 A Decision Tree of the sample tour using HD/MRE (0/100).

Table 8.2 Details about the Decision Tree of the sample run in Figure 8.5.

Trip	Depart date	Trip length in days	Days skipped so far	Possible trip so far	Depart day of week 1 = Mon, 7 = Sun	Catch avail (branch. factor)	Fisherman behavior	HD percent	Selected catch ID	Catch	Desir. 3 = highest 2 = okay 1 = fallback	Catch count	Payout catch count* Desir.	Site	Round trip distance (km)	Effort = ((RTD/MPG)*RE)/catch weight in kgs
1	29-Feb-84	2	0	1	3	8	MRE	0	511	pampano	3	48	144	San Vicente de Canete	18	0.818
2	02-Mar-84	2	1	3	5	11	MRE	0	533	chancho marino	1	1	1	Santa Bárbara	10	0.200
3	04-Mar-84	2	2	5	7	4	MRE	0	857	tollo	2	3	6	San Vicente de Canete	18	0.491
4	06-Mar-84	2	3	7	2	7	MRE	0	868	lenguado	2	13	26	Santa Bárbara	10	0.600
5	08-Mar-84	2	4	9	4	12	MRE	0	877	lengudo	2	179	358	San Vicente de Canete	18	0.083
6	10-Mar-84	2	5	11	6	7	MRE	0	885	bonito	3	60	180	Los Leones	32	0.188
7	12-Mar-84	1	6	13	1	2	MRE	0	77	lorna	2	48	960	Faro	1	0.001
8	13-Mar-84	2	6	14	2	5	MRE	0	894	chancho marino	1	5	5	Asia	56	0.134
Performance (sum of first 8 trips)													1680			2.516

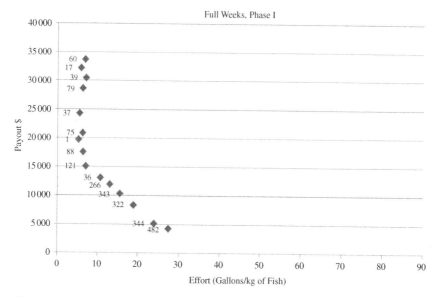

Figure 8.6 Pareto Front for Payout (Goal 1) and Effort (Goal 2).

Nondominance

The Pareto Front is a curve that reflects the best possible trade-off between conflicting goals that agents can make. This front is produced by the non-dominated sort – in which a point is nondominated if there is no other point that produces an increase in one goal without a decrease in the other. The non-dominant tours produced from a simulation run are plotted and form a Pareto Curve here.

To compare and assess the results, we begin with a comparison between each of four scenarios for Phase I in the next section. Each scenario corresponds to a sequence of trips generated in the phase by fishermen using a particular strategy (Full week, No Sundays, MTW, and ThFriSat) in terms of the two goals. Here, we begin with the Full Week Scenario where every day of the week is an available stop on the fishermen's itinerary for the given phase.

Figure 8.6 gives the Pareto Frontier for Fishermen whose tours can take place on all seven days of the week in Phase I, the Residual El Niño. Notice that in this phase, the presence of targeted fish dominates the need to invest in more resources to achieve a successful trip. Recall that in the base case for Effort such that a successful trip is one that brings back a catch. All of the trips in our database represent successful trips in that regard.

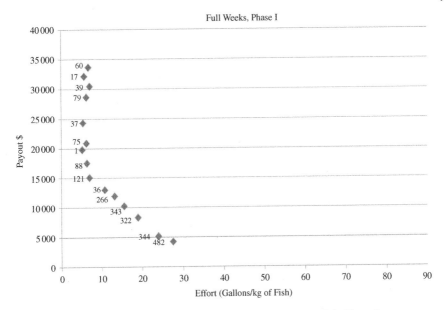

Figure 8.7   The Pareto Front for Payout vs. Effort for the Full week in Phase I.

What this curve means is that many targeted catches can be found within a short distance from Cerro Azul during the time of March through June. This is the conclusion of the El Niño, which is moderated by the fact that it is the tail end of summer and beginning of fall. Warmwater fish are enticed to remain in the area even though the warming phase of El Niño has diminished. It suggests that a productive sequence of trips in terms of Payout will be more dependent on timing than on location. Once fishermen are required to put more resources into the tour in this phase, the Payout drops exponentially (Figures 8.7 and 8.8).

The Experimental Results

Introduction

The agent-based model of artisanal fishing was used to generate tours through the trip graph over a given phase and a corresponding set of days of the week. A Pareto Curve of nondominated points is produced for each phase and each

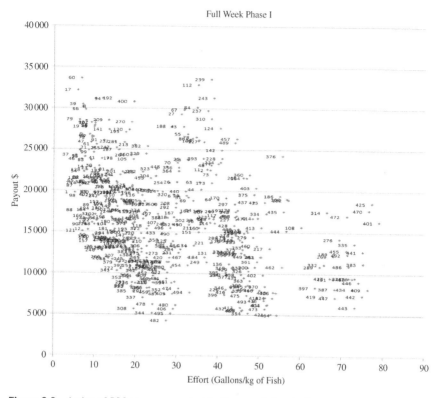

Figure 8.8 A plot of 500 tours generated in the search for the Pareto Front.

Days of the week scenario (3 * 4). These curves are compared to identify the decision-making adaptations made by agents to the changing local climate produced by ENSO.

Full Week, Pareto Frontier

Phase I: (March through June 1984). While the other two phases each last about a year, this is only one-third of a year. If the same pattern played out in the missing two-thirds, the maximum total would reach at least that of La Niña (120 000). Payout declines exponentially with increased effort, which suggests that fishermen did not have to venture far from Cerro Azul to achieve the expected payout in el Niño. Sustainable fishing activity could then easily be performed nearby Cerro Azul. For Phase II to achieve similar total payout (120 000) they need to take more trips and invest more resources to produce a successful trip. There is less exponential drop with distance from Cerro Azul. In Phase III they can still get to 120 000 but need more resources than Phase I but less than Phase II (Figure 8.9).

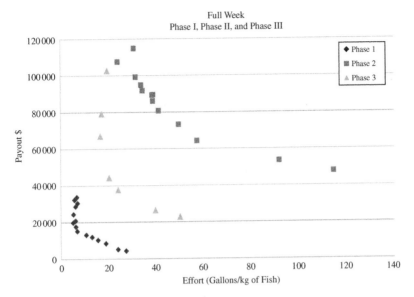

Figure 8.9   Full Week, Pareto Frontier with all Three Phases.

No Sundays, Pareto Frontier

Results are similar to Full Week since few trips went out on Sundays. In addition, often there was not an official there to record trips that went out and came back then. In general, Back to Normal had less exponential drop, which suggests that it was an easier curve to plan for as an agent. Phase II still needed to expend almost twice as many resources to sustain a successful fishing trip (Figure 8.10).

Monday, Tuesday, Wednesday, Pareto Frontier

Phase I stayed close to Cerro Azul and took in about half of the Full day's amount. We can see an exponential drop. Phase II exhibited a steep drop near Cerro Azul but gradual with increased effort, signifying it is necessary to plan for trade-offs. It is as if there were only limited slots near Cerro Azul and others had to just go farther even at the beginning of the week. Phase III exhibits a drop in payout with increased effort, so they stayed closer to Cerro Azul (Figure 8.11).

Thursday, Friday, Saturday, Pareto Frontier

Phase I: There was a steep drop off with effort so they stayed close to Cerro Azul. They were able to get more in the second half of the week. There was a learning curve for targeted catches. Phase II: There was more Payout than the other two phases but

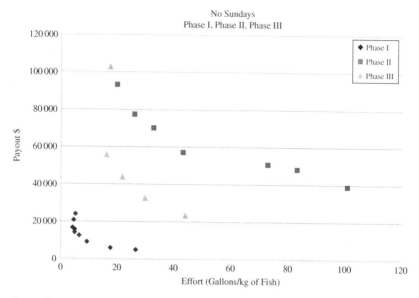

Figure 8.10 No Sundays, Pareto Frontier, with all three Phases.

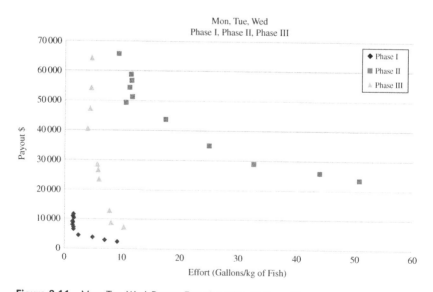

Figure 8.11 Mon_Tue_Wed, Pareto Frontier with all three Phases.

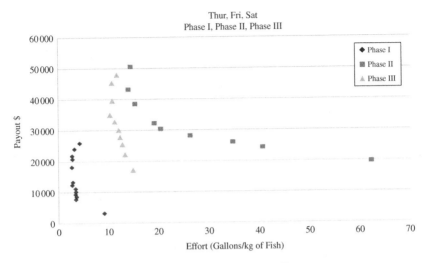

Figure 8.12 Thur_Fri_Sat Pareto Frontier with all three Phases.

more effort was exerted. There was a gradual trade-off between the two goals, which suggests that more knowledgeable planning is needed to support more resource expenditure. Phase III: There was an extreme drop in Payout with Effort like in Phase I, but effort is twice as much (Figure 8.12).

Summary of Experimental Results

A profitability target optimum of 120 000 units emerged. Agents tried to attain that in each phase. However, this was at a cost. The maximum effort needed to produce a successful trip increased from the El Niño to La Niña for example. To sustain their fishing endeavor, more resources were invested. Different fishing strategies based on both phases and days of the week emerged. Clear differences in Monday–Wednesday trade-offs versus Thursday–Saturday emerged. The La Niña Pareto Front had a more gradual decline in profitability with increased effort which suggested that more care was taken in the planning process to sustain fishing activities in this transitional phase.

Statistical Validation

Overall Performance Comparison

The agent-based model produces some interesting emergent behaviors. Those behaviors appear to correspond to patterns extracted from the data via analytics. In terms of the model results, can the patterns be explained by a simple linear regression model, which assumes a correlation between the goals? Or do the model results, based on the trip data support the notion of conflicting goals? If there is evidence for conflicting goals, then the results of the simulation should be better expressed as a non-linear curve that reflects the basic trade-off between them.

In this section, we use the CAPSO system to generate a hyperbolic curve (an NP-HARD problem) to fit the data produced by the model in each Phase Day of the Week scenario and compare its fit with that of an optimal linear model for that same data. This test is done by comparing the differences of each model prediction for each data point and testing to see if the difference is statistically significant using an *F*-test.

Hypothesis

Null Hypothesis (H0)

There is no statistical difference between the models at a given level of significance.

If this is rejected, then it suggests that the nonlinear trade-off between the conflicting goals produce a better prediction of the data. The level of significance selected here is 0.01, for testing. Testing how well does the line fit the data was done with a Residual plot. All computed points were used, not just the nondominated ones to test the relationship over the entire search space. The Coefficient of determination, r_2, Residual – difference between observed value (the Payout), and the predicted Payout for each simulation data point are given in Figure 8.13–8.15.

Figure 8.16 shows the distribution used to test the difference between the hyperbolic and linear model predictions. The distribution of the *F*-statistic is used to indicate the acceptable and rejection regions when the difference in residuals for a pair of functions exceeds a particular value of *F* (Tables 8.3 and 8.4).

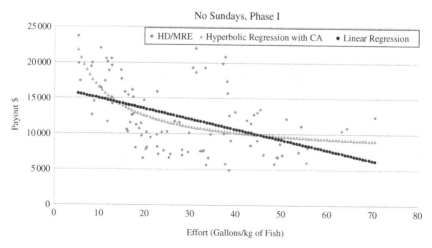

Figure 8.13 Curve fitting for Payout, Effort using No Sundays in Phase I.

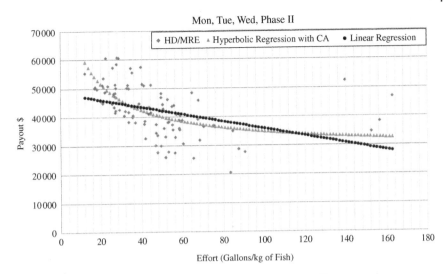

Figure 8.14 Curve fitting using for first half of the week, Phase II.

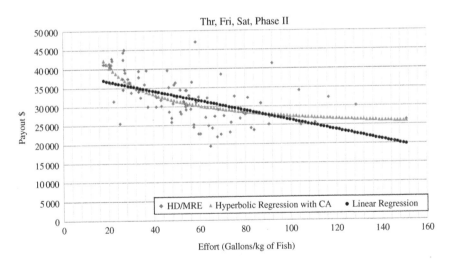

Figure 8.15 Curve fitting using for second half of the week, Phase II.

Summary

The CAPSO system was used to produce a hyperbolic model for the simulation results. The predictions of that model were compared with those for an optimized linear model using the F-test on the residuals of the predictions. The results show that in ALL Phases and ALL Days of the Week comparisons, the hyperbolic model was a better fit (alpha $= 0.01$) than the linear one.

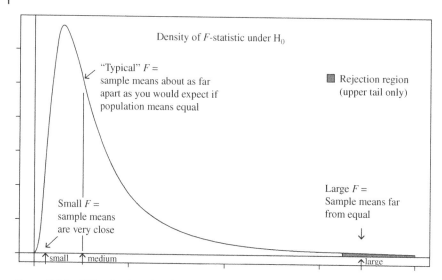

Figure 8.16 *F* Distribution showing Acceptance and Rejection Regions.

Table 8.3 Critical value for *F*-test at different significant levels of alpha.

Significant level α	$\alpha = 0.05$	$\alpha = 0.01$	$\alpha = 0.001$
$F_{(\alpha, df1, df2)}$	3.07	4.8	7.5

Table 8.4 Statistical value for (*F*-statistic) for Phase I, II, and III.

Case of fishermen trip durations	Phase I El Niño	Phase II La Niña	Phase III back to normal	$F_{(\alpha, df1, df2)} = 4.8$ For $\alpha = 0.01$
Full week	13.35	25.60	16.08	Ho: are rejected for all phases
No Sundays	23.90	29.91	18.36	
Mon, Tue, and Wed	6.31	24.75	21.31	
Thur, Fri, and Sat	7.27	37.25	14.73	

Conclusions and Future Work

Conclusions

Our results suggest that indeed the collective economic response of the fishermen demonstrates an ability to respond to the unpredictabilities of climate change, but at a cost. It is clear that the fishermen have gained the collective knowledge over the years to produce a coordinated response that can be observed at a higher level (Pareto Front). In fact, the first ENSO was recorded in Peru in 1602, so the behavior of artisanal fisherman here can be viewed as an accumulation of expertise over centuries. Of course, this knowledge can be used to coordinate activities only if it is communicated socially within the society. Although our data do not provide any explicit information about such communication, there is some indirect evidence that the adjustments in strategy are brought about by the increased exchange of experiences among the fishermen.

The Pareto distributions seem to suggest dominant and successor waves of strategies during the week that may be associated with the length of time over which the simulation window is conducted. These waves were suggested to represent how subsequent trips were influenced by knowledge brought back by agents from trips the days right before that trip. For example, Dr. Marcus recalls one brother talking to another brother about his fishing experiences. This knowledge might be shared with close blood relatives or might be conveyed in general to others. Our discussion of analytics in section "Data Mining at the Macro, Meso, and Micro Levels" suggested that indeed there were at least two waves (learning curves) present in terms of the amount of catches returned in certain phases relative to certain types of catches.

Future Work

The model used here is just a biobjective model, but the results suggest that there may be evidence for other subgoals in the acquired dataset. Future work would be to expand the hierarchy of goals for agents. There were gaps in some of the Pareto fronts. It is suggested that they represent an environment of physical constraints that make optimal decision-making in those regions problematic (infeasible). Future work will be to investigate those areas of the curve to identify the reasons why. There is also potential to integrate a Virtual Reality Implementation to show fish movement dynamics using a Fish Visualizer. In addition, we plan to take advantage of the Social Network capabilities of Cultural Algorithms to attempt to model the impact that knowledge acquisition by the fishermen and its subsequent distribution has on strategic decision-making.

References

1 Reynolds, R.G. (1979). *An Adaptive Computer Model of the Evolution of Agriculture.* PhD Thesis. Ann Arbor: University of Michigan.
2 Reynolds, R.G. (1994). An introduction to cultural algorithms. *Proceedings of the Third Annual Conference on Evolutionary Programming*, San Diego, CA, USA (24–26 February 1994).

3 Holland, J.H. (1975). *Adaptation in Natural and Artificial Systems.* Ann Arbor, MI: University of Michigan Press.

4 Marcus, J. (2016). *Coastal Ecosystems and Economic Strategies at Cerro Azul, Peru: The Study of a Late Intermediate Kingdom. Memoir 59.* Ann Arbor, Michigan: Museum of Anthropology, University of Michigan.

5 Wirth, L. (1925). *A Bibliography of the Urban Community*, 161–228. Chicago: University of Chicago Press.

6 Jayyousi, T. (2012). *Bringing to Life an Ancient Urban Center at Monte Alban, MEXICO: Exploiting the Synergy Between the Micro, Meso, and Micro levels in a Complex System.* PhD Thesis. Detroit: Wayne State University.

7 Stanley, S.D., Kattan, K., and Reynolds, R.G. (2019) CAPSO: a parallelized multi-objective cultural algorithm particle swarm optimizer. *2019 Proceedings of IEEE Congress on Evolutionary Computation*, New Zealand (10–13 June 2019).

9

CAPSO: A Parallelized Multiobjective Cultural Algorithm Particle Swarm Optimizer

Samuel Dustin Stanley[1], Khalid Kattan[1], and Robert G. Reynolds[1,2]

[1] Computer Science Department, Wayne State University, Detroit, MI, USA
[2] Museum of Anthropological Archaeology, University of Michigan, Ann Arbor, MI, USA

Introduction

CAPSO stands for "Cultural Algorithm Particle Swarm Optimizer." It is a multiobjective optimization system that combines elements from Cultural Algorithms (CAs) [1], Particle Swarm Optimization (PSO) [2], and Vector-Evaluated Genetic Algorithms (VEGAs) [3]. For benchmark evaluation of the CAPSO system, we provide results from several experiments with well-known test problems in multiobjective optimization. The CAPSO system contains several different knowledge sources in its Belief Space that vie for the control of the population of agents. Here we investigate the relative importance that each Knowledge Source (KS) has in the decomposition process relative to various types of benchmark-constrained multiobjective optimization problems.

It was felt that constrained problems would be especially good targets for search by a knowledge-driven system such as CAPSO. This is because extracted patterns from the current Pareto front approximation can be used to direct parallel flows of PSO agents to exploit related similarities in other parts of the search space. Each agent in the PSO population is considered as a vector and its modification in each generation is controlled by knowledge in the Cultural Algorithm Belief Space through a VEGA selection process.

The CAPSO population space algorithm borrows its elite selection process from VEGA (Vector-Evaluated Genetic Algorithms). VEGA was originally devised in the 1980s by David Schaffer [3] as a type of genetic algorithm for doing multiobjective problems in which the elite is comprised by admitting a certain percentage

This work was supported by NSF grant # 1744367.

of the top scorers for each individual objective function taken singly in turn. This is the way that the population elite are chosen in CAPSO's population space algorithm. In standard implementations of VEGA, various genetic operators such as mutation and crossover are used to generate a decent "spread" of individuals so as to partially compensate for the fact that the elite are chosen from the objective functions taken singly. CAPSO, too, uses such genetic operators, but unlike standard VEGA, individuals in CAPSO are additionally able to take advantage of CA knowledge from the various knowledge sources in the belief space. All-in-all, the CA dovetails well with VEGA because VEGA's simplicity works well in a hybrid parallel algorithm. Likewise, cultural knowledge from the CA is able to drastically ameliorate, and oftentimes entirely resolve, the specific shortcomings that come out of VEGA's simplicity.

Our goal here is to investigate the possible synergies that can arise between the interaction of the various CA knowledge sources in the creation and direction of parallel particle swarms during the search process. While exploratory knowledge sources tend to dominate search in unconstrained problems, exploitative knowledge sources are able to exploit search space patterns and symmetries in constrained problems. In CAPSO, the exploratory and exploitative knowledge sources can interact in parallel during the search process. We propose that during certain phases of the search process, a Knowledge Source can **dominate** another if it produces a point in the space that dominates points generated by another KS. The CAPSO system then uses the current dominance hierarchy to direct the parallel search by multiple swarms.

In this paper, we describe the CAPSO system and apply it to four constrained multiobjective optimization problems with differing Pareto front properties. We will show that the CAPSO system is able to adjust the roles of the knowledge sources to exploit the symmetries and patterns in each.

Multiobjective Optimization

Overview

Multiobjective Optimization is typically used in problems where there are two or more countervailing objectives.

Formulating a Multiobjective Problem

Typically, a multiobjective problem is specified with three components: The set of functions to be optimized, the set of constraint functions, and the parameters along with parameter ranges. In a multiobjective problem, "optimizing" the objective functions might mean minimizing all of them, maximizing all of them, or minimizing some and maximizing others. A general formulation of a multiobjective problem can be written as such:

Let $F : \{f_1, f_2, f_3, ..., f_n\}$ be the set of objective functions.
Let $G : \{g_1, g_2, g_3, ..., g_m\}$ be the set of constraint functions.
Let $\vec{x} = x_1, x_2, x_3, ..., x_k$ be the vector containing the parameters.
Let $\left[r_{i_1}, r_{i_2} \right]$ be the range for each parameter x_i.

It may be that the various knowledge sources possess differential abilities in the decomposition of space during the problem-solving process. Our goal in this chapter is to investigate how knowledge sources in the Belief Space can learn to work together to effectively solve multiobjective problems.

Cultural Algorithms

Background

Cultural Algorithms (CAs) were originally created by Dr. Robert Reynolds in the 1970s [4, 5]. In creating CAs, Dr. Reynolds drew an analogy between group learning and the tendency of group knowledge acquired in the past to influence current decisions by individual members of groups [1].

CAs were originally devised by Dr. Reynolds while working with Dr. John Holland on research on Genetic Algorithms (GAs). When Reynolds was working on the GA research project, he was not sure how much that the GAs were actually learning. His solution was to create a "scorecard" for the GA to formally keep track of the knowledge that it was uncovering. Eventually, Reynolds realized that his "scorecard" functioned as a social "memory" for the population, and that it could not only receive knowledge from the genetic algorithm but also could provide knowledge to the genetic algorithm to guide its progress.

Eventually, Reynolds called this shared social memory the *belief space* and proposed the name *cultural algorithms*. Reynolds and his fellow CA researchers realized that this "scorecard," this "belief space," could be attached just as well to other algorithms besides genetic algorithms (e.g., particle swarm algorithms, agent-based systems), and could collect from and provide knowledge to them in just the same manner. Hence, today the name *cultural algorithm* has been expanded to *any* algorithm or population-based framework that uses a belief space and facilitates coevolution between the population and belief space.

Overview

Formally, CAs contain a *Population Space* which is influenced by a *Belief Space* via a *Communication Protocol*. The Population Space is defined as a set of solutions to the problem, which have the ability to evolve from generation to generation. The Belief Space can be defined as the collected set of experiential or domain knowledge sources. Each of the Knowledge Sources has the ability to influence individual agents in the population space according to their relative degrees of past success in directing the population. The following is a general statement of a generic CA:

1) The Population Space and Belief Space are initialized.
2) The Population members, agents, are evaluated through a **fitness** function, and the population is ranked.
3) a) The agents with the highest rankings are allowed to influence the belief space through the **Acceptance** function. This tends to produce more generalized solutions.
   b) In some Cultural Algorithms, the population members ranked *lowest* are also allowed to influence the belief space by providing various forms of *negative* information (Tabu's) that worked to specialize solutions.
4) The Knowledge Sources are **updated** with this new knowledge.
5) The knowledge sources then interact with each other to **influence** the agents in the population and to direct their modifications. Evolutionary Operators can be applied to at least some of the children to produce mutated variants of their parents.
6) Steps 2 through 5 are repeated until a stop condition is reached.

A schematic version of this process can be seen in Figure 9.1.

Acceptance Step

Depending on the individual cultural algorithm being used, either all individuals in the population space will be allowed to influence the belief space, or only some. The acceptance function is in charge of determining the set of agent experiences that are able to influence their set of collective beliefs. Oftentimes, the acceptance function is specified in terms of a percentage. An example might be "The best 10% of individuals according to the fitness function will be allowed to influence the belief space." [7] In CAPSO, the top 15% of scorers for each objective are allowed to influence the belief space.

Belief Space Update Step

In the update function, the knowledge received through the acceptance function is encoded into the belief space. Also during this step, knowledge that is obsolete or otherwise no longer relevant can be discarded from the belief space. One way of doing this is through a function that uses certain criteria to identify obsolete knowledge and remove it from the belief space [8, 9]. Another way is by having a

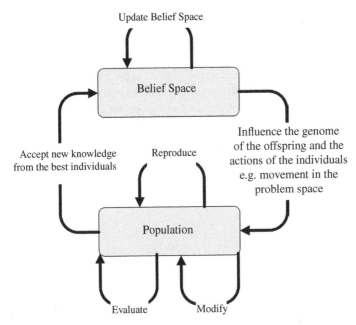

Figure 9.1 Cultural Algorithm Schema [6]. *Source:* Reproduced with permission of ResearchGate.

competition during the update step in which the new knowledge that was just received and the preexisting knowledge already in the belief space vie against each other. The winners remain in the knowledge base and the others either removed or modified.

Influence Step

In the influence step, the different Belief Space knowledge sources cooperate and/ or compete with each other to influence agents within the Population Space. Some of the different methods that have been used are simple random selection [10], a weighted roulette mechanism, an auction mechanism, [11] or a complex game [7].

When a population agent calls the influence function, an influencer knowledge source is selected through a mechanism such as those described above, and an individual in the belief space corresponding to that knowledge source is selected or randomly generated, and the population agents' values are "pulled toward" those of the individual within the belief space.

Knowledge Sources

CA researchers usually divide knowledge sources into five traditional categories: Situational Knowledge, Normative Knowledge, Topographic Knowledge, Domain Knowledge, and Historical Knowledge. Because CAPSO is designed to deal with problems with unusual and even very discontinuous search space topographies, it does not use traditional topographic or Domain Knowledge, and its formulations of Situational and Historical Knowledge are slightly different than what is in the usual literature. A description of the CAPSO knowledge sources follows in the next section.

CAPSO Knowledge Structures

CAPSO supports all five types of knowledge sources traditionally used in Cultural Algorithms. However, each has been tailored for its role in our hybrid system. Topographic knowledge, in particular, has been modified to allow for the control of multiple swarms of agents in parallel via threading. This allows swarms to be spawned in productive areas and removed from unproductive ones during the search process. Each of the five knowledge sources is now described in more detail.

Situational Knowledge

At the beginning of the program, CAPSO generates a number of initial guesses (exemplars) and assigns a selection probability to each of them. Each of these initial guesses can be thought of as a vector-point in hyperdimensional space. When Situational Knowledge is chosen as a knowledge source, CAPSO chooses one of these exemplars and produces a randomly weighted average between the exemplar and the velocity of the individual that called the influence function. The individual that called the influence function then has its velocity changed to this weighted average.

During the update step, CAPSO checks to see if any accepted individual's velocity is sufficiently close (i.e., within 1%) to an exemplar velocity within the Situational Knowledge container. If so, the chance that this exemplar will be chosen to be selected from the situational knowledge container in the future is incremented by 1%, and the exemplar itself is changed to a randomly weighted average between its old value and the velocity of the aforementioned accepted individual.

For example, if a particle whose velocity is $\langle 1, 2, 5 \rangle$ calls Situational Knowledge, and the Situational Knowledge Source chooses an exemplar velocity of $\langle 8, 9, 4 \rangle$, and the random weight chosen is 0.3, then the new velocity for the particle will be $0.3 \cdot \langle 1, 2, 5 \rangle + 0.7 \cdot \langle 8, 9, 4 \rangle = \langle 5.9, 6.9, 4.3 \rangle$.

Normative Knowledge

CAPSO's Normative Knowledge container contains a range for each of the parameters in the problems. When Normative Knowledge is selected, a velocity is randomly generated from within the ranges contained in the Normative Knowledge source. Then, as for the individual who called the influence function, its velocity is changed to a randomly weighted average between its old velocity and the generated one.

During the update step, for each population agent that influenced the belief space, a simple average is taken between the population agent's velocity within each dimension and the nearest edge of the Normative Knowledge interval for that dimension. That edge is then changed to the result of this simple average.

Historical Knowledge

CAPSO's Historical Knowledge container has a number of velocities that have adjoined elite particles in the past. Each of these historical velocities also contains the latest time in the past in which it was accepted or reaccepted into Historical Knowledge. During the Influence step, when Historical Knowledge is selected as a knowledge source, CAPSO randomly selects one out of all the velocities in the Historical Knowledge container. Then, as for the individual who called the influence function, its velocity is changed to a randomly weighted average between its old velocity and the chosen velocity.

During the Update Step, the entire Historical Knowledge container is checked and if any historical velocity has not been accepted or reaccepted in over 500 generations, it is removed from the Historical Knowledge container.

Domain Knowledge

The Domain Knowledge container contains points believed to be on the boundary of the search space. If a particle selects Domain Knowledge as its knowledge source, a point is selected from the Domain Knowledge container, and a target velocity is generated equal to the vector difference between the location of the point on the boundary and the current location of the particle. Then, the particle's velocity is changed to a randomly weighted average between its old velocity and the target velocity.

During the Acceptance Step, for each solution set newly accepted into the Pareto Front, a location is created from a randomly weighted average taken between the point in the search space corresponding with said solution set and the closest other point in the search space that corresponds to another solution set within the Pareto Front. Each of these locations is then placed within the Domain

Knowledge container. During the Update Step, if any point on the Pareto Front dominates any point in the Domain Knowledge container, the dominated point is removed from said container.

Topographic Knowledge

Topographic Knowledge is the only one that governs how the algorithm searches through the search space as a whole rather than governing individual agent behavior. Topographic Knowledge works on a recursive "Drill-Down" basis. If the algorithm is searching within a certain portion of the search space and it discovers a parameter set that corresponds to either an entirely new point for the Pareto Front or a point that dominates another point within the Pareto Front, the Topographic Knowledge component will divide the aforementioned portion of the search space into four equal subportions, and the algorithm will recursively search within those subportions.

Tracking Knowledge Source Progress (Other than Topographic)

In situations where an evolutionary algorithm is used in a single-objective problem, a "learning curve" is typically used to track the progress of the algorithm. It is typically a plot of the best-achieved fitness function value versus the number of generations elapsed. For this problem, we cannot use that methodology because our final deliverable is a Pareto Front rather than a single best-achieved value, so we have come up with an alternate methodology to track the progress of the algorithm: If a solution set (represented by a point in vector space) is added to the Pareto Front and it does not dominate any existing points in the Pareto Front, a raw score of 5 is added to the total score for the knowledge source currently influencing the particle that achieved that point (10 if it is the first point ever added to the Pareto Front). However, if a point is added to the Pareto Front and it *does* dominate one or more existing points within the Pareto Front, the total score for the knowledge source currently influencing the particle that achieved the new point is incremented by the absolute value of the vector distance between the new point and the closest dominated point.

The above is how progress for knowledge sources other than Topographic are tracked. Progress for Topographic Knowledge, because it is the only KS that governs search space subdivision rather than individual agent behavior, is tracked in a different way which is described later in Section "Multiple Runs."

CAPSO Algorithm Pseudocode

The CAPSO system is a hybrid system composed of a Particle Swarm and Vector-Evaluated Genetic Algorithm population component operating under the control of a Cultural Algorithm framework. The guiding principle in its design is to keep each as vanilla as possible to facilitate their interaction and support explicit parallelism in the search process.

The **Main** function recursively calls **SearchInSpace** to generate a new swarm thread. A swarm population is associated with that thread via a call to **PopSpaceAlg**. PopSpaceAlg is in charge of updating the swarm associated with the thread. If any swarm ever goes *maxGensWoImprov* generations without improving the Pareto front, it is removed and the thread associated with it is joined with the main thread. If on the other hand it survives for a number of generations equal to the subdivision threshold ("subdivThresh"), then four child threads are spawned each containing an offspring particle swarm, each of whose territory consists of one-fourth of the parent swarm's old territory. After this act of reproduction, the parent swarm dies (is removed) and the thread associated with it is joined with the main thread.

In PopSpaceAlg, selection of an elite takes place via the VEGA method: The population's agents are ranked according to their performance vis-a-vis each individual objective function taken in turn. If an agent is in the top $1/7$ of performers for any of the objective functions, it is added to the elite. Genetic operators (i.e. Crossover, Mutation, and Vector-Weighted Average) are then used to create a new generation with an adequate amount of agent "spread."

CASteps is then called and accepts a certain number of points, elite, into the Belief Space to update it. It then applies the knowledge sources to selectively modify the remaining ones based on their relative performance using a weighted Roulette Wheel mechanism.

The process continues recursively until all swarm threads have finished and have joined with the program's main thread. In that case, the system can be restarted with a new random swarm but still using the acquired knowledge from the currently completed run and any previous runs that reside in the Belief Space. In the problems described below, most were solved in one pass with a second and third try producing no new points. Only SRN benefited from second and third iterations as shown in Figure 9.11 and it is described in the next section. There, the existing front was successfully refined in each of the subsequent two steps.

```
Function Main()
    pFront = ParetoFront.Initialize()
    CA.Initialize()
    SearchInSpace(initSearchSpace)
```

```
#The last line here is recursive and will continually
#subdivide the search domain and "drill down" into each
#subdivision until specified stop conditions are reached.

Function SearchInSpace(topographicCell):
  particleSwarm = ParticleSwarm(topographicCell)
  t = Thread(func = PopSpaceAlg, arg = particleSwarm)
  If t adds at least one new point to ParetoFront &&
  maxRepeats is reached by PopSpaceAlg:
    newSubspaces = DivideIntoEqualPortions(subspace)
    foreach sSpace in newSubspaces:
      searchInSpace(sSpace)


Function PopSpaceAlg(partSwarm):

  numRepeats = 0

  DO:
    #Particle Swarm Movement Step
    Foreach indiv in partSwarm:
      indiv.position += indiv.velocity

    #Pareto Front Update Step
    Foreach indiv in partSwarm:
      If no pFront members dominate or equal F(indiv):
        pFront.Add(F(indiv))
        If F(indiv) dominates any items in pFront:
          indiv.knowSource.increment(domBonus)
          Remove dominated item(s) from pFront
            Else: #discovery bonus is awarded
          indiv.knowSource.increment(dscvBonus)

    #Particle Swarm Elite Selection Step
    elite = SelectElite(VEGA Method, select top 1/7 of
        performers according to each individual obj function.)

    #Particle Swarm Velocity Update Step
    Foreach indiv in partSwarm and not in Elite:
      Rnd0 = random(0, 1)
```

```
Rnd1 = random(0, 1)
Rnd2 = random(Rnd1, 1)
Rnd3 = random(Rnd2, 1)

If rnd0<rnd1: #both crossover and mutation
   Indiv.velocity = Crossover(elite.pickrandom().
   velocity, indiv.velocity)

   Indiv.velocity = Mutation(Indiv.velocity)

Else If Rnd0<Rnd2: #(crossover but no mutation)
   Indiv.velocity = Crossover(elite.pickrandom().
   velocity, indiv.velocity)

Else If Rnd0<Rnd3: #(mutation but no crossover)
   Indiv.velocity = Mutation(Indiv.velocity)

Else If Rnd0<Rnd4 #(weighted average)
   Indiv.velocity= vectorWgtAvg(elite.pickrandom().
   velocity, indiv.velocity)

Else: #Neither crossover nor mutation

CASteps(partSwarm, elite)

UNTIL (++numRepeats == subdivThresh)
OR no pFront Improvement for maxGensWoImprov gens
```

```
Function CASteps(particleSwarm, elite):
   CA.Acceptance(elite)
   CA.Update()


#CA Influence Step
For each indiv in particleSwarm but not in elite:
   indiv.knowSource = CA.ChooseKnowSource( situational,
   normative, historic, or domain)

   targVeloc= CA.Influence(indiv, indiv.knowSource)
   indiv.velocity=vectWtAvg(indiv.velocity, targVeloc)
```

Multiple Runs

When CAPSO undertakes an experiment involving multiple runs, it automatically deletes the population component at the end of each run, but retains both the Pareto Front and the cultural component. This allows CAPSO to continually accumulate both Pareto Front points and cultural knowledge over cumulative runs of the same problem.

In experiments involving multiple runs, CAPSO tracks Topographic Knowledge progress. As the system finds out where the better approximations there are for the Pareto Front, less and less new points will be added to the Pareto Front in the subsequent runs. The Topographic Knowledge component will thus be prompted to subdivide the search space into fewer subspaces in the subsequent runs, and hence less threads should have to be used in each subsequent run. We can thus chart the number of threads used in each run to track Topographic Knowledge progress.

Comparison of Benchmark Problems

We have chosen four well-known benchmark problems in constrained multiobjective optimization to compare our results against some of those achieved by other researchers and methodologies. The benchmark problems we have chosen are CONSTR, SRN, TNK, and KITA. The Pareto front for each of the four has different patterns and symmetries. It was felt that the solution of each would benefit from the applications of collected knowledge to efficiently direct the CA search process for the Pareto front. Our interests here are in how the several knowledge sources can contribute to the solution process. For certain types of problems, does one knowledge source tend to dominate over others in producing effective agent trajectories toward a solution? Are there synergies between knowledge sources that result from their interactions during the search process?

Results for each of these are shown in the following sections. We have used the same program parameters for all of these benchmark experiments, shown in Table 9.1:

Table 9.1 Experimental results.

Particles in Swarm	1000
Number of Initial Guesses for Situational Knowledge	40
Nonimprovement Cutoff Threshold ("maxGensWoImprov")	3 generations
Subdivision Threshold ("subdivThresh") (If this threshold is hit, the subspace currently being searched will be subdivided and new threads will spawn subswarms in each of the subdivisions as described in the pseudocode.)	30 generations
Number of Runs	3

CONSTR

1) *Problem Formulation*
   Minimize:
   $f_1 = x_1$
   $f_2 = (1 + x_2)/x_1$

   Subject to:
   $g_1 = x_2 + 9x_1 - 6 \geq 0$
   $g_2 = -x_2 + 9x_1 - 1 \geq 0$

   Parameter Ranges:
   $x_1 \in [0.1, 1.0]$
   $x_2 \in [0, 5]$

2) *Problem Overview:* CONSTR was first proposed by Kalyanmoy Deb [12]. CONSTR's Pareto Front is constrained on the right side by x_1's parameter range, it is constrained on the left side by constraint g_2, and it is constrained on the bottom by a combination of x_2's parameter range and constraint g_1. What makes this problem interesting is that a portion of the unconstrained Pareto Optimal region is infeasible. Therefore, the constrained optimal Pareto front is a concatenation of the first constraint boundary and a portion of the unconstrained optimal Pareto front.

3) *CAPSO's Solution for CONSTR* (Figure 9.2):

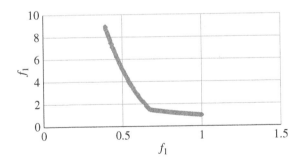

Figure 9.2 CAPSO's Pareto Front for CONSTR.

4) *CONSTR Results Discussion:* CONSTR was Historical Knowledge's worst performance out of the four problems. This is most likely because the parameters corresponding to the Pareto Front (Figure 9.3) form two distinct intersecting

lines with a very abrupt transition between the two. Any Historical Knowledge gained through the discovery of one of these lines is useless in intuiting the other (Figure 9.4).

On the other hand, CONSTR was Situational Knowledge's best performance among the four problems, reaching nearly 50% dominance among the four knowledge sources (Figure 9.5). This is probably because there happened to be two (or more) initial guesses corresponding to the correct velocity "moves" needed to discover the two lines (Figures 9.6 and 9.7).

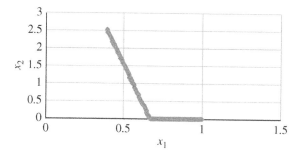

Figure 9.3 CONSTR Parameters Corresponding to the Pareto Front.

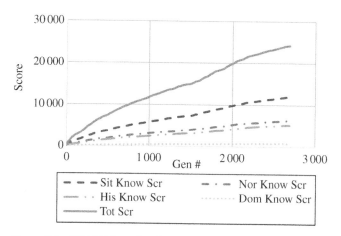

Figure 9.4 CONSTR Learning Curves.

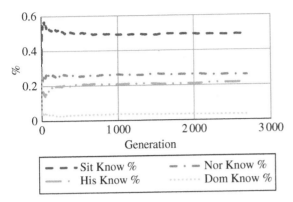

Figure 9.5 Proportion of each Knowledge Source within Weighted Roulette Wheel versus Generation Number for CONSTR (i.e. Knowledge Source Dominance).

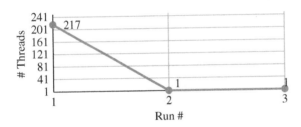

Figure 9.6 CONSTR: Number of Threads Per Run (Topographic Knowledge Source Progress).

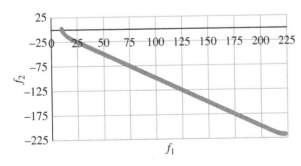

Figure 9.7 CAPSO's Pareto Front for SRN.

SRN

1) Problem Formulation

   Minimize:

   $$f_1 = (x_1 - 2)^2 + (x_2 - 1)^2 + 2$$
   $$f_2 = 9x_1 - (x_2 - 1)^2$$

   Subject to:

   $$g_1 = x_1^2 + x_2^2 - 225 \le 0$$
   $$g_2 = x_1 - 3x_2 + 10 \le 0$$

   Parameter Ranges:

   $$x_1, x_2 \in [-20, 20]$$

2) *Problem Overview:* SRN was first proposed by N. Srinivas [13]. The parameter space in SRN is bounded at the top by the edge of a circle whose equation is given by g_1 and is bounded at the bottom by a line whose equation is given by g_2. SRN is a difficult problem due to the large search space and the large number of particle moves needed to flesh out the entire Pareto Front (see Figure 9.8).

3) *CAPSO's Solution for SRN*: See Figure 9.7.

4) *SRN Results Discussion:* In our evaluation of SRN, Historical Knowledge was the best-performing knowledge source. This is probably because the set of parameter pairs corresponding to the Pareto Front (Figure 9.8) is mostly composed of a thick central "shaft." This "shaft" can be discovered through making similar back-and-forth velocity motions that can be stored within the Historical Knowledge space (Figures 9.9–9.11).

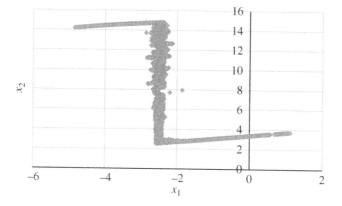

Figure 9.8 SRN Parameter Values Corresponding to Pareto Front.

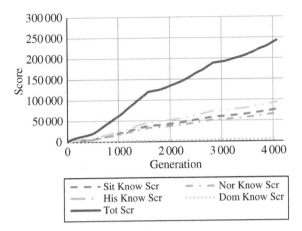

Figure 9.9 SRN Learning Curves.

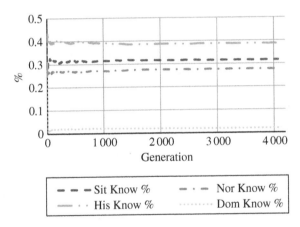

Figure 9.10 SRN Knowledge Source Dominance.

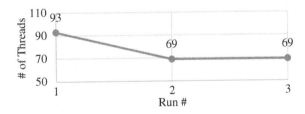

Figure 9.11 SRN Threads Per Run (Topographic Knowledge Progress).

TNK

1) *Problem Formulation*

Minimize:

$f_1 = x_1$

$f_2 = x_2$

Subject to:

$g_1 = -x_1{}^2 - x_2{}^2 + 1 + 0.1\cos(16\arctan(x_1/x_2)) \leq 0$

$g_2 = (x_1 - 0.5)^2 + (x_2 - 0.5)^2 - 0.5 \leq 0$

Parameter Ranges:

$x_1, x_2 \in [0, \pi]$

2) *Problem Overview:* TNK was first proposed by M. Tanaka [14]. TNK's second constraint, g_2, designates as infeasible any solution set that is outside a circle whose center is at (0.5, 0.5) and whose radius is $\sqrt{2}$. The effect of this constraint is to "clip" the Pareto Front so that the leftmost and rightmost ends are slightly shorter than they otherwise would be. The first constraint designates as infeasible any solution set lying inside a hypotrochoid whose formula is given by g_1. TNK's Pareto Front has two discontinuities. The first is caused by the fact that the portion of the hypotrochoid going from $x_1 \in (0.195, 0.459)$ lies up and to the right of the portion going from $x_1 \in (0.056, 0.186)$, the latter thus dominating the former. The second discontinuity is caused by the fact that the portion of the hypotrochoid going from $x_2 \in (0.173, 0.460)$ lies directly above the portion going from $x_2 \in (0.057, 0.173)$, the latter once again dominating the former. Because $f_1 = x_1$ and $f_2 = x_2$, TNK is unique here in being determined wholly by its constraints, g_1 and g_2. Figure 9.12 is provided below to show how g_1 and g_2 interact with one another to produce TNK's Pareto Front.

3) *TNK Ideal Pareto* Front: See Figure 9.12.

4) *CAPSO's Solution for* TNK: See Figure 9.13.

5) *TNK Results Discussion:* TNK is an interesting problem not only because the Pareto Front is disjoint, but because each of the functions are simply set equal to each of the parameters (i.e., $f_1 = x_1$ and $f_2 = x_2$), and thus the graph of TNK's Pareto Front (Figure 9.12) is exactly the same as the graph of the parameter values used to achieve it (Figure 9.13). Historical Knowledge was the best knowledge source in our evaluation of TNK, finishing with around 32.6% dominance among the four knowledge sources. This is probably because even though the Pareto Front is disjoint, there are some parts which are extremely similar to other parts. For instance, the portion stretching from $f_1 \in (0.05, 0.2)$ is extremely similar in shape and slope to the portion stretching from $f_1 \in (0.8, 0.92)$. Thus, Historical Knowledge used to fully discover one of these could be reused to fully discover the other (Figures 9.14–9.17).

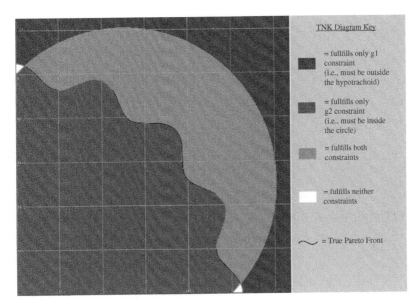

Figure 9.12   TNK Ideal Pareto Front.

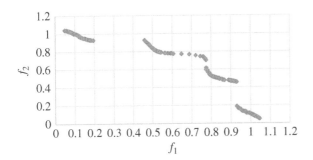

Figure 9.13   TNK Pareto Front.

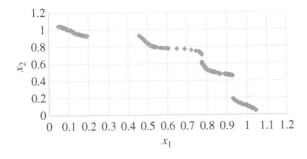

Figure 9.14   TNK Search Space.

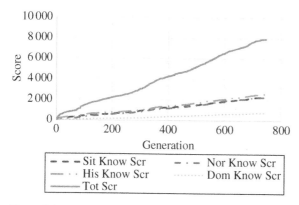

Figure 9.15   TNK Learning Curves.

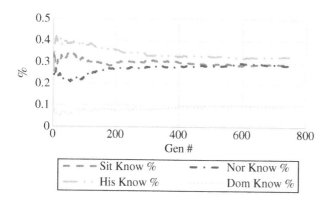

Figure 9.16   TNK Knowledge Source Dominance.

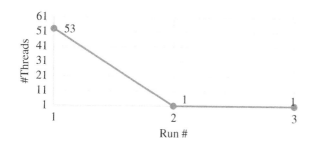

Figure 9.17   TNK Number of Threads Per Run (Topographic Knowledge Source Progress).

KITA

1) *Problem Formulation*

Maximize:

$$f_1 = -x_1^2 + x_2$$
$$f_2 = x_1/2 + x_2 + 1$$

Subject to:

$$g_1 = x_1/6 + x_2 - 13/2 \leq 0$$
$$g_2 = x_1/2 + x_2 - 15/2 \leq 0$$
$$g_3 = 5x_1 + x_2 - 30 \leq 0$$

Parameter Ranges:

$$x_1, x_2 \in [0, 7]$$

2) *Problem Overview:* KITA was first proposed by H. Kita [15]. Out of the four benchmark problems that we evaluated, Domain Knowledge most came into play in KITA.

3) *CAPSO's Solution for KITA:* See Figure 9.18.

4) *KITA Results Discussion:* KITA was Situational Knowledge's best-performing problem because the parameter values corresponding to the achieved Pareto Front almost entirely corresponded to a single line with domain $x_1 \in (0, 3)$ and with a slope of -2.167. The velocity "moves" needed to "flesh out" this line after its initial discovery would thus logically correspond with this slope, which is a fact very easily remembered by Historical Knowledge. In our evaluation of KITA, Historical Knowledge finished with around 43.4% dominance, way ahead of the other knowledge sources.

Domain Knowledge finished third out of the four knowledge sources for KITA. KITA was the only problem where Domain Knowledge did not finish last out of the knowledge sources. In general, Domain Knowledge is usually the least-dominant knowledge source because it is effectively the "clean-up crew," which polishes up Pareto Fronts that have been achieved by the other knowledge sources. This is because it acts almost like a "stem cell" in that it can work as either an exploitative or exploratory knowledge source depending on the situation (Figures 9.18–9.22).

Figure 9.23 shows KITA's true Pareto Front (right) along with the corresponding parameter space (left). KITA's Pareto Front contains a "tail," line segment $\overline{YZ}$, which has domain $f_1 \in [-3, -20]$ and where f_2 is always equal to 8.5. KITA's "tail" is very difficult for optimizers to handle because it is in fact a very long Weakly Pareto-optimal line. With conventional multiobjective optimization approaches, it is possible to "wipe out" points within the Weakly Pareto-Optimal region $(\overline{YZ})$ by achieving any point with a higher f_1 value and a just barely higher f_2 value, even if it is very far away. The "wiped out" points are often extremely close to optimal.

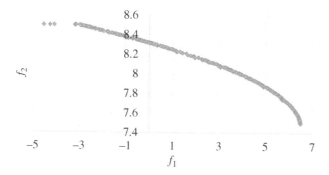

Figure 9.18 KITA Pareto Front.

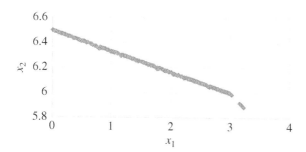

Figure 9.19 KITA Parameter Values.

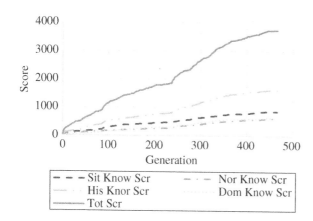

Figure 9.20 KITA Knowledge Source Scores.

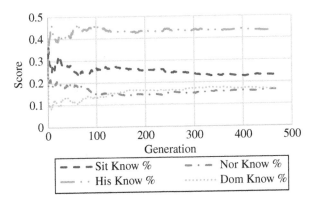

Figure 9.21 KITA Knowledge Source Dominance.

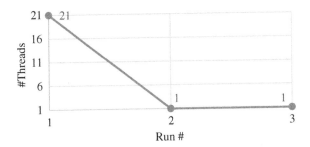

Figure 9.22 KITA Threads Per Run (Topographic Knowledge Progress).

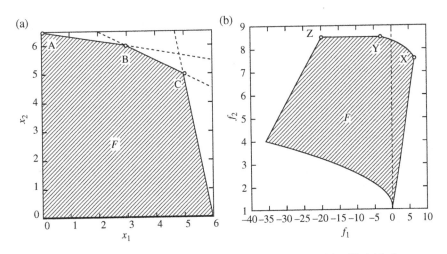

Figure 9.23 KITA Feasible Region. (a) Feasible Region in the Decision Variable Space and (b) Feasible Region in the Objective Function Space. *Source:* Taken from [15]. Reproduced with permission of AAAI.

The core problem lies with the fact that conventional multiobjective optimization approaches, including CAPSO, want to continually produce solutions that are stronger and stronger, whereas Weakly Pareto-optimal solutions are in some sense weaker and weaker, despite the fact that they are not suboptimal solutions. Optimization with Weakly Pareto-optimal zones is still an open topic of research. That being said, CAPSO was still successful in achieving at least a few of the Weakly Pareto-optimal solutions within the "KITA tail."

Overall Summary of Results

In this work, we investigated the role of Knowledge in directing the "flow of agent traffic" in the generation of Pareto Optimal fronts using the Cultural Algorithms framework. Knowledge sources can function to "explore" the search space or "exploit" it. While some are primarily exploratory (normative and topographic), others are primarily exploiters (situational and historical). Domain knowledge occupies a hybrid category, where like a "stem cell" it can be either exploratory or exploitative depending on the context.

Four traditionally difficult multiobjective constrained optimization problems were investigated using our hybrid CAPSO model. In many cases, exploratory knowledge sources are the first to dominate the search process. However, here the explorative knowledge sources (normative and topographic) are dominated almost from the start by the exploitative knowledge sources (situational and historic). Exploitative knowledge sources dominated in all four of the cases. In fact, historic knowledge was the top performer in three of the four cases, while situational was the top performer in CONSTR.

Overall, Situational Knowledge was the dominant knowledge source for one out of the four of these benchmark problems (CONSTR). It was followed by Normative knowledge there. Since the Pareto front in CONSTR was produced by the concatenation of two different fronts, the exploratory knowledge source was needed to deal with the separate components. For the other three (SRN, TNK, and KITA), Historical Knowledge was the dominant knowledge source followed by Situational Knowledge. In these cases, History knowledge was able to exploit symmetries in the different fronts. Future work will investigate in more detail how Pareto front structure affects knowledge dominance in Cultural Algorithms.

Other Applications

Earlier in Chapter 8, CAPSO was used to analyze trends in a study of the impact of El Niño and climate change on artisanal fisherman behavior from the early 1980s in Cerro Azul, Peru. In that study, CAPSO was used to perform nonlinear regression analysis on the results of different fishing strategies produced by fishermen in different scenarios weighing the two countervailing objectives of payout in the form of quality-weighted fish catches versus effort in the form of fuel used, distance travelled, and other expenditures [16].

CAPSO is also currently involved in an upcoming work, which will be centered around using multiobjective optimization to plan archaeological expedition seasons. In that work, CAPSO controls a number of expert system rules, which can flag locations in the region of expedition interest. CAPSO is set to tune these rulesets with the countervailing objectives of minimizing the number of locations flagged while simultaneously maximizing the number of training set structures contained within the whole set of flagged locations. Running this problem through CAPSO results in a Pareto Front containing (number of locations predicted, number of structures therein) ordered pairs as points, along with corresponding rulesets as parameters for each point. CAPSO's rulesets are then plugged into a visualizer program which prints out from these a series of visual expedition plans that archaeologists can select from based on their time and budgetary constraints. An example of expert system rules that can be used for Archaeological site location can be found in Chapter 10.

References

1 Reynolds, R.G. (1994). An introduction to cultural algorithms. *Proceedings of the 3rd Annual Conference on Evolutionary Programming,* San Diego, CA, USA (24–26 February 1994).

2 Eberhart, R. and Kennedy, J. (1995). A new optimizer using particle swarm theory. *Proceedings of the Sixth International Symposium on Micro Machine and Human Science,* Nagoya, Japan (4–6 October).

3 Schaffer, J.D. (1985). Multi objective optimization with vector evaluated genetic algorithms. *Proceedings of an International Conference on Genetic Algorithms and their Applications,* Pittsburgh, PA, (24–26 July).

4 Reynolds, R.G. (1978). On modeling the evolution of hunter-gatherer decision making systems. *Geographical Analysis* 10 (1): 31–46.

5 Reynolds, R.G. (1979). An adaptive computer model of the evolution of agriculture for hunter-gatherers in the valley of Oaxaca, Mexico. PhD Dissertation. University of Michigan, Ann Arbor, MI.

6 Jin, J. (2011). Path planning in reality games using cultural algorithm: the land bridge example. M.S. Thesis. Wayne State University, Detroit, MI.

7 Reynolds, R.G. (2018). *Culture on the Edge of Chaos: Cultural Algorithms and the Foundations of Social Intelligence.* Cham, Switzerland: Springer.

8 Stanley, S.D. (2013). Analyzing environmental change and prehistoric hunter behavior through a 3D time-lapsed model with level auto-generation and cultural algorithms. M. S. Thesis. Wayne State University, Detroit, MI.

9 Stanley, S.D., Salaymeh, A., Palazzolo, T., and Warnke, D. (2014). Analyzing prehistoric hunter behavior with cultural algorithms. *Proceedings of the 2014 IEEE Congress on Evolutionary Computation*, Beijing, China (6–11 July).

10 Peng, B. (2005). Knowledge and population swarms in cultural algorithms for dynamic environments. PhD Dissertation. Wayne State University, Detroit, MI.

11 Reynolds, R.G. and Kinnard-Heether, L. (2013). Optimization Problem Solving with Auctions in Cultural Algorithms. *Memetic Computing* 5 (2): 83–94.

12 Deb, K. (2001). *Multi-Objective Optimization Using Evolutionary Algorithms*. New York: Wiley.

13 Srinivas, N. and Deb, K. (1994). Multiobjective optimization using nondominated sorting in genetic algorithms. *Journal of Evolutionary Computation* 2 (3): 221–248.

14 Tanaka, M., Watanabe, H., Furukawa, Y., and Tanino, T. (1995). GA-based decision support system for multicriteria optimization. *1995 IEEE International Conference on Systems, Man and Cybernetics. Intelligent Systems for the 21st Century*, Vancouver, Canada (22–25 October).

15 Kita, H., Yabumoto, Y., Mori, N., and Nishikawa, Y. (1996). Multi-objective optimization by means of the thermodynamical genetic algorithm. *International Conference on Parallel Problem Solving from Nature*, Berlin, Germany (22–26 September).

16 Kattan, K. (2019). The use of cultural algorithms to learn the impact of climate on local Fishing Behavior in Cerro Azul. PhD Dissertation. Wayne State University, Detroit, MI.

10

Exploring Virtual Worlds with Cultural Algorithms

Ancient Alpena–Amberley Land Bridge

Thomas Palazzolo[1], Robert G. Reynolds[1,2], and Samuel Dustin Stanley[1]

[1] Department of Computer Science, Wayne State University, Detroit, MI, USA
[2] Museum of Anthropological Archaeology, University of Michigan, Ann Arbor, MI, USA

Archaeological Challenges

The field of archaeological study and research faces numerous challenges in regards to the availability of research sites. Archaeological sites represent past peoples and cultures that have been weathered by the forces of time, nature, and humanity itself, and sites that are still intact are often restricted in terms of accessibility [1]. What had once been a coastal city with a ripe fishing population and shipyards may now be entirely submerged underwater due to rising water levels and geological upheaval. Figure 10.1 shows a hunting blind found by archaeologists under Lake Huron in Michigan.

Submerged sites are at the mercy of the elements and the indigenous species as well. Invasive mussels can adhere to and destroy surfaces of solid rock. Plants growing up through cracks and push apart the most secure of structures. The temperature changes from the onset of the yearly seasons can cause structures to expand and shrink, cracking apart, and losing cohesion. In addition, site accessibility and location is often a problem. Specialized and expensive diving equipment combined with an uncertain schedule due to unpredictable weather events that can cancel an entire day's planned work in a single stroke means a risky gamble on a reward that is likely obscured by layers of underwater species and plant life.

This work was supported by NSF grant #1744367.

Figure 10.1   An Underwater Archaeological Site.

Similarly a site which was once the site of an indigenous people's struggle to survive may still be relatively easy to access in terms of physical effort but as new nations rise and fall over the course of time and borders are redrawn over and over again, archaeologists may find themselves barred entrance for political reasons. Governments that wish to have their historical sites investigated by their own teams, tension over borders and property lines, and arguments about what party found relics would belong to can keep teams from even getting close to an area that is vital for research. An example of such events is given by the excavations of an ancient fort in Syria that had to be abandoned due to heavy antigovernment protests, and with the construction of the nearby Halabiyeh hydropower dam, the site is now underwater [2].

The most frightening aspect to those seeking to uncover and preserve archaeological treasures is the very human element. The older a site gets, the more difficult it becomes for an untrained person to recognize it for what it is. Figure 10.1's stone hunting blind would appear to the untrained eye to be just a collection of large rocks. However, they are in fact one of the oldest archaeological finds in North America that remains largely intact. One of the reasons for this is the fact that it is difficult to find even for the trained observer. It is entirely possible that similar structures had existed across North America, only to be hauled away and broken up by early settlers looking to clear farmland and extract materials for crafting their own homesteads. A grim recent example is the ancient Great Wall of China, a world-renowned wonder of the ancient world which is slowly vanishing as it is used to rebuild houses and roads, destroying sections of it to make passage easier, and spraying it with graffiti. It is estimated that only a third of the original wall still exists today, and that number is getting smaller every day [3].

Figure 10.2 shows Dr. John O'Shea from the University of Michigan holding an ancient artifact that is over 8000 years old. To an untrained diver who might happen on such an object, they would be hard-pressed to discern it from any regular driftwood or remnant of a modern-day wreckage. There are a number of indicators of archaeological sites that are difficult to recognize. A rounded stone may have been used to grind food for meals, and rocks cracked by the intense heat of a fire may be signs of a camp [4]. Microdebitage, some as small and fine as grains of sand, are remnants of flint knapping, a means of shaping tools and weaponry such as arrowheads. It is typically ignorance rather than maliciousness that can cause vital archaeological evidence to be lost forever by an unassuming, simple

Figure 10.2 Dr. John O'Shea Pictured with an Ancient Artifact.

gesture. As such, archaeologists are hard-pressed to both discover and preserve these sites and artifacts as quickly and efficiently as possible before they are lost to either nature or man. But at the same time, it is important that the manner in which the discovery is made is carefully cataloged and documented, a process that becomes even more difficult when the discovered location is underwater [1].

To aid in these endeavors to study and preserve the history of mankind, the Land Bridge Project, under the direction of Dr. Robert G. Reynolds, has developed a digital toolset, which allows for these previously undetected sites to suddenly be as close at hand as the keyboard of a computer. The project uses NOAA data to create a framework that allows for virtual interaction and exploration aimed at generating sites of interest that may yield real-world finds in an effort to increase the efficiency of an archaeological team's research. The Land Bridge Project also uses simulated, AI-driven agents, and because of this it can not only model animal behavior but also allow for the simulation and modeling of cultural elements. Being able to model and experiment on ancient social interactions is a tool rarely available and highly desirable to archeologists looking to test theories [5].

Generalized Framework

Virtual Archaeology is by no means a new technology. There are two main categories that Virtual Archaeology fits into. The first is a way to educate and illustrate known archaeological information for a wide variety of users, typically aimed at those without a background in archaeology. Virtual tours of ancient temples, allowing students to try their hand at reassembling a digital representation of a shattered artifact, and taking part in a cultural exchange from the past are designed with a user-friendly interface, and simplified information navigation with a non-academic user in mind [6]. Yet this representation is only a sophisticated documentation of work that is already been done, a flashy presentation of discoveries already made.

The second category is a more complex simulation that exists for the purpose of aiding research as a sophisticated toolkit. Virtual Archaeology has been used to simulate ancient societies in an attempt to recreate migration patterns and discover possible answers to few very complex questions. For example, Virtual Archaeology has been used to model the migration of the Anasazi people, using simulated agents who reproduce the household needs of food and kinship with other households, moving perhaps when they no longer have access to those necessities [7].

The framework developed in the Land Bridge Project is an attempt to focus not only on the displaying of what has been found but also to enable the user to take part in actual, active research in an attempt to find a genuine, real-world location that is the likely site of an archaeological find. That means exposing the user to a tremendous amount of information in a way that it is not overwhelming or alien, but rather enticing and familiar. The system begins with over 200 gigabytes of raw data that can first be fed into a preprocessor which sorts and checks the information, and while in this preprocessor a series of algorithms and equations are run to expand the knowledge base by extracting additional information. As there are various sources and pieces of information available, one of our goals is sorely needed interoperability with existing virtual archaeology systems which vary so dramatically from one another that a focused system of data validation and exploration is a top priority [8].

This information is then passed into a visual system, which grants the user both a three-dimensional, first-person view of the world, and a two-dimensional, top-down view as well. Once the user becomes situated with the virtual world and its features, such as the dips and drops in the terrain to be explored and the rush of water against the coastline, the next step in the framework becomes readily available to them, digital creatures with which to populate the virtual world they are exploring. Their behavior then becomes a new source of information that can be given to another function to generate data that the archaeologist can make use of to refine their own real-world searches.

All of this is presented via a simple user interface that is designed for everyone from a casual user to a first-time student to a seasoned archaeologist. As a tool, this software is capable of generating actual information that can be used for real-world study, and it is also capable of expanding beyond its initial native test bed of the Alpena–Amberley Land Bridge. Some of the world's most inaccessible and dangerous regions, such as the Bering Strait crossing, a hypothetical submerged Land Bridge that could have once connected Russia and Alaska, will be virtual regions, which a user may explore from the comfort of an armchair rather than in the freezing, turbulent waters of the Bering Strait (Figure 10.3) [9].

The Land Bridge Hypothesis

This goal can be accomplished by a number of components working together to shuttle data around the system behind the scenes while the user looks at a graphical user interface that puts each piece of information at their fingertips. The original NOAA data used for the Alpena–Amberley Land Bridge area, which will be examined in detail in a later section, is over 270 gigabytes of textual data. One of the most essential aspects of a GUI is to reduce the complexity between the raw data to be processed and the user [10]. To reduce the overwhelming size for the user, the GUI initially displays a visual of the entire landscape at low resolution. It is from this landscape that the user can select which area to view in greater detail. This landscape the user's seeing represents a two-dimensional array of all of the

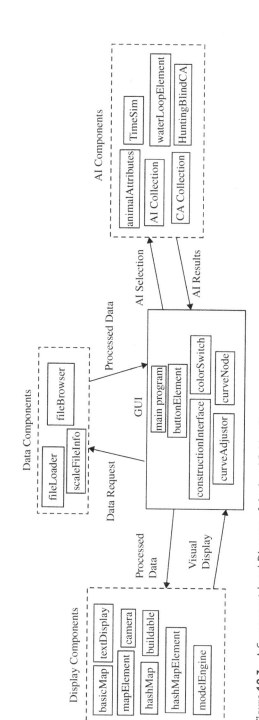

Figure 10.3 A Component-Level Diagram of the Land Bridge Program.

available files. By making their selection, the user chooses which collection of files they wish to view. Once they finalize their selection, the user is given the option to choose at what variable scale they wish to view the information.

At this point, the GUI component takes the user's data request and sends the coordinates and specifics to the data component. The data component, which not only contains the pathway information to access the files but also the necessary preprocessing algorithms to deal with and assemble their data, takes the user's request specifications and forms an array of processed data out of the individual files requested. This merged piece of processed data is returned to the GUI component, whereupon it is immediately passed along to the display component. The display and GUI components differ significantly in that while they are both concerned with displaying information, the GUI displays information about how the user may control their virtual environment. The display component is what determines how the information about the virtual environment is actually displayed. This includes generated two-dimensional maps through various calculations and three-dimensional maps, extrapolated from height data.

It is important that while the user is able to feel a real-world effect from their actions (i.e., button feedback, audio feedback, system adjustment) that they still maintain a sense of reversibility [11]. So while the GUI component allows them to press buttons and manipulate where data are displayed and how, it does not allow them to directly manipulate the data. The user is never in danger of creating some scenario from which they are unable to reclaim previous data or unable to undo a manipulation they have made. This sensation of an ability to manipulate data without its destruction gives the user a greater sense of freedom and exploration in their work. The more relaxed a user is with a piece of software, the more quickly they might adapt to it and take advantage of its capabilities. Any piece of complex software is judged not only on its capabilities but how long it takes the average uninitiated user to be trained to use it [12]. A promising piece of software with a yearlong window of training before it can be properly used is something that would likely deter the average user.

The Land Bridge software is designed with a wide range of users in mind. Although the results created by the software are detailed enough that they can be used by real-world, highly trained archaeologists, the interface is designed with an uninitiated user in mind [13]. This variation in end-user profiles has focused the Land Bridge Project in a way that there is a visual simplicity combined with a computational complexity. Users can proceed as deeply into the available information as they wish and extract as much data as they can understand [14]. There is even a capacity for a user unskilled in archaeological work (but with some interest in it) to supply useful data to an actual archaeologist by running their own experiments.

The most complex component of the software is the AI component. There are numerous levels of artificial intelligence at work in the software as well as a number of different approaches to tactics, strategy, and use of data. More detail on the AI-driven processes will be given in a later section, but here it must be specified that the AI component uses an iterative approach that allows the software to build on itself through several layers, each layer contributing to another piece of information that can be fed into the next, more complex technique.

First, a hierarchical, cell-structure-based approach is used. Similar techniques have been used to build randomized worlds in games [15], where a series of linked cells have data shared between them to generate new layers of data. Similarly, in this project's approach, the heights of individualized cells are used to calculate the directional slope of a cell. The directional slopes and their severities can be used to calculate how water flows between the cells to generate a water map. This water layer of information in turn provides the information used to calculate the vegetation layer of information. Thus, the cells work together to form an interconnected mesh of information that generates new data with each subsequent layer, and these layers can be fed to AI-driven agents to yield even more complex patterns [16].

Once the system has generated the layers of information to feed into the AI component, several stages take place as each agent feeds on information delivered from other agents. This all begins with a top-level hierarchical assembly. A highly scaled, low-resolution version of the entirety of the Alpena–Amberley Land Bridge data is used, first broken into several smaller cells.

As can be seen in Figure 10.4, this initial coarse read can be viewed as a series of 16 distinct cellular regions. Each of these regions has the same dimensions, except for regions 15 and 16 that were included to show more information on the Canadian edge and are not included in the topmost step. In addition, each region has a series of viable boundaries along each edge that an agent may use to pass from one region into another. For example, in Figure 10.4, it can be seen that region 9, located approximately at the center of the Land Bridge, has several very narrow expanses near the southwestern point of the region. This means that any agent seeking to move through region 9 into regions 11 or 12 would need to pass through this viable boundary. This collection of boundaries effectively creates a series of checkpoints the agents MUST pass through to proceed from one end of the Land Bridge to the other. By subtly adjusting at which points in these boundaries the agents pass through, their progress can be scored based on variables such as total distance covered and survival rates calculated from caloric needs versus caloric consumption.

Using the Cultural Algorithm it is possible to maximize these scores across the top-level, low-scale version of the Land Bridge, which will be discussed in more

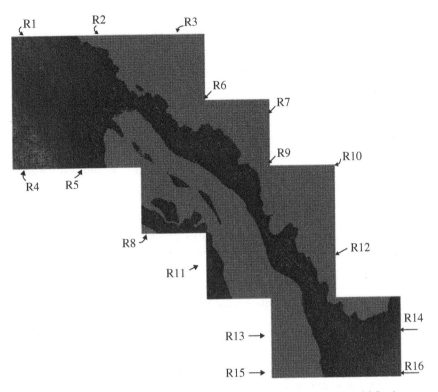

Figure 10.4 The Low-Scale Top-Level Scan of the Land Bridge Data with 16 Regions.

detail in later. After establishing these highest-ranking pathways, they will become checkpoints in the more fine-grained view of the landscape where agents will be able to make use of variable strategies to attempt to maximize their scores. This next level of strategy introduces new tactics and works with the data more in-detail. In the future, it is possible to bring actual human users into the loop as a potential hazard for caribou agents to contend with, allowing users themselves to become a step in this process.

After these tactical and strategic levels of establishing routes through the landscape, the pathways of the agents form another layer of information that allows the AI component to establish areas of potential archaeological interest. The Cultural Algorithm can take these potential areas and rank them based on various rulesets, which will be explored in detail in the section Identifying Good Locations. It is this layer of information which yields data that an archaeologist may find most interesting, as it can be tied in to real-world coordinates.

Origin and Form

NOAA stands for the National Oceanographic and Atmospheric Administration, an American scientific agency that comprises numerous laboratories and divisions to research the oceans, weather, effects on the environment, geodetic surveys, drought information, and more. It is thanks to their constant surveying work and research as well as that of Dr. John O'Shea of the University of Michigan that the Land Bridge Project gained access to a sonar scan of the lakebed of Lake Huron. The result of this sonar scan was over 270 gb worth of data, comprising Easting and Northing coordinates, and heights. Easting and Northing is a standardized system of measurement used in the NOAA surveying data, based on set UTM (universal transverse Mercator) locations. The reasons for using these locations over something more familiar such as latitude and longitude are two fold. For example, the distance between Easting and Northing coordinates remains consistent regardless of location, while latitude and longitude may differ at times due to the curvature of the Earth. NOAA themselves even study the effect of terrain decay and geological events on where latitude and longitude lines lay.

The UTM location that accompanies the project's Easting and Northing coordinates is 16T, an indicator which places a fixed location (approximately in an Eastern part of Michigan). The Easting and Northing coordinates then correspond to metric distance from that fixed location. For example, an Easting of "500" would mean a point exactly 500 m east from the fixed points, while a Northing of "42" would mean 42 m north from the fixed location. The NOAA survey sampled height data at every meter, meaning the resulting collection of information provides an incredibly detailed look at the entire region below Lake Huron. This also means a tremendous amount of data as at its longest point Lake Huron is 332 000 m long, and at its widest point 295 000 m long [17].

At each point, the project has a reading of height data in meters, such that the difference between any two surveyed points is their difference in meters. So for example, a measurement of 8.6 in one location and 4.2 in another indicates a difference of 4.4 m total. There is at this stage to be noted one problem that arises in the collected data. Though accurate and painstakingly collected, the movements of the sonar array caused a rake-like disruption in the data. This causes a very slight amount of noise that can be observed when certain data are extracted and rendered into visible form, most notably the flow direction data. This will be mentioned in the section "Putting Data to Work" when the flow direction data are discussed in depth.

As it is a daunting task for most commercially available computers to open and maintain several hundred gigs of data at a time, it is necessary for the project to compress the data through selective scale sampling. It was mentioned previously in this chapter that the user, from the GUI component, is able to select a scale at

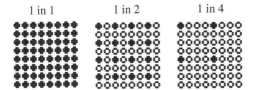

Figure 10.5 An Example of the Scaling Sampling.

which they wish to view the data that is then incorporated into the request sent to the data component. The number which the user selects indicates a "1 in X" rate of sampling. As each individual file present in the NOAA collection comprises a square kilometer of data, which means there is a 1000 by 1000 grid of single meter data points in every collection. In a raw, unaltered file, there are only three pieces of data making up each of the 1 000 000 data points. For a typical view, a user may choose to view 100 files at once, leading to 100 000 000 data points. On top of that, each data point then has additional information calculated for it from the previously mentioned layers of data, including vegetation, flow direction, and water accumulation.

So to ease the strain on the system, the user's scale choice reduces the size of the data by sampling smaller pieces within the data. As seen in Figure 10.5, a scale of 1 in 1 skips nothing, reading all available data. The first reduction, scale of 1 in 2, collects only a single piece of data in every $2\,m^2$; 1 in 4 collects only a single piece of data in every $4\,m^2$; and so on. Thus, a scale of 1 in 250 means that between each data point is a distance of 250 m. The files are read, the unwanted data points are discarded, and the remaining data points are assembled into the two-dimensional array that will be used by the system.

Putting Data to Work

After scaling the two-dimensional array of data points comprising Easting and Northing coordinates and the heights, the program can start to extrapolate additional data. The first thing that is created is the topographical map. This grid is specifically a collection of just the height points rendered into chromatic form to display a difference in height.

As can be seen in Figure 10.6, the basic topography map is the sum total of all height data in the two-dimensional array rendered into a greyscale shading scheme, with the brighter hues (as see in the lower-right corner) representing the higher points, and the darker hues representing lower points. As this display is relativistic, the maximum for the selected collection of data is the brightest shade, and the minimum is the darkest. Converting the height into the shading scheme

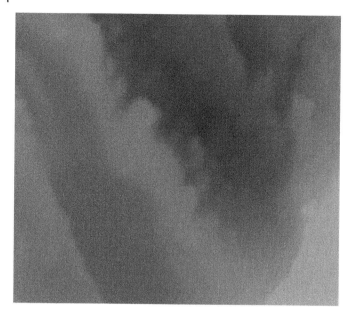

Figure 10.6   The Topography Map.

is done by creating a ratio based on a given position's selected height, which is then subtracted from the maximum height in the height array. This is then divided by the maximum height minus the minimum height. The program then takes the resulting ratio and subtracts it from one to invert it, due to the way shades are displayed in the program, with a scale of zero being black to one being brightest shade.

$$shade = 1 - \left(\left(heightMax - currentHeight \right) / \left(heightMax - heightMin \right) \right) \quad (10.1)$$

This allows the user to view the heights as seen in Figure 10.6. The topographical map also displays the water data, which is determined in two ways. First is the user-defined lake-level water, which is set at levels as discerned from geological records of approximately 10 000 years ago, which gives the simulated landscape a border along the edges of the Land Bridge, and makes a number of cut-off points visible as well. The user can raise and lower this level to make the simulation more representative of alternate time periods by associating the time period with the level the lake's water would have been at according to past data. However, these lake levels are not calculated, but rather culled from previously existing research into the rise and fall of the lake levels due to the encroachment and later retraction of glaciers changing the shape of the what is now Lake Huron.

In Figure 10.7, it is possible to view the two separate water elements together. The large, dark mass in the upper right of the figure is the edge of the Land Bridge

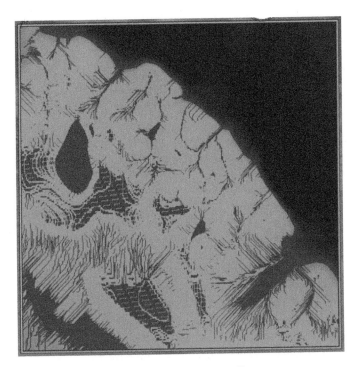

Figure 10.7 The Topography Map with Water Elements.

defined by the user-defined lake level. The more intricate waterways and forms in the rest of the figure come from several additional layers of calculation used to determine how water flows and collects in the various natural deformations of the virtual landscape.

The first step in calculating these flows is to extrapolate flow-direction data from the height data that were viewed previously in Figure 10.6. The Direction Equation takes the input of four points of height, where each point located at one corner of a square and extrapolates from those heights which direction has the most dominant slope. The meaning of dominant slope is that should a perfectly spherical object be placed on the square and free of friction to only be drawn by the force of gravity, it would invariably roll in the direction of the dominant slope.

To first establish the direction, the program must generate two vectors, one for X (East to West) and one for Y (North to South). Given a square of land on the map with four points, one at each corner, from those the program can establish four average heights. One corresponding to each line segment of the square, so that every line segment has a stored piece of data that represents the average of each of the two nodes it is attached to.

By calculating the ATAN2 of the greater of the two heights subtracted from the lesser of the two heights, with the initial map scale used to determine the distance between the points and then dividing by Pi/2, we are given a percentage ratio that is then multiplied by 9.8 as a marker for gravity. The logic behind this is that if the slope is so severe that it approaches being a straight drop, then the force of acceleration would be based on gravity alone. If the ground were perfectly flat, then there would be no measured accelerative force due to gravity as the object would not have a direction to roll in. In the case of the two opposite average heights being equal, then there would be no vector for that particular direction, indicating no shift in height from the two points.

The basic function used appears as follows:

In the case of $AverageHeightX1 > AverageHeight\,X2$, *then:*
$xAcclFactor = 9.8 * (ATAN2((AverageHeightX1 -$
$AverageHeightX2), InitialScale)\,/\,(Pi\,/\,2))$
In the case of the $AverageHeightX1 < AverageHeightX2$, *then:*
$xAcclFactor = -9.8 * (ATAN2((AverageHeightX2 -$
$AverageHeightX1), InitialScale)\,/\,(Pi\,/\,2))$
If the two values are equal, then xAcclFactor is set to 0.
The equations are identical for computing the yAcclFactor,
only that AverageHeightX1 and AverageHeightX2 are replaced
with AverageHeightY1 and AverageHeightY2. (10.2)

Once these values are calculated, before storing them it is important to flip them. This flip was done to correct the output just before it is passed on to other equations that use it. This complication comes about as a result of the use of ATAN2, and in future versions may be improved on to lessen the complexity of the equation and remove the need for flipping the values. However, this version has been confirmed to produce correct outputs. The verification taking place when it was given a series of sample landscapes where the resulting directions the land sloped was in the predicted direction.

The flip that occurs is to store the resulting yAcclFactor as the given element's xAccl and store the NEGATIVE of the resulting xAcclFactor as the given element's yAccl. The two resulting vectors, xAccl and yAccl, may then be used to calculate a third vector between them that indicates direction.

Figure 10.8 serves as a visualization of how the X and Y vectors of the landscape produce the direction of flow for a given area of land. As the Y vector indicates which direction (and with how much magnitude) an object would roll off in the North or South direction, and the X vector indicates the same for the East and West directions, coupling them together results in a new vector which points out the actual direction an object would roll off of the slope.

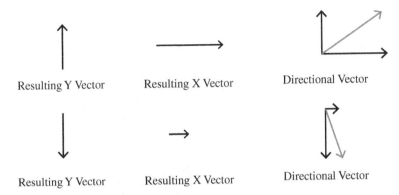

Resulting Y Vector   Resulting X Vector   Directional Vector

Resulting Y Vector   Resulting X Vector   Directional Vector

Figure 10.8 An Example of Calculating Vectors.

Originally, the resulting vector was then placed within one of eight cardinal directions by comparing it to a collection of angles, which divided a circle into eight equally sized areas, with one set being North, another being Northeast, East, Southeast, etc. It became possible to feed the results of the Direction Equation into an equation similar to the grayscale equation seen previously, set to a range of the seven primary colors. To accomplish this, the angle of the vector was calculated by ATAN2(yAccl,xAccl), then Pi was added to it to result in a range between 0 and 2 * Pi. This information is then similarly grey-scale coded as the topography and used to generate the flow direction map (Figure 10.9).

The program now has the deformation of the landscape given by each data point's height attribute, and the direction and magnitude of that direction given by the flow-direction equation, and it is now possible to calculate how water will flow and accumulate throughout a given landscape. Water is treated as if it were a spherical object with a limited supply of mass, as each movement across the virtual landscape depletes it somewhat, simulating natural absorption and dispersion of water. The faster it can move from one region to another, the more intact it stays, whereas once it begins to decelerate it loses more of itself. On either exhausting its supply of mass, encountering an edge of the map or reaching a previously set iterative level (used to reduce processing strain), the water object ceases its journey from its initial cell. This process is then repeated, with a water object originating at each and every grid cell in the array and its movements dictated by the heights and flow directions it encounters. Each cell that the water object passes through records two pieces of information. First, a singular instance of the water object's passage is incremented. Secondly, the calculated speed of the water object as it passes through the location is stored as well and averaged with any previously existing water speeds on that object.

As seen in Figure 10.10, visualizing this information by means of applying Eq. (10.1) to the count of water objects to each area, along with a cut-off point for

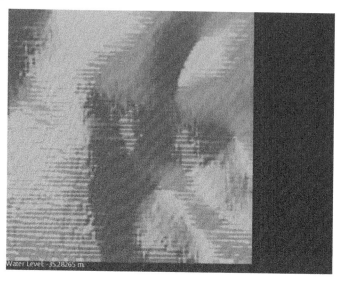

Water Level: 35.28265 m

Figure 10.9 The Flow Direction Data Represented on a Map.

the total number of water objects that are allowed in a single grid space, allows the user to see a number of lines cascading away from highest points and gathering at the lowest points on the grid. These most dramatic points become standing water objects and rivers. It is only those grid points that reach the maximum cap for possible water objects that become denoted as water objects for later calculations.

To formally make these water calculations, the assumption is made that all objects have no initial velocity, leaving their initial direction and speed to be determined by the grid space they begin on. It first checks to see if there is an accelerative vector in the X direction (East to West). If there is not, the algorithm quickly steps out of the calculations and goes to check the Y direction. If it still finds no accelerative vector, it simply assumes that the water object cannot escape the square it has landed on, makes notation about it having landed on that square, and then proceeds to the next grid space with a new object.

If there is an accelerative vector on the given segment of land, then when the object initially has no velocity the accelerative vector is simply added to the velocity. To simulate the time spent in any segment, the following information is used. First the Water Distance is set to match the initial map scale, so that regardless of the distance in meters between any two grid spaces, the equation produces realistic results based on the distance covered. Second, a rudimentary Countdown is set to zero.

After each calculation of acceleration, the program subtracts the Countdown from the Water Distance and stores it as the new Countdown. Each time the equation loops, it adds one to the Countdown. In this way, the distance traveled winds up acting as the timer, determining how much effect a given grid space can have on a water object.

Figure 10.10   A Visualization of the Water Object Data.

This is the accelerative force application applied to the *X* vector:

```
while (!getOutQuick && (countDown < waterDistance))
        {
        if (xVelocity == 0)
        {
            if (xAcceleration == 0){ getOutQuick = true; xSign = 0; }
            else
            {
                xVelocity+ = xAcceleration;
                if (xVelocity > 0 && xSign == 0) xSign = 1;
                else if (xVelocity > 0 && xSign == -1)
                { xSign = 1; countDown = (int)waterDistance - countDown; }
                if (xVelocity < 0 && xSign == 0) xSign = -1;
                else if (xVelocity < 0 && xSign == 1)
                { xSign = -1; countDown = (int)waterDistance - countDown; }
            }
        }
        else
        {
```

$$xVelocity+=xVelocity+(xAcceleration*(1f/Math.Abs(xVelocity)));$$
$$xVelocity=xVelocity*decelerant;$$
$$if(xVelocity>0\ \&\ \&xSign==0)xSign=1;$$
$$else if(xVelocity>0\ \&\ \&xSign==-1)$$
$$\{\ xSign=1;countDown=(int)waterDistance-countDown;\}$$
$$if(xVelocity<0\ \&\ \&xSign==0)xSign=-1;$$
$$else if(xVelocity<0\ \&\ \&xSign==1)$$
$$\{\ xSign=-1;countDown=(int)waterDistance-countDown;\}$$
$$\}$$
$$countDown+=1;$$
$$\}$$

(10.3)

The Y vector has the equation applied the same way, as such it will not be reproduced here. The decelerant is used to slow down the object and can be seen as the force of friction slowing the object down. Without the decelerant, the water object would act as though it were on a frictionless surface and continue to glide along with even the most minor accelerative vector applied to it.

Once the added accelerative X and Y vectors have been determined and the object has been given a new velocity, the leaving angle is calculated by ATAN2(yVelocity,xVelocity), which gives the angle the water object should leave the grid space by. The direction by which the object leaves can be determined by the following series of logical comparisons:

$$if(leavingAngle>(-MathHelper.Pi/8f)\ \&\ \&leavingAngle<=(MathHelper.Pi/8f))$$
$$\{offsetX+=1;\}$$

$$if(leavingAngle>(MathHelper.Pi/8f)\ \&\ \&leavingAngle<=$$
$$MathHelper.PiOver4+(MathHelper.Pi/8f))\{offsetX+=1;offsetY-=1;\}$$

$$if(leavingAngle>MathHelper.PiOver4+(MathHelper.Pi/8f)$$
$$\&\ \&leavingAngle<=2f*MathHelper.PiOver4+(MathHelper.Pi/8f))$$
$$\{offsetY-=1;\}$$

$$if(leavingAngle>2f*MathHelper.PiOver4+(MathHelper.Pi/8f)$$
$$\&\ \&leavingAngle<=3f*MathHelper.PiOver4+(MathHelper.Pi/8f))$$
$$\{offsetX-=1;offsetY-=1;\}$$

$$if(leavingAngle>3f*MathHelper.PiOver4+(MathHelper.Pi/8f)$$
$$leavingAngle<=-(3f*MathHelper.PiOver4+(MathHelper.Pi/8f)))$$
$$\{offsetX-=1;\}$$

$$if (leavingAngle <= -(MathHelper.Pi / 8f) \& \&leavingAngle >$$
$$-(MathHelper.PiOver4 + (MathHelper.Pi / 8f)))\{ offsetX+=1; offsetY+=1; \}$$

$$if (leavingAngle <= -(MathHelper.PiOver4 + (MathHelper.Pi / 8f))$$
$$\& \& leavingAngle > -(2f * MathHelper.PiOver4 + (MathHelper.Pi / 8f)))$$
$$\{ offsetY+=1; \}$$

$$if (leavingAngle <= -(2f * MathHelper.PiOver4 + (MathHelper.Pi / 8f))$$
$$\& \& leavingAngle > -(3f * MathHelper.PiOver4 + (MathHelper.Pi / 8f)))$$
$$\{ offsetX-=1; offsetY+=1; \} \tag{10.4}$$

The offsets determined by this are then used to establish the new grid space which the current object will move into, and then the procedure repeats. Before the current grid space is left for the new one, a quick action is performed to increment a value on that segment of land, to indicate water has been there. It is this accumulated data for each grid space that is seen in Figure 10.10.

By combining this accumulated standing water body information that has been calculated through the above equations with the user-defined lake-level information, there is a sufficiently diverse collection of water with which the program can next define the vegetation level of information. It must be noted that the vegetation layer is defined as a lush opportunity for vegetation rather than concrete assurance that a plant exists in a given area. Ranging from zero to one, vegetation data dictate the odds of a rich growth of foliage in a given area. Whereas a rating of zero would indicate a stark landscape devoid of any noteworthy plant life, a rating of one indicates a grid space that should be bursting with all the necessary conditions to support a variety of plants, and thus should contain sufficient vegetation for an agent that requires such vegetation for survival.

Several equations are used to calculate the vegetation, the first of which determines how hospitable a grid space may be for vegetation. This is done using two values, the flow direction, and its magnitude. Logically a grid space is more hospitable for a plant to thrive on if it is not located on a severe slope, so the closer a grid space is toward being perfectly flat, having a magnitude of zero, the more hospitable it is for plant life. However, the greater the magnitude of the flow direction, that is to say the more severe the slope, the more likely it is that the facing direction of the slope should have some influence on the plant. A plant with continuous exposure to the sun throughout the day, which is to say a slope facing in a southern direction, will profit more than a facing which only receives the sun through half of the day. This produces the Eq. (10.1) to determine how hospitable the slope of the land itself is.

$$VegetationLevel = \left(angle * grade + \left(1 - grade\right)\right) * \left(1 - grade\right) \qquad (10.5)$$

This gives the hospitality of the terrain and will allow the calculation of the vegetation content of it provided it meets the second requirement, proximity to water. First, tap-root distance of approximately 6 m is used for plants similar to those present 10 000 years ago to estimate the maximum possible distance from the user-submitted lake level that a grid space may be and still be capable of reaching the water [18]. From a minimum distance of zero (at which plants would be partially submerged) to the maximum of 6 m, a scale is set from zero to six and places the grid space's height in relation to them to equate a value between zero and one. This is then multiplied by Eq. (10.5) to receive our vegetation data.

While the coastal vegetation yield is calculated thusly, the vegetation data for the standing bodies is done based on distance from the bodies themselves. Again using the 6-m tap-root data, this time it is used as a distance horizontally rather than vertically calculating how far adjacent grid spaces are from the standing water bodies and rivers calculated previously. The program performs the same multiplication and combines this information with that of the coastal information (with a cap of one when combining the two values to avoid exceeding the maximum vegetation data).

As can be seen in Figure 10.11, once this data have been calculated it can be seen that a visible spread that coincides with the positioning of the water bodies

Figure 10.11 A Visualization of the Vegetation Data.

and the coastal area appears. It is important to note that the rate of vegetation decreases very quickly as soon as a grid space is submerged, which is why the very visible forms of the water bodies can be seen in stark white outline in comparison to the darkened forms of the vegetation. Again, the vegetation uses Eq. (10.1) to convert its range of zero to one into a gradient from white to black, those areas most conducive to growth of plants denoted by the darkest of shades and those stark areas easily visible as bright white.

Having performed these layers on layers of calculations, there is now a large amount of extrapolated data available to the program. What began initially as a two-dimensional array of data points consisting solely of the Easting and Northing coordinates and height has the addition of flow direction, magnitude of slope, water bodies, the average speed of the water occupying those bodies (used to differentiate between rivers and bogs), and vegetation. This wealth of information can now be used to produce a significant variety of influences on intelligent agents, and these agents themselves will form yet another layer of information.

Pathfinding and Planning

In work previously done by James Fogarty, much effort has been made to establish pathways across the Alpena–Amberley Land Bridge, albeit in much smaller scope than is currently being used [19]. The purpose of this research continues in this chapter to discern the movements of groups of Paleo-indians to yield useable data for archaeologists. It accomplished this in a similar manner to the Land Bridge Project's recent work, establishing the movements of simulated herds of caribou which could then be hunted by the simulated humans (Figure 10.12).

As the primary intelligent agents to populate all of the simulations are the caribou themselves, their herd mechanics must be properly replicated to properly replicate the real herds themselves. A tremendous number of creatures can lead to a high processing overhead which can slow down calculations, and as such flocking methods that allowed a herd to move as a singular being were used initially. Using variables that controlled the separation and attraction between members of a larger cohesive agent (consider the herd itself to be a singular agent comprising numerous smaller agents), it was possible to make large, dynamic herds move with a fluid nature through the landscape [20].

Elements of Fogarty's original work were imported into the new system and improved on. The initial pathfinding technique used to first traverse a small area was the A* technique, which relies on collecting adjacent nodes, establishing scores for those nodes comprising the lengths it took to reach them plus the estimated lengths it will take to reach the goal from them, and then proceeding through those nodes and assigning parental nodes until the goal node is discovered [21]. For early

Figure 10.12   An Image from James Fogarty's Program.

work this was satisfactory, but basic A* yielded unnatural paths that had harsh turns and decidedly mechanical patterns. It is from the initial combined influence maps [19] that the program set up a selection of variable weights which drive the agents to prefer various paths based on the weighting.

Another problem with A* is the processor power needed on a particularly large area. As the subject matter is absolutely massive, Figure 10.13 showing only a miniscule portion of the entire Land Bridge, it becomes necessary to make goals to ease the processing load of the A* [22]. The flags in the image represent sub-goals that the A* algorithm seeks to find a path to, rather than allowing it to attempt to find a path through every possible node from start to finish. In this way, the program can reduce processing costs significantly.

As previously noted, the A* algorithm can yield unnatural paths. These can be smoothed noticeably using kinematics. The idea behind kinematics is to take the decidedly unnatural, mechanical results of something such as A*, and apply the real-world steering motions of a real animal to make the simulated movement much closer to that of the actual creature the agent is based on [23]. Using a variety of steering variables and controls in combination with the herd dynamics [20], the program takes the generated A* path and assigns the herd to follow it as a series of goals and guideposts, with the kinematics being responsible for steering them toward the next node of their journey. This yields much more realistic paths with smooth curves and turns. However, care must be taken to ensure the kinematics sync up with the given scale of the map to prevent infinite loops when the kinematics cause an agent to continuously overshoot their goal.

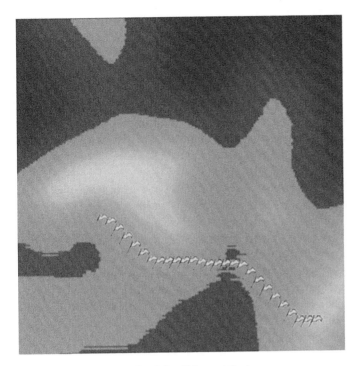

Figure 10.13   An Example of the A* Spaced Goals.

The next step after the A* and the kinematic herd is one that makes use of the genetic algorithm. With the genetic algorithm, the program determines an initial chromosome that will represent the movement variables of a herd, and a viable mutation rate for each element of the chromosome to ensure that the other randomly generated agents will not be ludicrously incompatible [24]. After initializing a population of agents, they are set to follow the A* algorithm with their varied kinematics, then rank those who successfully reach the goal based on their speed.

As previously described in section "Putting Data to Work", the system was able to extrapolate a wide selection of differing variables, such as height, vegetation, and water bodies from the initial landscape. Giving the agents access to all of these variables allows more realistic modeling of their movement and behavior, as well as refinement and smoothing of their kinematics. Once the program has a variety of data that can be used to weight the influence maps, it allows the agents to then have their weighting system decided by chromosomes evolved through the genetic algorithm.

In the work done by Jin Jin [35], a genetic system is used to refine the motion of the agents through repetition and evolution. Each agent is an entire herd as described before, and their score is determined by two factors. First is the caloric intake of the herd, and second is the total distance the herd has covered in their trek from the start to goal positions. By having two opposing elements of the score, as typically encountering vegetation requires straying from a straight path, the herd agents are able to improve (or worsen) their scores by adjusting how they weight the attraction to the various elements of the Land Bridge. Multiple herds are run at the same time and for multiple generations the number of which the user may specify, and when the system has completed running these generations, a printout is made available to the user to view the statistics.

After running these various agents and improving how realistically they move through the use of A*, kinematics, and the genetic algorithm, the grid spaces that make up the array now have information within them denoting whether or not an agent has passed through it. After each pass in the genetic algorithm, the map is erased, so the final pass that is recorded is of those herd agents who are the off-spring of the most-fit previous generations. The layers of information have been fed into these steps to generate this new layer of information, a simulated migration path of the caribou-based agents that traverse the virtual landscape. The program can now take this information and apply the next level of extrapolation to it to yield useable, real-world data.

Identifying Good Locations: The Hotspot Finder

The next step in the extrapolation, the Hotspot Finder, takes the collection of all data collected thus far and uses it to establish a collection of points of interest that may correlate to real-world sites that contain actual artifacts. This step makes use of the Cultural Algorithm to collect and interpret data, and the Cultural Algorithm will be examined in more detail in section on "Cultural Algorithms".

As specified earlier when calculating the water body data, the lake level is a user-defined attribute that may be altered while the system is running. Differing lake levels were equated with the time expanse for which the Alpena–Amberley Land Bridge was a viable passage from the two masses of land that now make up modern-day Michigan and Canada. By repeatedly running the hotspot finder, there was first created a GA optimized group of herd agents that could traverse the viable landscape. On top of that, the hunter hotspot finder then placed its own hunter agents on the field, which would score themselves based on proximity to the herd agent pathways, as well as proximity to one another, and landscape height.

The pathways were then erased, the lake level altered to reflect the next year (typically done in groups of five years at a time in the interest of processing speed), the herd agents rerun to generate new paths, and then the hotspot agents were reevaluated with these new paths. Those hotspot agents who were able to either improve or maintain their score, or avoid falling beneath a certain level, were given more of a total score that ensured their persistence for the next generation of the system. As can be seen in Figure 10.14, even for a smaller sample of the Alpena–Amberley Land Bridge, this can yield exceedingly varying herds. Typically those agents who were constantly near the migration routes and located on high ground to avoid the encroaching water of the temporal cycle tended to score higher than most.

Figure 10.15 shows the results of running the hotspot finding algorithm over a succession of simulated years as the water levels rise and fall. The expanse of land covered by this particular run of the hotspot finder is the same as that which appears in Figure 10.16, a small section of the Alpena–Amberley Land Bridge, which has had actual artifacts discovered on it. In Figure 10.15, the collection of points represent those hotspot agents and their resultant scores placed into a selection of rankings. In Figure 10.15, in the center of the image is a larger white box surrounding one of these agents. This box represents a coinciding real-world artifact find that matches up with the find predicted by Land Bridge Project.

In Figure 10.16, the black caribou icons on the map point to a number of locations where actual artifacts have been found. By comparing Figure 10.16 with Figure 10.15, it is possible to notice similarities in the clustering of found artifacts and scored hotspot agents. It should be noted that though Figure 10.16 denotes found artifacts, the entire area depicted in the figure has yet to be thoroughly explored, so those artifacts shown on the map may not as of yet represent all artifacts present.

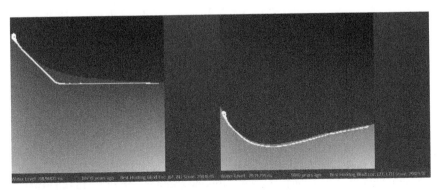

Figure 10.14 An Example of the Temporal Difference in the Hotspot Finder.

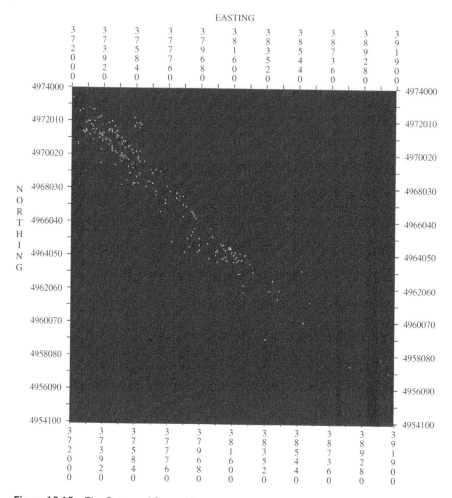

Figure 10.15   The Output of Samuel Dustin Stanley's Hotspot Finder.

With more artifacts discovered, there are more opportunities for validation and adjustment of the hotspot finder. In Figure 10.17, the filled square images represent the most highly scoring points, the empty squares with a range less than that, the filled diamonds further down the ranking, and the lowest ranking but still significant spots being the hollow diamond shapes. The dotted boxes appearing in the image denote the location of real-world artifacts discovered by Dr. O'Shea and his team. It should be noted that several of the real-world artifacts and several of the simulated-world artifacts overlap with one another, and those found artifacts without a corresponding simulated-world artifact are typically located in close proximity to a highly scoring hotspot element.

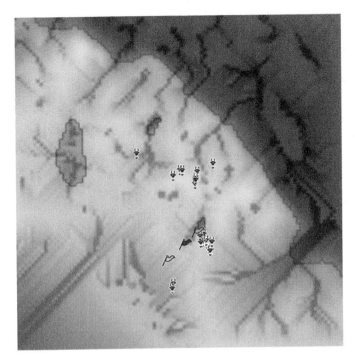

Figure 10.16 Area 1 with Superimposed Artifact Markers.

The Cultural Algorithm can be used to simulate a societal group, groups of hunters looking to move to more appealing landscapes that promise greater resources [25]. The software at this level has gone beyond the traditional category of virtual archeological program, which allowed the user to casually explore a simulated world [6]. Here, it has also now been used to make actual reportable information which can be of use to real-world archaeological and paleontological teams as they plot their new expeditions to search for more artifacts [7] while still maintaining the user-friendly interface of the first category. Allowing such results from such a simple interface allows for a greater user experience as users can go beyond simply viewing information that is already been collected, but can generate their own which could someday lead to real discoveries in the field.

Everything discussed up until now, the A*, the kinematics, the genetic algorithm, and the cultural algorithm, when taken together can be computationally expensive. Initially the Land Bridge Project could only run such programs on an extremely small section of the simulated Alpena–Amberley Land Bridge. This limited view also produced limited results as elements that existed beyond the borders of the sampled areas, such as herd entry and exit points, had to be estimated on limited information.

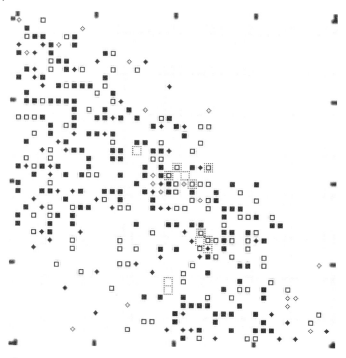

Figure 10.17   A More Recent Run of the Hotspot Finder.

Figure 10.18 shows the whole of Lake Huron with the raised Alpena–Amberley Land Bridge visible. However, the area that has been examined thus far has been limited to the small box seen in the center of the image. This initially is due to processing power as machines capable of processing this much information are not regularly available for testing and design purposes. Also, as the software is designed with the common user in mind, the average person does not have access to a super-computer capable of doing such work, but rather would prefer to have such a program available to them on their tablets and portable devices. As such, the Land Bridge Project is targeting a new hierarchical technique to perform which will reduce processing time while allowing access to the entire Alpena–Amberley Land Bridge, as well as any hypothetical landscape that might be used in the future.

Cultural Algorithms

In the previous section we discussed identifying likely artifact locations through the use of Cultural Algorithms. The section had to do with extrapolating those locations from the given information, but more importantly it was necessary to do

Bathymetry of Lake Huron with Topography

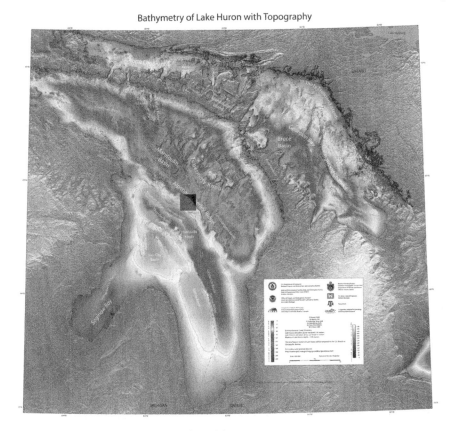

Figure 10.18 A Visual of the Investigated Area.

more than refine and optimize the data through successive evolution through the genetic algorithm. It became necessary to extract cultural rules that could serve as a "heritage mechanism" to form consistent knowledge that can be present throughout the entire simulation [26].

In the following sections we will describe how Cultural Algorithms are used here in more detail [27]. It is a dual-inheritance algorithm that allows for the social fabric of humanity to be added into the computations, with rulesets that can be shared among the hunter [28]. Typically there is also an associated element of social interface, which is to say a means by which data are distributed. An example of this is a soldier with important information who cannot relay this information until he reaches a communications station, and only those soldiers with access to the other end of the station's network will receive this information. For the purposes of this simulation, there is no limiting communications network. Influence from the Belief Space is capable of occurring at any point; however,

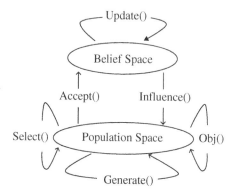

Figure 10.19 A Visualization of the Cultural Algorithm.

Accepting into and Updating of the Belief Space is limited to take place at the end of a single generation (Figure 10.19).

As defined by Reynolds, "the experience of individuals selected from the population space is used to generate problem solving knowledge that can reside in the belief space" [29]. It is this continuous depositing of knowledge and the subsequent retrieval of knowledge that can yield the emergence of highly complex behaviors.

As previously discussed, the population space is an evolving system, where agents are ranked and allowed to generate new members of the species if they score sufficiently, the Genetic component of the AI is in action here [30]. With the addition of the belief space of the cultural algorithm on top of this, the system now has the ability to have ideas which can transcend generations and outlive their creators, much in the same way humans have the capability to pass on knowledge to future generations. An acceptance function acts as a gateway to bring new ideas into the belief space, and an influence function distributes those ideas out into the population so that the hunter location can make use of them [31].

There are a number of knowledge sources which make up the belief space, each corresponding to a type of knowledge. They are normative, topographic, domain, temporal, and situational [32]. The normative domain, which concerns itself with desirable ranges of data, is used by the agents to limit which areas of the map they establish themselves in. In the hotspot finder this keeps them from placing themselves in any submerged range of locations, an important distinction as during the processing of the hotspots, the user-defined lake level will both raise and fall, and grid spaces which were once above water may suddenly be submerged.

For the domain-specific knowledge, there is a ruleset imposed on the human agents that causes them to work to move away from one another, on the supposition that hunting blinds located too close to one another run the risk of one hunter interfering with another. The last specific piece of knowledge used to predict hotspots is the temporal. Here the system uses a range of time over which the Alpena–Amberley Land Bridge existed by raising and lowering the lake levels to reflect the approximate state of the test bed as it would have existed several thousand years ago. In this way, the system can identify those agents who have withstood the test of time, despite the fact that as the water rises and falls previously viable test locations will become impossible to use due to being submerged.

Cultural Algorithm Mechanisms

There are three major mechanisms associated with the Cultural Algorithm, which allow an interface between the Population Space and the Belief Space. The first two, the influence and acceptance functions, deal with information being passed back and forth between the two spaces and the third, the update function, deals with the improvement, adjustment, and evolution of the ideas held in the Belief Space [33]. Acceptance deals with determining which agents are able to submit information into the Belief Space. It is not necessarily the highest ranking agents on one singular metric, as the collection of possible information that makes up the Belief Space can sometimes be best suited by gathering information from a wider variety of agents. If a metric is composed of multiple objectives that do not always coincide and may be in opposition (such as speed versus vegetation consumed), it is sensible then to accept new information not only from those agents who scored the most highly in the overall metric but also those agents who had the highest ratings for the separate objectives, in the hopes that their information can be used by those agents who are skewed more toward one objective and need improvement on another.

The influence function determines which agents need information distributed among them. For example, the most highly scoring agents may have no need for information whatsoever, whereas a lower scoring agent may have a tremendous need. But as noted above it is entirely possible for an agent to need specific information in regards to how they specifically are assessed in the given metric. So, for example, an agent requiring information to improve the speed with which they travel will specifically receive knowledge about that given source. In this way an agent is able to extract from the procured data a "process diagram" to assist them in seeking improved results by following the examples of those that came before them [32].

As the Cultural Algorithm in a dual inheritance system, meaning that not only does the Population Space benefit from the chromosomes of its parents but also their knowledge as well, it makes sense that the knowledge comprising the Belief

Space is repeatedly measured and validated just as the agents in the Belief Space [34]. This is where the third main mechanism comes in, the update function. Using this function, knowledge in the Belief Space can be graded on its accuracy, frequency of use, difference in result from its use, etc. In this way, each successive generation of agents in the Population Space will not be trapped using faulty information. Shared knowledge that leads to a decrease in score can be updated to be less frequently used or removed entirely, thus keeping the Belief Space full of up-to-date, useable information.

The Composition of the Belief Space

The Belief Space is where knowledge is stored that can then be distributed among the agents. Knowledge is an abstract concept in and of itself, and so it is converted into five different domains in which it can be encoded. The categories cover normative, domain-specific, situational, temporal, and spatial knowledge bases, and each piece of knowledge can be sorted into one of these five categories.

The normative knowledge category has to do with preferable standards of behavior, what would be seen as normal for agents to do. An example of normative knowledge in the Land Bridge Project is the known behaviors of caribou and hunters encoded into rulesets that govern their movement and placements. Domain-specific knowledge has to do with that knowledge, which can be categorized as having to do with a specific agent's endeavor or skill. For the purposes of this project, the focus is on archaeological and paleontological domain-specific knowledge, using real-world discoveries made in these fields and techniques such as studying the relationship between the major food source species and the hunter.

Situational knowledge is a category wherein a measured response can be stored for a given situation. For example, a situation can be defined as an agent being surrounded by eight data points at any location on the grid, if those points are higher, lower, or equivalent to the data point in the grid they currently occupy, and if any of those points are impassable water obstacles. Recognized configurations can be stored and recalled from the Belief Space, the previous actions that yielded favorable outcomes being repeated.

Temporal knowledge is recorded information of previously discovered data and results. For example, when the system discovers hotspots that might be possible hunting sites, it is able to compare these hotspots to those hotspots predicted in earlier searches, and rank them based on which of them occupy recurring locations, and which of them are newly discovered.

The final category is spatial knowledge is information about the topographical nature of the problem. This can be about viable ranges, indicative elements that exist in the topology, such as a small sampling that can indicate a more major feature like a waterfall [35]. A major example of this comes in the program's ability to quickly divide up the data points into viable and non-viable locations. As the system is dealing with a computationally expensive amount of data, being able to discount any unnecessary data points as soon as possible to increase the processing speed in a boon. To this effect, the system is able to determine which data points are non-viable based on their being completely submerged throughout the entire simulated lifetime of the project. As these locations will never be above the water's surface at any point in the lifespan of the Alpena–Amberley Land Bridge test bed, it does not have to spend computational power allowing pathfinding algorithms and hotspot placing algorithms to examine these locations.

In future work, the Land Bridge Project will expand the role of the cultural algorithm in the software as it works to bring in actual humans who can take the place of a simulated hunter, storing their actions and strategies and making it available to future, simulated hunters. The system can also use real-world archaeological discoveries of artifact locations to expand the domain-specific knowledge, allowing the simulation to improve its ability to recognize the location of a potential artifact location.

Future Work

The current evolution of the software is a Unity-based model that can more readily handle upgrades and more devices. Previous builds relied on XNA, a system which is no longer supported as readily as it once was, while Unity is now heavily supported and capable of being exported to a number of systems including handheld devices such as tablets and smartphones.

One of the major goals of the newly upgraded build is not only that it will be capable of handling the entirety of the Alpena–Amberley Land Bridge instead of just running its more advanced agents on smaller sections of it, but it will also be able to work with any additional landscapes the user might provide. The previously mentioned Bering Strait is one feasible example of what the work may entail someday, including coastal areas, danger zones humans cannot safely walk in, politically contested areas, and even extraterrestrial landscapes such as scan data of other planets. The remainder of this paper will deal with the current extensions that are being made within the current Unity platform to support this more general functionality.

Path Planning Strategy

One component of the system will focus on a hierarchical view of the entirety of the Alpena–Amberley Land Bridge, allowing the charting of a path from one end to the other and back again. In Figure 10.4, it can be noted that the current areas of interest can easily be broken down into approximately 14 larger squares. These squares themselves have viable borders that denote their entrance and exit points that are above-water and accessible, and the first step would be to view them simply as 14 connected, adjacent squares. On finding a path through these squares, the system can then view them in greater detail.

By examining Figure 10.20, it is possible to see the borders denoted as slashes of white, signifying viable access points between one cell and another. It is possible to

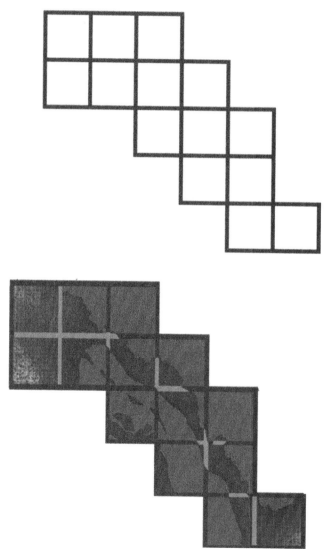

Figure 10.20 The Alpena–Amberley Land Bridge Broken into Large Sections.

use these borders as subgoals for a large A* algorithm that can seek to cross from the top left to the bottom right, going in both directions depending on migration season. By adjusting the points at which the agents leave and arrive at these subgoals, they can be scored based on the time spent to cross the Land Bridge, as well as vegetation consumption and overall herd health, determined by time spent in lower heights that are likely to be host to insects and hazardous terrain.

Once the system has established a route for the agents to walk on their migratory routes, it will be able to use this information to establish more subgoals within each area based on those locations which are constantly encountered regardless of start and end goal positions. By saving these areas, the system can then view the entirety of the landscape at finer resolution using these subgoals to massively reduce the necessary computational overhead that would undoubtedly come from a pathfinding algorithm operating on such a large collection of data.

Local Tactics

Having established a collection of subgoals, the system will be able to create a reactionary system for the agents, allowing attractive and detractive elements of the map to sway their paths as they proceed toward their subgoals. It is possible to consider that based on the perception of caribou agents, their migration paths may change significantly due to their orientation [36]. As it can be established that some elements, such as hunting blinds, may have been disguised to be attractive to a caribou-based agent, one that came into such an agent's view would act as an attractor. Meanwhile, a site where a caribou had died either due to predation or injury from uncertain terrain would act as a detractor for another group traveling through.

It is possible that the fluid nature of the herd can even cause injury or force an alternate path, as the herd has its own natural physics that allow for an altering shape to deal with an altering environment [37]. For example, a herd agent proceeding through a known high risk area may adapt its form to a more protective circular shape to protect its young. This larger shape will require wider pathways to maintain, meaning it is likely a herd agent adapted to this shape will avoid a narrow pathway between water obstacles that will force the herd agent into an unwanted shape (Figure 10.21).

As the needs of the herd agents change during their migration across the virtual landscape changes, so too will their formation alternate to better serve those needs. When low on food, the agents will realign into a foraging formation. This formation gives the group a wider swath over the landscape, allowing them to see further and detect the influence of nearby vegetation with greater efficacy than that of the speed formation, one designed specifically to cut through narrow paths

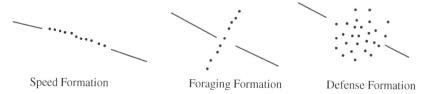

Speed Formation   Foraging Formation   Defense Formation

Figure 10.21 A Collection of Possible Formations.

at the expense of a shorter range of vision for the entire herd agent. A realistic herd that seeks out food, attempts to minimize injury, and is attracted to generated points of interest would make use of all of these formations to its benefit, but this would also give birth to new paths that would variate away from following specifically to a given subgoal. This will be operationalized in subsequent sections.

Detailed Locational Information

As previously detailed in section "Putting Data to Work", the system can use the data from established agent migration paths to postulate new likely hotspots where it is likely to find evidence of an ancient human establishment of some sort, such as a hunting blind or a bone cache. With new advancement in local tactics, however, these generated hotspots themselves become information that can be fed back into the system due to their attractive and detractive natures, allowing the system to form a looping system that evolves and expands as it discovers new possibilities.

As seen in Figure 10.22, each iteration of the strategic pathway alteration discussed in section "Local Tactics" can yield additional migration herd agent data that can be used by the hotspot finding algorithm. Each extrapolated, hypothetical archaeological site can then yield data, which can result in changes for the migration route data. Understandably this could yield an infinite loop of data generation and alteration, so there needs to be a termination point, an optimal value set that the system can attempt to approach with each loop.

For this particular section sustainability will be examined, the idea that while a simulated caribou herd may be attacked and culled by hunters, it is essential that a certain percentage of caribou survive the migration across the entirety of the Alpena–Amberley Land Bridge to allow for propagation of the herds to replace the members that get killed off or die due to dangerous terrain or starvation. If the hotspot algorithm produces too many efficient hypothetical hunting spots, the herd may be overharvested by human agents causing caribou to die out rather than make a return migration. This would be terminally devastating to the native hunters, and so such a situation must be avoided. Therefore, the entire system

Figure 10.22 A Diagram of the Flow of Data, Starting with the Hierarchical Pathway.

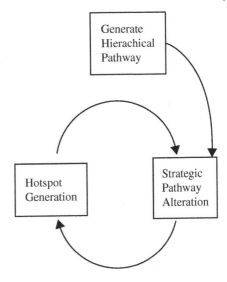

would work to achieve the highest hunting score possible while leaving the minimum number of caribou necessary to ensure constant migration back and forth.

Extending the CA

To accomplish this drastic advancement in complexity of both the hotspot algorithm and the strategic pathways of the caribou-simulating agents, the system will employ the Cultural Algorithm to increase the capabilities of the agents. The caribou-simulating agents will have the hierarchical path to use as guideposts from one area to the other, but they will be able to maintain a consistent scoring mechanism across the entirety of the Land Bridge based on the previously stated metric of sufficiently remaining herd members necessary for propagation and sustainable migration. The system can calculate this by estimating the average number of females per herd, the length of gestation periods, and the time to maturation of a newly born caribou to breeding age. If these numbers cannot be satisfied, the system can rule that a herd's score yields unsustainable results.

To improve these results, the Cultural Algorithm allows the most highly scoring herds to have their information available to other herds. As several herds with differing genomes will proceed across the landscape in the style of the Genetic Algorithm discussed earlier, the system will also keep track of decisions they make according to these genomes, as well as their results. Although the overall scores of the herd depend on vegetation consumed, distance traveled, and members remaining, it will also keep track of which herds that scored the highest on these individual aspects as well as their total overall score.

A decision in this case will be the reaction to given stimulus in a given scenario. If one of the lower scoring herds scored lowly due to its vegetation decisions, during its next trial it will seek out the rulesets established by a herd which exceeded beyond all others in the vegetation consumption field. Of all of the herds, the herd with the highest vegetation score previously will be ranked above the others based on this metric, and those decisions it made in the previous region will be saved as a form of rulesets. These decisions will be defined as the reaction to a given scenario based on the influence of the surrounding objects, such as water obstacles, vegetation, and hotspot objects such as hunting blinds. The herd using this information will adjust its pathway based on what the highly scoring herd did in the same situation. Thus, the swarm of agents can be guided by one particular knowledge source in the belief space that could yield new improvements to the overall score [33].

If adhering to these decisions increases the herd's overall score in the next region, this piece of information from the highly scoring vegetation-seeking herd will be given points toward validity, which will increase its ability to remain with each successive region's results. As each region is completed, there will be new scores for each of the herds, and it is possible that some herds will overtake others in terms of their scores. However, it is entirely possible that the decisions of the herds which now reside in the Belief Space are still of great use to the herd, and it will not be replaced if its score is sufficiently high to have survived the test of time.

The total number of decisions a herd can make from the start of one region to the other can be estimated, and it can be decided how great a disparity there is between the given herd's score and the most highly scoring herd's score, specifically whichever herd the current herd is attempting to emulate. Again for this example, consider the low-scoring herd which did not consume enough vegetation to score as highly as the herd which did. The higher this disparity, the greater the odds of the new herd querying the Belief Space for the other herd's tactics. So if a herd is only slightly behind another in terms of its score, it is less likely to rely on that herd's available decisions.

This can be applied to all aspects of the metric including, survival, consumption, and speed. Those decisions made will be denoted and later scored based on the change in the total metric of the herd as it reaches the next region. The greater the change in score (either positively or negatively), the greater the change in decision's standing in the belief space. If a score falls too low, a decision is effectively removed from the belief space to keep the decision searches more efficient for the active herds. So thus a collection of decisions made earlier in the migration may persist longer if it proves itself to be useful. When the herds complete the migration from one end to the other, it will be possible for the system to view these ranked decisions and see which ones are held by the highest system based on their scores, and the difference in scores of the herds that use them.

These decisions will remain even though at the end of a migration the herds will genetically repopulate and variate their chromosomes. They will still have access to the decisions of past herds and use those decisions as they travel back. Random mutation will ensure that some herds will initially ignore past advice but will soon seek it once they have begun establishing their own scores along the route. As each herd will be able to choose how to update itself based on its own individual needs rather than the needs of all herds, it will have the benefit of a complex web of information linked together but separate, allowing for finding new possible optimal routes and patterns [38, 39].

Meanwhile, the hotspot finder will likewise be upgraded to recognize scenarios. As more real-world artifacts are discovered, more and more information is gathered on the nature of the various artifacts. Hunting blinds are just one sort of artifact, while there are things, such as bone caches, and tanning pits. Each of these artifacts may be studied for its placement with regards to various elements surrounding it. Since the coordinates of each placement are known, it is possible to discern the attributes surrounding it, such as slopes, proximity to water body objects and migration paths, and proximity to other artifacts. As this information is extracted, it can be fed into the hotspot finder to generate additional finds and a more complete report of information when it finishes running.

As the final goal of this project is to generate a user-friendly distributed system, which can be designed for more than just the initial Alpena–Amberley Land Bridge test bed, the ability to generate new rulesets on the fly from user input and refine agent movements and decision-making will become vital. It will be especially useful if the system can use such information to generate artifact and species templates that can be used in different environments. For example, designing the necessary decision properties of migratory birds or aquatic species to allow specific species to be saved and distributed to users as additional information that they can use to populate their own simulated environments. This information can be combined with artifacts that are introduced into the environment, and then extrapolated and reproduced by the hotspot finder. This will enable the casual armchair archaeologist access to a tool which is capable of genuine discovery.

As the system is capable of recreating interactions between various species and social groups across a wide range of time, it can also be useful for modeling long-term effects of disturbing one species or another in the food chain [13]. This yields yet another potential user base as current interest in deep-sea mining is currently viewed as potentially massively harmful toward the complex biological structures that exist in potential mining areas [40]. Using the software, it would be possible to map a site out, distribute a population of agents representing the local flora and fauna, and then insert a disruptive object similar to the repulsive elements that cause agents to flee from a given site to see what the resultant effect of these events done in a long-term scale would be.

Human Presence in the Virtual World

Despite recent advancements in processing speed and algorithm design, modern computers cannot come close to emulating the actual thought processes of a real human being. Even the most impressive supercomputers such as Japan's K computer can currently only manage one second of one percent of human mental capacity [41]. In the past, a casual user's interaction with a virtual archaeology system was limited to an nonconsequential role in the environment such as reassembling a trinket, or pretending to be a member of Roman society. However, none of these events affected a change in a meaningful way by the human's presence. The data remained the same, the results were from those which were preselected to happen, and when completed the program yielded no additional information from the user's time spent with it.

However, the Land Bridge Project is looking to bring the human into the loop. The simulation of ancient hunters has been discussed previously. But, no amount of simulation will equate to a 1 to 1 simulation of a real human being who is running around and doing what they wish. So for the next step beyond the increased intelligence of the algorithms and their output, the system is taking what used to simply be a roaming camera that had no more effect than a ghost on the world, and making it a real, physical thing in the simulated world.

The user will become a human in the loop, an virtual presence that can interact with other objects in the world in a meaningful way. From diverting herds to hunting them down with the simulated hunters, even acquiring and placing objects it finds, such as acquiring the materials necessary to make artifact sites or by the construction of hunting blinds by moving the rocks that would comprise it. They will be able to attempt to hunt their own game, kill it with primitive means, and then cook it to sustain their virtual life. In this way, the user will have the option of not just viewing the world from an omniscient seat high in the sky but also the ability to get down among the simulated world and explore it as someone walking on it would actually discover it.

It is a naturally occurring pattern in agents driven by cultural algorithms for leaders and followers to emerge, generally those agents who score the highest which then leave behind information in the Belief Space that the other agents can use to improve on themselves [42]. By having an actual human working with the AI-driven agents, it is possible for the human to take the role of leader and leave behind invaluable information that can then be used by the agents in future work.

In addition to exploring the world of the past as a hunter, the user will be able to explore the world as a researcher as well. With modern-day drone technology, it will be possible for users to sync up the virtual world with the real world, and compare the conditions and elements which comprise it. In this way, the user will be able to compare what is with what was, and even view their drone

Figure 10.23 A Side-by-Side Display of a Single Area Viewed in Two Timescapes.

companion exploring the world with them. By walking away from the drone, it is possible for a user to explore an area more thoroughly in the simulated world, than in the possibly risky environment of the real world. As seen in Figure 10.23, anchoring the two views of the world together with the existence of an artifact, one simulated and one real, can help the user to visualize the world as it was while exploring the present-day world. This cyberphysical system allows for real-time abstraction of information that can then be presented to the user manning the system controls [43].

This can also assist with navigation for bulkier drones which do not always have full 360° freedom of movement and vision. Checking behind the drone for obstacles and dangers before moving it could save professional archaeologists a tremendous sum of wear and tear on their expensive devices and increase the speed of their work as well. Importantly, using this tandem system will lead to increased safety and efficiency, an essential aspect of any cyberphysical system [44]. As the archaeological process itself can be viewed as a complex system, this integration can lead to a gain in all steps of the process.

Increasing the Complexity

As mentioned in section "Human Presence in the Virtual World," the user will have the option of becoming a physical element in the simulated world, a "real" thing which can interact with the simulated agents and environment. It was also mentioned that even the most sophisticated, most powerful systems in existence can only simulate the working of the human mind for a matter of seconds. However, the introduction of a real human mind can suddenly offer a simulation the necessary insight to integrate an actual human into the simulation, such that it would react as we would expect a human would.

The human finding the initial hierarchical pathway, traveling as a member of the herd, is described in section "Path Planning Strategy." A human being would likely travel in a given direction, seeking based on what they can see, and straying when they see something interesting. Given a set fuel limit in the form of starvation based on food encountered in the route would limit how much wandering they would perform.

After that, comes the loop of sections "Local Tactics" and "Detailed Locational Information." As the hunters and caribou interact with one another to maintain a sustainable hunting and migrating cycle, a real human attempting to hunt the caribou in each area would likely devise strategies that a computer could not and enact them in ways the system would have to react to. As the system works to react and stores this new information via the cultural algorithm, it is possible this new information could be stored and used even when the human is no longer in the loop, when it is just a simulation running in an attempt to still improve itself.

Similarly, the user could take control of the herd in an attempt to evade the hunters, working only from its point of the simulated world around it, attempting to lead its herd to survival while keeping track of where it is going. These actions could then be saved as detailed in section "Local Tactics," such that the cultural algorithm could then have access to the works of the human mind that was guiding the herd, and use it to further guide simulated herds in the future when the human is absent.

It is not just the presence of the human in the loop which would have a beneficial effect, but the remnants of the human in the loop which will allow the system to store their contributions afterwards. Similar to how it has been demonstrated that a user will have the capability to generate actual useful reports that can lead to real-world findings, the human participating in the simulations will have the opportunity to yield new information that the cultural algorithm's belief space can store for future use. It can improve on it for future users, or possibly being distributed among all users such that the more users the system has, the more complex the assembled strategies of all of the human users.

It has now been demonstrated how the system has evolved and will continue to evolve. It has taken the idea of virtual archaeology in both of its forms, highly user-friendly but ultimately unyielding of useful information and intensely complex form but delivering reportable data, and combined them into a system capable of generating complex information from a user with only limited experience and the curiosity to explore the simulated world.

Updated Path-Planning Results in Unity

Previously we have provided the basic building blocks for caribou path planning relative to a small component of the Land Bridge. In this section full migrations across the Land Bridge have been computed for both migration seasons of Spring and Fall. These migrations were generated using optimized weightings produced by the Cultural Algorithm for both A* and A*mbush, the structures of which will be described here. In addition, the new Dendriform A*mbush pathfinding algorithm will be described as well.

The underlying purpose of this research is to develop a toolkit, which will aid in the archaeological work of scientists, especially those dealing with restrictive areas in which casual visitation and investigation are limited due to geographical location, environmental hazards, governmental restriction, and budgetary concerns. Such systems are inherently complex in nature. They can be viewed and understood at different levels of granularity or detail. A toolkit that deals with these systems will need to support hierarchical levels of abstraction. Thus, it is necessary for the toolkit to take readily available data about a given landscape and use that data to create a hierarchical model through which the original landscape to be investigated can be replicated during different levels of spatial and temporal abstraction [13].

After recreating the landscape as a simulated model, it is then necessary to populate this landscape with guiding elements, which would dictate the flow of life during the given time period. For this research project, the two major life forms in question are the ancient hunters that dwelled in what is now North America, and the caribou which migrated across the Alpena–Amberley Land Bridge. As these caribou were the lifeblood of the groups which hunted them, the accurate replication of the herd movements is necessary to accurately replicate the movements of the hunters themselves so that they can accurately envision not only their environment but also the creatures that dwell within it [16].

Through the design of artificially intelligent agents who can closely mimic the migration decision processes of the caribou traveling across the landscape for their biannual migration patterns, it is possible to establish likely routes, avoided areas, waypoints, and more. With the use of a social-motivated learning algorithm, the Cultural Algorithm, to optimize how various factors influence the decision-making process, it is possible to create an AI-driven caribou agent who can work toward a sustainable migration pattern. A sustainable migration pattern being one that will ensure that any given herd will not wipe itself out through excessive consumption of available resources.

The Fully Rendered Land Bridge

When this research was first initiated, the viable scope over which experimentation would be conducted on was several small subsets of the section of landscape data now known as Region 7. Region 7 is depicted with its adjoining regions, which comprise the entirety of the Land Bridge in Figure 10.24.

Using the data points collected by the National Oceanic and Atmospheric Administration, it was possible to replicate the Alpena–Amberley Land Bridge

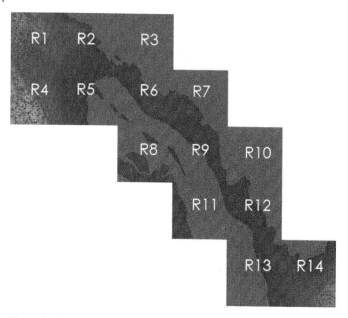

Figure 10.24 The Regional Sections of the Alpena–Amberley Land Bridge.

[45]. Originally smaller, more easily computed locations were focused on as described earlier due to system limitations. But, as programming systems and engines advanced from Microsoft's XNA to Unity Technology's Unity Engine, it became possible to load and use the entirety of the NOAA data. This allowed the generation of a full virtual landscape that replicated the Land Bridge at any given point in time [19].

The transition from XNA to Unity also resulted in the ability to make use of Unity's three-dimensional topographical rendering capabilities, functions which originally had to be hand-coded into the original work. However, it also became necessary to use Unity's rendering system to interpret data about the landscape itself. The engine was capable of understanding topography as a three-dimensional image, but without any rules dictating how physics and life would interact on such a landscape. Figures 10.25 and 10.26 depict the original XNA rendering of a small subsection, and Unity's rendering of the entirety of the Land Bridge.

The original hydrological and vegetation systems created for the XNA prototype were used to calculate vegetation growth rates and areas in which water would collect and flow as discussed earlier, and then these data were imported into the Unity version. Through the combination of Unity's rendering capabilities and the computed data, it became possible to create a landscape which could readily have physical water objects and vegetation placed on it that could then be used to establish nutritional sources and hazardous locations for artificial agents.

Figure 10.25   The Land Bridge System on Microsoft's XNA.

Figure 10.26   The Land Bridge System on Unity.

Pathfinder Mechanisms

The initial mechanism used to guide caribou across the Land Bridge landscape was the basic A* pathfinding algorithm discussed earlier. The A* pathfinding algorithm is an adaptation of Djikstra's algorithm, that systematically explored a search space without the algorithm being aware of the goal's location [46]. The difference between A* and Djikstra is A*'s ability to score a node's feasibility in terms of actual and estimated distance from a goal, similar to how a GPS can inform a driver of approximately how far away their destination is at any given point. Typical A* is designed with a singular goal that the agent navigates toward, but this was altered to allow for a navigational goal. Agents can be assigned one of eight different compass directions, such as North or South-West, to move toward, and so long as a path lead in that direction, it would be considered viable.

This allowed simulated caribou agents to move across the terrain in search of nutrition or the avoidance of effort more freely than a defined point destination. As the landscape was divided into explorable regions, it was possible for an agent to exit along any edge of a given region provided it leads them closer toward their directional goal. The exit point of one region would then become the entry point of an adjoining region, where the A* would continue along its route.

By then stitching together these optimal paths found through each of the regions, the end result was to produce a continuous route over the entire Land Bridge. This route could then be given a score focused on effort, risk, and nutrition. Effort in the form of distance traveled and altitude traversed, nutrition gained by passing through areas calculated to have vegetation in them, and risk associated with low-lying areas. An example of a generated Fall migration can be seen in Figure 10.27.

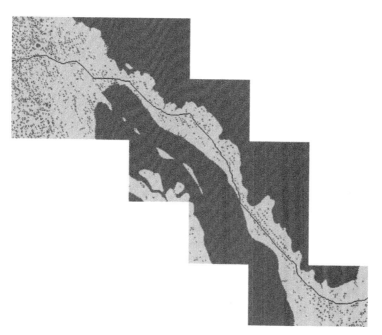

Figure 10.27 A Full A* Path from Alpena to Amberley, through 14 Regions.

However with this algorithm, it must be noted that any subsequent path starting from the same initial location will take the exact same route given the same influencing weights used by the previous A*. As there is no variation in the environment due to the presence of the agents, there is no variation in the movements of subsequent agents.

To rectify this, an enhanced form of A* known as A*mbush was utilized. Originally developed to simulate the movements of SWAT-Team-like squads of agents looking to surround and ambush a given target. It was determined that such agents should not follow one another's route exactly but rather diverge from previously taken paths to take up new routes toward the same given goal [47]. This was done through the use of disincentives placed in the path of each agent. These disincentives would make each part of the path less inviting to the next agent, causing them to take the next available optimal path (Figure 10.28).

A*mbush's use of disincentive to spread agents was replicated through the manner in which the caribou agents would devour all resources in their wake, leaving no vegetation behind for subsequent herds to graze on. Even with the exact same weighted influences controlling the algorithm, each additional herd of simulated caribou would follow a different path to compensate for the lack of vegetation caused by the previous herd's grazing.

In some regions the agents would diverge slightly, as can be seen in Figure 10.29. It can be noted that in the map on the right, two of the herds followed closely along the vegetation-rich coastline. The third herd, finding this area now stripped of vegetation, diverted drastically toward the center of the landscape in search of food. This new optimal path taken by the third herd also brings the simulated caribou closer to known artifact locations that indicated the presence of hunters in the real world.

To replicate the natural divergent, spreading nature of herds, it was necessary to run a number of herds in A*mbush resulting in wider and wider spreading paths. However, a problem arose from A*mbush. For a typical caribou herd, there is an optimal route, and then numerous branches off of the main route as those caribou which follow further behind stray from the main herd in search of more food once they can no longer sustain their own caloric needs.

The result is a tree-like pattern, similar to a vascular system or a Lindenmayer system, where branches and sub-branches can spread out as dictated by the influences of the environment [48]. While A*mbush can made herds diverge, the fact that those initial caribou spread disincentive at a constant rate means all divergence happens at a singular location, and all branches stem from a single spot.

An adaptation of A*mbush called Dendriform A*mbush takes this into account and yields a more natural spread of agents. This is similar to what is seen in Figure 10.30, while simultaneously dealing with the problem of a system computing the positions of numerous agents at any given time [49]. While the initial herd

- **A* Pseudocode:**
- *Place starting point in OPEN list*
- *As long as there are points in the OPEN list:*
  - *Find node with the lowest travel cost.*
  - *If found node is Goal, end loop and save path.*
  - *Else, Find all possible neighboring nodes.*
  - *If neighbor's in the CLOSED list, ignore.*
  - *If neighbor's not in the OPEN list, add them.*
  - *If that neighbor's tentative path score is better than what's recorded, record them now. If not, put them on the CLOSED list.*

- **A*mbush:**
- *Place starting point in OPEN list*
- *As long as there are points in the OPEN list:*
  - *Find node with the lowest travel cost.*
  - *If found node is Goal, end loop and save path.*
  - **CREATE DISINCENTIVE ALONG SAVED PATH.**
  - *Else, Find all possible neighboring nodes.*
  - *If neighbor's in the CLOSED list, ignore.*
  - *If neighbor's not in the OPEN list, add them.*
  - *If that neighbor's tentative path score is better than what's recorded, record them now. If not, put them on the CLOSED list.*

Figure 10.28 Comparative Pseudocode of A* and A*mbush Algorithms.

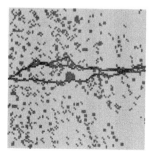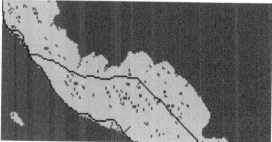

Figure 10.29 Image of Three Consecutive A*mbush Herds.

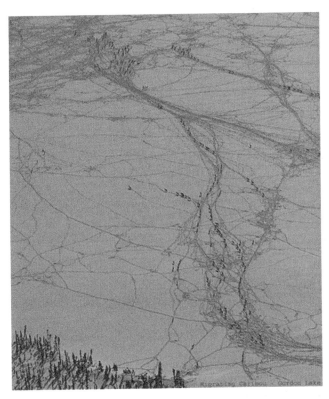

Figure 10.30   Natural Caribou Migration Pathways as seen from Above.

follows the optimal A* path, the branching herds each follow an optimal A* path as it would exist in the world after the previous path's vegetation consumption (Figure 10.31).

The initial reference frame is the starting number of simulated caribou in the herd, and an initial stored stock of calories. Movement across the land bridge will cost calories based on the effort rating, which is composed of the distance traveled and the difference in altitude between points. The total calorie cost for the herd to make a movement is the cost needed to move to a location times the number of caribou in the herd. If this cost cannot be met, then the herd is divided and a waypoint is placed at this point in the path. A herd that reaches a point where it cannot be sufficiently divided to cover calorie costs will be considered dead, having starved to death.

Once the end of the initially computed path is reached, the algorithm returns to the first established waypoint with those cast-off agents, and a new Dendriform A*mbush path is calculated. It should be noted that the initial agents were running in A*mbush form, so this original optimal path has had its vegetation rating

O **Dendriform A*mbush:**

O *Initialize Number of Agents, and Current Calories Stored*

O *Place starting point in OPEN list*

O *As long as there are points in the OPEN list:*

> O *Find node with the lowest travel cost.*
>
> O *If found node is Goal, end loop and save path.*
>
> O *Create disincentive along discovered path.*
>
> > O **Decrement Calories Stored While Traversing Path**
> >
> > O **If Predicted Calories Stored is Less Than Calorie Needs*Agents**
> >
> > O **Set Divergence Waypoint and Halve Agents.**
> >
> > O **Repeat Until Exit Point Reached.**
>
> O *Else, Find all possible neighboring nodes.*
>
> O *If neighbor's in the CLOSED list, ignore.*
>
> O *If neighbor's not in the OPEN list, add them.*
>
> O *If that neighbor's tentative path score is better than what is recorded, record them now. If not, put them on the CLOSED list.*

Figure 10.31   Dendriform A*mbush Pseudocode.

reduced due to grazing. For the next herd, it is now an unlikely optimal path for the remaining agents, who will follow a new path starting from their initial waypoint. Again, should this new group of agents find its caloric stores insufficient, it will set a waypoint, discard half of its agents, and continue.

The result of this is an optimal path with multiple branches en route, and each of those branches in turn can have subbranches as well. For the test-run depicted in Figure 10.32, it was set at 100 caribou, with 100 calories. Because of this, the system immediately calculated a starvation scenario and divided the herd up several times from the initial point as it costs more calories to move a herd of that size than was available.

Once divided, the herds were able to shore up their calorie counts by grazing along the way. The leftmost branching herd in Figure 10.32 took the relatively lush area nearest the lake in this scenario, and was content and had no further need to subdivide. The herd in the center took the high-route which had less nutrition available, causing another starvation scenario making it branch off into the three herd lines.

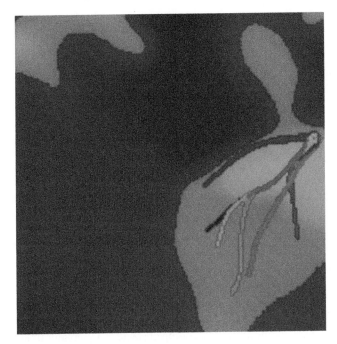

Figure 10.32 An Example Dendriform A*mbush Run.

The full distance that could be traversed and the size of the map in this test run was limited while testing the capabilities and likely number of branches that could be generated by Dendriform A*mbush. Given that herds may also consume a surplus of calories, it could be possible in the future to add a surplus flag to a given path, which could reduce the disincentive effect of A*mbush and lead to other branches moving back toward the optimal path.

One major advantage of using Dendriform A*mbush is that it is able to form a balance between the exploitative and explorative aspects of the Cultural Algorithm's belief spaces. As the two concepts of exploitation and exploration are typically in contrast to one another, using the optimal path as an exploitable baseline with the starvation points as exploration gateways, it is possible to make use of both concepts to maintain a balance as the system strives toward optimization [50].

Results

The influences that control all three pathfinding algorithms, A*, A*mbush, and Dendriform A*mbush, are Effort, Risk, and Nutrition. Effort is a combination of distance traveled and difference in altitude between two points over the distance

Figure 10.33 An Example of a Heavily Effort Weighted Path.

between them. An ascent of a 45° grade will have the same caloric cost as a descent along a 45° grade of the same distance, and will thus be treated identically in terms of effort value.

As seen in Figure 10.33, which mimics the topography of two side-by-side hilltops, with the influence heavily skewed to favor effort. As effort is dictated by distance traveled and difference in height over short distances, agents will attempt to circumnavigate large differences in height. The agents will attempt to maintain their present elevation provided that the difference in effort between the distance it takes to circumnavigate an ascending or descending obstacle is not greater than the effort necessary to scale the obstacle.

The Risk influence comes from an assessment of a given data point's height with regards to the height of its eight neighbors. The more of a data point's neighbors that are at a relatively superior altitude, the riskier the given data point is. The more neighbors that are below a data point's height, the less risky the point is. Thus, the most risky location is a depression where there is likely to be standing water and larger concentrations of mosquitoes, while the least risky location would be an overlooking hilltop with a commanding view of its surroundings.

As seen in Figure 10.34, a data point with the majority of its neighbors lower than itself will be dubbed a low risk, such as the central data point on the left. The central data point on the right of Figure 10.34 would be regarded as high risk due to the majority of its neighbors being at a higher elevation than itself. The more heavily the influence of risk is weighted on the heuristic, the more agents will avoid lowlands and make an effort to reach higher points such as hilltops.

The Nutrition influence is the last of the three, and it is concerned with the amount of vegetation a data point replicating an area of land holds. The vegetation is calculated based on the proximity to water (both horizontal distance from standing water and vertical distance from lake level), the severity of the landscape's slope, and the orientation of the slope with regards to exposure to the sun, Southern exposure being the most beneficial to greater growth.

Figure 10.34 Three Examples of Risk.

Figure 10.35 An Example of a Heavily
Nutrition Weighted Path.

As shown in Figure 10.35, a heavy emphasis on the nutrition influence will cause the path to skew toward those areas rich in vegetation. Currently, vegetation can only be altered by consumption by herds and alterations in the lake level due to time periods. But, in the future its growth rates will be assigned due to the season the simulation is taking place in, either the bountiful fall migration or the scarce spring migration. However, the vegetation rating currently describes how capable an area is of supporting vegetation, not the actual content. When an A*mbush agent moves through a vegetation area, a separate value is reduced while the area's vegetation potential is not altered. Vegetation can over time regrow, and the vegetation potential is used as a cap for a given data point.

To test the possible range of the path outcomes across the various influences, a full series of migrations were run across the land bridge, replicating the directions that would be followed in both the Spring and Fall migrations. Among these initial migrations was a series of every permutation of zero influence and maximum influence between the Effort, Risk, and Nutrition respectively, resulting in a series of paths that defined likely boundaries for paths within. These initial tests were done without A*mbush, so each migration traveled over a pristine landscape.

Figure 10.36 depicts the boundaries of each of the eight runs for each season. All variations of the influences fell within those shaded areas with the lightest shaded region representing the Fall migration from Alpena to Amberley (top left to bottom right) and the slightly darker areas areas representing the Spring migration from Amberley to Alpena (bottom right to top left). The dark thin patches situated between the two represent their overlap.

In addition to testing the variation that could be caused by the alterations of the influences, these test runs also served to identify some of the pathway boundary effects that are caused by the regional borders used to subdivide the land bridge into smaller parts. These are most prominent at the extremities with larger areas, but become much less intrusive in the interior parts of the land bridge.

After the establishment of this series of boundaries as a baseline for comparison, the Cultural Algorithm was used to optimize the weighted influences with a heuristic focusing on caloric consumption. The Cultural Algorithm uses a group

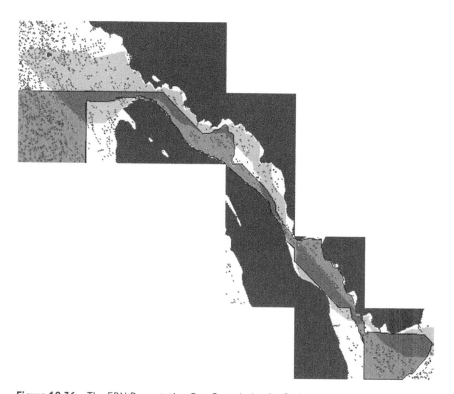

Figure 10.36 The ERN Permutation Run Boundaries for Spring and Fall.

of five knowledge sources to observe and influence the movements of the simulated caribou as described earlier. Each knowledge source differs in how explorative or exploitative it is with the available data, either spreading out in search of a new optimal solution or refining a previously found optimal solution. Each knowledge source is able to influence a number of agents, and the influence exerted by each source expands and shrinks based on the success or failure experienced by its agents [51].

The score any simulated herd could achieve is calculated by a combination of calories lost in movement across a region, subtracted from the calories acquired through the consumption of vegetation. The higher the resulting number, meaning the most calories still retained at the end of the migration, the greater the score of that particular herd.

The Cultural Algorithm's five knowledge sources would each use aspects of successful herds to suggest new search criteria to the agents, in this case specific combinations for the Effort, Risk, and Nutrition values to be used [51]. In this case, the Situational Knowledge source, which kept a record of the most successful past herds and then made only minor alterations to a known high-scoring permutation of values, performed the best through the varying landscapes.

In total, there were 40 full migrations run, divided into 20 migrations for each season, and then further divided into 10 migrations for either A* or A*mbush in that season. After being given an initial starting point at either the Alpena or Amberley boundary on the map, and being given the goal direction to seek a path toward, the CA would run for 100 generations with each of the CA's belief spaces exploring different variations of the possible weights of the influences, of which there were one million possible permutations. This was done to find the optimal weighting of the three influences in each region, for each migration.

The optimal influence for the run would be recorded and the point at which it exited the region would be noted, and that point would become the entry point into the adjoining region. It should be noted that due to the general compass direction being sought rather than a specific point, this meant it was possible for the pathfinder to find alternate routes out of a region. For example, when seeking a southeastern migration route, a route might be found that left a region toward its eastern neighbor, while other routes may have been found that left toward its southern neighbor. These alterations were noted and stored in the resulting statistics tables.

Tables 10.1 and 10.2 are depicting the statistics recorded from one of the 10 CA optimized migrations from Alpena to Amberley:

- Calories indicate the number of calories spent in transit.
- Distance indicates the distances in meters it took to traverse the given region.
- Avg Slope indicates the average severity of slope encountered across the region in degrees.

Table 10.1 Table of an A* Alpena-to-Amberley CA Optimized Migration (part 1).

	Calories	Distance	Avg slope	Min slope	Max slope	Avg veg	Avg risk	Dist to lake
R1	8060	23488.44	1.04	0	7	0.75	0.15	61.13
R2								
R3								
R4	3070	8096.19	0.96	0	3	0.66	0.38	36.82
R5	10500	26199.75	0.5	0	5	0.89	0.7	11.33
R6	11580	29202.79	1.58	9	7	0.92	0.62	12.62
R7	5860	17513.46	1.27	0	5	0.76	0.63	25.04
R8								
R9	10740	29720.54	0.74	0	4	0.93	0.76	11.76
R10								
R11	200	353.55	0	0	0	0	0	1
R12	10650	33094.91	0.76	0	5	0.93	0.57	16.08
R13	2440	5724.87	1.62	0	8	0.89	0.57	4.1
R14	11120	28770.8	0.9	0	6	0.94	0.75	8.13
Total	74220	202165.3	9.37	9	50	7.67	5.13	188.01
Avg	118.75	323.46	0.94	1.44	5.552	0.89	0.6	18.52

- Min Slope and Max Slope indicate the minimum and maximum slopes traversed in that path.
- Avg Veg indicates the average vegetation rating of the cells traversed.
- Avg Risk indicates the average risk in cells traversed.
- Dist to Lake is the average vertical distance from lake level the agents were at during travel.
- Effort, Risk, and Nutrition columns indicate the percentage of the weight exhibited by a particular influence.
- Exit location denotes the *XY* coordinates where the path left the region.
- Exit region indicates what region the departing path arrived in.
- # of cells in paths indicates how many data points were traversed across a landscape.
- Score is the result of the heuristic described above which is calories consumed minus calories expended, compared to the "ideal" traversal of no caloric exertion and full caloric consumption.

It should be noted that in some of the smaller regions, such as R11 which can be seen in Tables 10.3 and 10.4, the region was so small that the agents barely spent

Table 10.2 Table of an A* Alpena-to-Amberley CA Optimized Migration (part 2).

	Effort	Risk	Nutrition	Exit location	Exit region	# of cells in path	Score
R1	0	5	77	(72,99)	4	73	0.3874
R2							
R3							
R4	17	4	97	(99,11)	5	28	0.8123
R5	19	11	93	(99,9)	6	100	0.6306
R6	1	7	79	(99,52)	7	100	0.4328
R7	66	10	81	(50,99)	9		0.5248
R8							
R9	18	4	54	(98,99)	11	100	0.7163
R10							
R11	10	67	55	(99,1)	12	2	5
R12	12	0	45	(83,99)	13	99	0.7416
R13	12	0	9	(99,11)	14	21	2.0351
R14	1	3	83	(99,25)	EXIT	102	0.6341
Total	156	111	673			625	11.915
Avg	9.34	4.99	70.65			1	0.019064

any time there at all, and the proximity to lake level was so high that the vegetation rating was also quite large, resulting in a surplus of calories in these choke points.

It should be noted in these results, which are typical of all of the A* CA Optimized results, that the Nutrition influence was prioritized over both Effort and Risk in reaching the highest possible goals. Also, those rows which are devoid of data represent regions in the land bridge which were not entered at any point by any of the optimal paths.

The calculation of the scores for the A*mbush runs was slightly different. As A* did not decrease available vegetation, all repeated runs could benefit from the vegetation and their scores could be gauged against one another. But if this same method were to be used in A*mbush, then there would never be a herd that could top the path taken by the initial herd before any of the vegetation was devoured. Thus, it was necessary that for each generation the highest possible score for that particular generation was considered and NOT compared to the highest possible score overall, which would always be higher in the previous generation when more food was available.

Table 10.3 Table of an A*mbush Alpena-to-Amberley CA Optimized Migration (part 1).

	Calories	Distance	Avg slope	Min slope	Max slope	Avg veg	Avg risk	Dist to lake
R1	6030	17720.57	1.6	0	8	0.45	0.37	66.77
R2								
R3								
R4	5190	12457.11	0.38	0	3	0.33	0.65	43.36
R5	10760	26406.85	0.76	0	9	0.78	0.92	16.33
R6	10900	30134.76	0.9	0	4	0.73	0.77	20.54
R7	5740	16952.8	1.25	0	5	0.78	0.52	24.71
R8								
R9	10500	29720.55	0.5	0	4	0.81	0.86	16.4
R10								
R11	200	353.55	0	0	0	0	0	1
R12	10850	33448.46	0.85	0	10	0.86	0.75	15.11
R13	2360	5517.77	1.24	0	3	0.9	0.64	4.24
R14	11140	28770.8	0.92	0	6	0.94	0.76	8.11
Total	73670	201483.2	8.4	0	52	6.58	6.24	216.57
Avg	108.66	297.17	0.87	0	6.19	0.76	0.74	21.62

For the A*mbush migrations, it can readily be noticed that the calories expended are noticeably lower than in the A* runs, but the average vegetation encountered is also lower due to the vegetation having been consumed. Given that the A*mbush CA optimized migrations all favored an increase in the weighting of effort, prioritizing it over the weighting of nutrition, it can be assumed that due to the scarcity of food for the later generations that rather than attempt to waste precious energy seeking out food, it became more important to conserve what energy they had to start with.

The resulting A*mbush scores are lower, of course this is mainly due to being unable to increase their rankings dramatically through the consumption of large amounts of vegetation. The consumption rate was set at 100%, meaning those herds traveling through these regions essentially clear-cut any area they were traveling through leaving no vegetation for subsequent generations.

The Risk influence seems to be mostly ignored in this scenario as there is no possibility of death in these runs, just bad scores. But as the Dendriform A*mbush migration will be using a sustainable breeding population as its heuristic rather than consumed calories, and decreasing caloric stores that may result in agents

Table 10.4 Table of an A*mbush Alpena-to-Amberley CA Optimized Migration (part 2).

	Effort	Risk	Nutrition	Exit location	Exit region	# of cells in path	Score
R1	0	5	20	(50,99)	4	52	0.1742
R2							
R3							
R4	15	5	16	(99,2)	5	50	0.1927
R5	98	33	27	(99,4)	6	100	0.0957
R6	72	5	16	(99,56)	7	100	0.0937
R7	75	18	93	(50,99)	9	51	0.2179
R8							
R9	65	5	16	(98,99)	11	100	0.0958
R10							
R11	63	43	76	(99,1)	12	2	5
R12	70	0	27	(85,99)	13	100	0.0967
R13	89	12	79	(99,11)	14	21	0.4505
R14	6	5	89	(99,25)	EXIT	102	0.0906
Total	553	131	459	0	81	678	6.5078
Avg	55.58	9.70	38.45	0	0.12	1	0.009599

dying on the map. Thus, risk can become a much larger influence as not only will low lands be judged as risky but also those areas which now contain death sites of previous herds that starved to death in their attempts to cross the land bridge. If an entire branch dies off, then it is possible that its information may be lost to the next update of the CA as they are unable to donate to the communication pool the CA uses to disperse information [51]. Despite the dead branches being unable to report their methods, the herds should react critically to known death sites, altering their perception of the area and causing a divergence in future path-taking choices [36].

In addition to herd death, seasonal vegetation changes will also be included in future versions so that movement in the Spring will need to emphasize speed and minimization of effort with sparser vegetation, while the movement in Fall will be able to take advantage of lusher vegetation to consume en route. These migrational seasons should be comparable to the A* and A*mbush runs in terms of prioritizing effort and nutrition differently depending on their season's particular goals. In addition, they will be able to make use of the Cultural Algorithm's ability to phase-transition, where differing solutions can improve how a problem that changes for some reason (in this case, due to seasonal vegetation availability) [52].

With the Dendriform A*mbush splitting herds at starvation points, it can also use the differing seasonal vegetation rates to establish points of surplus where the consumption rate can be lowered, meaning more resources along a previously traveled path which can cause herds to join back together to mimic natural separation and cohesion [20]. The benefit of using this particular model is that it is a form of separation and cohesion done without numerous agents moving at once, rather a representation of numerous agents as they split apart and come back together.

Conclusions

The work performed has resulted in simulated caribou that more closely mirror the vegetation-consuming nature of their real-world counterparts, resulting in pathways that more closely resemble those generated by real caribou. Computing and analyzing the paths taken across the simulated land bridge has shown patterns reflecting how the system adapts to favor effort when nutrition becomes scarce due to grazing. This can be used for comparison with the seasonal growth system where the caribou in the Fall migration will have access to more vegetation than the Spring migration.

The Dendriform A*mbush shows promising replication of the branching patterns produced by caribou without the need to simulate every individual caribou that comprises a herd. It will be tested in future work on a larger amalgamation of regions 6, 7, 8, and 9 where two naturally occurring choke points to the North-West and South-East will act as entry and exit points, respectively. In addition, the Cultural Algorithm's heuristic will be changed to sustainable herd sizes needed for reproduction instead of a flat calorie intake count.

This research forms the first component of a three-step system, including the path planning system itself, a hunter-simulating ruleset analytical system known as the Deep Dive, and a user-interactive Virtual Reality system that allows the user to hunt caribou and place structures in the virtual landscape to aid in their survival on the simulated landscape.

The caribou pathways generated within this system form the lifeblood relied on by the hunters, which affects the rules used by the Hotspot Finder. The more accurate the caribou paths, the more accurately the Hotspot Finder will be able to replicate the decisions of an ancient hunter. The results of the Hotspot Finder and the Pathfinding System will then be used populate the Virtual Reality, giving the user artifacts to discover, and caribou to hunt.

References

1 O'Shea, J.M. (2002). The archaeology of scattered wreck-sites: formation processes and shallow water archaeology in western Lake Huron. *The International Journal of Nautical Archaeology* 31 (2): 211–227.

2 McDonald-Gibon, C. (2011). Syria upheaval halts excavation of ancient fort. *The Independent/UK*, October 14.

3 Doar, B.G. (2005). The Great Wall of China: tangible, intangible and destructible. China Heritage Newsletter, China Heritage Project, Australian National University.

4 Howey, M.C.L. and O'Shea, J.M. (2006). Bear's journey and the study of ritual in archaeology. *American Antiquity*: 261–282.

5 O'Shea, J. and Zvelebil, M. (1984). Oleneostrovski mogilnik: reconstructing the social and economic organization of prehistoric foragers in Northern Russia. *Journal of Anthropological Archaeology* 3 (1): 1–40.

6 Sideris, A. and Roussou, M. (2002). Making a new world out of an old one: in search of a common language for archaeological immersive VR representation. *Creative Digital Culture, Proceedings of the 8th International Conference on VSMM*, Korea (25–27 September 2002). IEEE Computer Society, pp. 31–42.

7 Kohler, T.A., Gumerman, G.J., and Reynolds, R.G. (2005). Simulating ancient societies. *Scientific American* 293 (1): 76–84.

8 Ryan, N. (2001). Documenting and validating virtual archaeology. *Archeologia e Calcolatori XII*: 245–273.

9 Elias, S.A., Short, S.K., Nelson, C.H., and Birks, H.H. (1996). Life and times of the Bering land bridge. *Nature* 382 (6586): 60–63.

10 Galitz, W.O. (2007). *The Essential Guide to User Interface Design: An Introduction to GUI Design Principles and Techniques*. Wiley.

11 Shneiderman, B. (1982). The future of interactive systems and the emergence of direct manipulation. *Behaviour & Information Technology* 1 (3): 237–256.

12 Karat, J. (1997). Evolving the scope of user-centered design. *Communications of the ACM* 40 (7): 33–38.

13 Stanley, S.D., Salaymeh, A.J., Palazzolo, T.J., and Warnke, D.M. (2014). Analyzing prehistoric hunter behavior with cultural algorithms. In: *2014 IEEE Congress on Evolutionary Computation (CEC)*. IEEE.

14 Wood, L.E. (1997). *User Interface Design: Bridging the Gap from User Requirements to Design*. CRC Press.

15 Compton, K. and Mateas, M. (2006). Procedural level design for platform games. *AIIDE Proceedings of the Second AAAI Conference on Artificial Intelligence and Interactive Digital Entertainment* June: 109–111.

16 Sweetser, P. and Wiles, J. (2005). Combining influence maps and cellular automata for reactive game agents. In: *Intelligent Data Engineering and Automated Learning-IDEAL 2005*, 524–531. Berlin, Heidelberg: Springer.

17 U.S. EPA (2012). *Great Lakes Factsheet No. 1*. U.S. Environmental Protection Agency, June 25.

18 Weaver, J.E. and Crist, J.W. (1922). Relation of hardpan to root penetration in the Great Plains. *Ecology* 3 (3): 237–249.

19 Fogarty, J., Reynolds, R.G., and Palazzolo, T. (2015). *Serious game modeling of caribou behavior across Lake Huron using cultural algorithms and influence maps.* Caribou Hunting in the Upper Great Lakes, Part I, Chapter 4, pp. 31–52.

20 Reynolds, C.W. (1987). Flocks, herds and schools: a distributed behavioral model. *ACM SIGGRAPH Computer Graphics* 21 (4). ACM.

21 Lester, Patrick (2005). A* pathfinding for beginners [online]. GameDev WebSite. http://www.gamedev.net/reference/articles/article2003.asp (accessed 8 February 2009).

22 Stout, B. (1996). Smart moves: intelligent pathfinding. *Game Developer Magazine* 10: 28–35.

23 Sims, K. (1994). Evolving virtual creatures. *Proceedings of the 21st Annual Conference on Computer Graphics and Interactive Techniques*, ACM.

24 Whitley, D. (1994). A genetic algorithm tutorial. *Statistics and Computing* 4 (2): 65–85.

25 Reynolds, R.G. (1978). On modeling the evolution of hunter-gather decision-making systems. *Geographical Analysis* 10 (1): 31–46.

26 Reynolds, R.G. and Chung, C.J. (1996). A self-adaptive approach to representation shifts in cultural algorithms. In: *Proceedings of IEEE International Conference on Evolutionary Computation*. IEEE.

27 Reynolds, R.G. (1994). An introduction to cultural algorithms. *Proceedings of the Third Annual Conference on Evolutionary Programming*, Singapore (February 2008).

28 Reynolds, R.G. and Ali, M. (2008). Computing with the social fabric: the evolution of social intelligence within a cultural framework. *Computational Intelligence Magazine, IEEE* 3 (1): 18–30.

29 Reynolds, R.G. and Ali, M.Z. (2007). Exploring knowledge and population swarms via an agent-based Cultural Algorithms Simulation Toolkit (CAT). In: *IEEE Congress on Evolutionary Computation, 2007*. IEEE.

30 Coppin, B. (2004). *Artificial Intelligence Illuminated*. Jones & Bartlett Learning.

31 Reynolds, R.G. and Peng, B. (2004). Cultural algorithms: modeling of how cultures learn to solve problems. In: *16th IEEE International Conference on Tools with Artificial Intelligence, 2004*. IEEE.

32 Franklin, B. and Bergerman, M. (2000). Cultural algorithms: concepts and experiments. In: *Proceedings of the 2000 Congress on Evolutionary Computation, 2000*, vol. 2. IEEE.

33 Iacoban, R., Reynolds, R.G., and Brewster, J. (2003). Cultural swarms: modeling the impact of culture on social interaction and problem solving. In: *Proceedings of the 2003 IEEE on Swarm Intelligence Symposium, 2003*. IEEE.

34 Reynolds, R.G. and Sverdlik, W. (1994). Problem solving using cultural algorithms. In: *Proceedings of the First IEEE Conference on Evolutionary Computation, 1994. IEEE World Congress on Computational Intelligence*. IEEE.

35 Jin, X. and Reynolds, R.G. (1999). Using knowledge-based evolutionary computation to solve nonlinear constraint optimization problems: a cultural algorithm approach. In: *Proceedings of the 1999 Congress on Evolutionary Computation, 1999*, vol. 3. IEEE.

36 Turner, A. and Penn, A. (2002). Encoding natural movement as an agent-based system: an investigation into human pedestrian behaviour in the built environment. *Environ Plann B* 29 (4): 473–490.

37 Van Den Berg, J., Patil, S., Sewall, J. et al. (2008). Interactive navigation of multiple agents in crowded environments. In: *Proceedings of the 2008 Symposium on Interactive 3D Graphics and Games*. ACM.

38 da Silva, D.J.A., Teixeira, O.N., and de Oliveira, R.C.L. (2012). *Performance Study of Cultural Algorithms Based on Genetic Algorithm with Single and Multi Population for the MKP*. INTECH Open Access Publisher.

39 Alami, J., El Imrani, A., and Bouroumi, A. (2007). A multipopulation cultural algorithm using fuzzy clustering. *Applied Soft Computing* 7 (2): 506–519.

40 Fairley, P. (2016). Robot miners of the briny deep. *Spectrum, IEEE* 53 (1): 44–47.

41 RIKEN, BSI (2013). *Largest Neuronal Network Simulation Achieved Using K Computer*. Wako: Press Release.

42 Reynolds, R., Peng, B., and Whallon, R. (2005). Emergent social structures in cultural algorithms. *Annual Conference of the North American Association for Computational Social and Organizational Science (NAACSOS 2005)*, pp. 26–28.

43 Sha, L., Gopalakrishnan, S., Liu, X., and Wang, Q. (2009). Cyber-physical systems: a new frontier. In: *Machine Learning in Cyber Trust*, 3–13. Springer.

44 Lee, E.A. (2008). Cyber physical systems: design challenges. In: *2008 11th IEEE International Symposium on Object Oriented Real-Time Distributed Computing (ISORC)*. IEEE.

45 Vitale, K., Reynolds, R.G., O'Shea, J., and Meadows, G. (2011). Exploring ancient landscapes under lake Huron using cultural algorithms. *Procedia Computer Science* 6: 303–310.

46 Cui, X. and Shi, H. (2011). A*-based pathfinding in modern computer games. *International Journal of Computer Science and Network Security* 11 (1): 125–130.

47 Fernández, K., González, G., and Chang, C. (2012). A*mbush family: A* variations for Ambush behavior and path diversity generation. *International Conference on Motion in Games*, Springer, Berlin, Heidelberg, pp. 314–325.

48 Goel, N.S., Knox, L.B., and Norman, J.M. (1991). From artificial life to real life: computer simulation of plant growth. *International Journal of General System* 18 (4): 291–319.

49 Leigh, R., Louis, S.J., and Miles, C. (2007). Using a genetic algorithm to explore A*-like pathfinding algorithms. In: *IEEE Symposium on Computational Intelligence and Games, 2007*. IEEE.

50 Črepinšek, M., Liu, S.-H., and Mernik, M. (2013). Exploration and exploitation in evolutionary algorithms: a survey. *ACM Computing Surveys (CSUR)* 45.3: 35.

51 Reynolds, R.G. (2018). Cultural algorithm framework. In: *Culture on the Edge of Chaos*, 13–25. Cham: Springer.

52 Reynolds, R.G. and Peng, B. (2005). Cultural algorithms: computational modeling of how cultures learn to solve problems: an engineering example. *Cybernetics and Systems: An International Journal* 36 (8): 753–771.

Index

IEEE Press Series on
COMPUTATIONAL INTELLIGENCE

Series Editor, **David B. Fogel**

The IEEE Press Series on Computational Intelligence includes books on neural, fuzzy, and evolutionary computation, and related technologies, of interest to the engineering and scientific communities. Computational intelligence focuses on emulating aspects of biological systems to construct software and/or hardware that learns and adapts. Such systems include neural networks, our use of language to convey complex ideas, and the evolutionary process of variation and selection. The series highlights the most-recent and ground-breaking research and development in these areas, as well as the important hybridization of concepts and applications across these areas. The audiences for books in the series include undergraduate and graduate students, practitioners, and researchers in computational intelligence.

Computational Intelligence: The Experts Speak. Edited by David B. Fogel and Charles J. Robinson. 2003. 978-0-471-27454-4

Handbook of Learning and Appropriate Dynamic Programming. Edited by Jennie Si, Andrew G. Barto, Warren B. Powell, and Donald Wunsch II. 2004. 978-0471-66054-X

Computationally Intelligent Hybrid Systems. Edited by Seppo J. Ovaska. 2005. 978-0471-47668-4

Evolutionary Computation: Toward a New Philosophy of Machine Intelligence, Third Edition. David B. Fogel. 2006. 978-0471-66951-7

Emergent Information Technologies and Enabling Policies for Counter-Terrorism. Edited by Robert L. Popp and John Yen. 2006. 978-0471-77615-4

Introduction to Evolvable Hardware: A Practical Guide for Designing Self-Adaptive Systems. Garrison W. Greenwood and Andrew M. Tyrrell. 2007. 978-0471-71977-9

Computational Intelligence in Bioinformatics. Edited by Gary B. Fogel, David W. Corne, and Yi Pan. 2008. 978-0470-10526-9

Computational Intelligence and Feature Selection: Rough and Fuzzy Approaches. Richard Jensen and Qiang Shen. 2008. 978-0470-22975-0 *Clustering.* Rui Xu and Donald C. Wunsch II. 2009. 978-0470-27680-8

Biometrics: Theory, Methods, and Applications. Edited by: N.V. Boulgouris, Konstantinos N. Plataniotis, and Evangelia Micheli-Tzanakou. 2009. 978-0470-24782-2

Evolving Intelligent Systems: Methodology and Applications. Edited by Plamen Angelov, Dimitar P. Filev, and Nikola Kasabov. 2010. 978-0470-28719-4

Perceptual Computing: Aiding People in Making Subjective Judgments. Jerry Mendel and Dongrui Lui. 2010. 978-0470-47876-9

Reinforcement Learning and Approximate Dynamic Programming for Feedback Control. Edited by Frank L. Lewis and Derong Liu. 2012. 978-1118-10420-0

Complex-Valued Neural Networks: Advances and Applications. Edited by Akira Hirose. 2013. 978-1118-34460-6

Unsupervised Learning: A Dynamic Approach. Matthew Kyan, Paisarn Muneesawang, Kambiz Jarrah, and Ling Guan. 2014. 978-0470-27833-8

Introduction to Type-2 Fuzzy Logic Control: Theory and Applications. Jerry M. Mendel, Hani Hagras, Woei-Wan Tan, William W. Melek, and Hao Ying. 2014. 978-1118-278291

Fundamentals of Computational Intelligence: Neural Networks, Fuzzy Systems, and Evolutionary Computation. James M. Keller, Derong Liu, and David B. Fogel. 2015. 978-1119-214342

Simulation and Computational Red Teaming for Problem Solving. Jiangjun Tang, George Leu, and Hussein A. Abbass. 2020. 978-1-119-52717-6

Cultural Algorithms: Tools to Model Complex Dynamic Social Systems. Robert G. Reynolds. 2021. 978-1-119-40308-1

Printed and bound by CPI Group (UK) Ltd, Croydon, CR0 4YY